If you would like to contact the Association the details are as follows:
South West Coast Path Association,
Unit 2, Bowker House, Lee Mill Bridge, Ivybridge, Devon, PL21 9EF
Tel: 01752 896237

Chairman: chair@southwestcoastpath.org.uk
Administration: hello@southwestcoastpath.org.uk

Published by: The South West Coast Path Association
ISBN: 978-0-907055-27-3

© South West Coast Path Association 2018
Designed by Ingrid Kendall, Paignton.
Map imagery by Luke Smith.
Printed by Deltor Communications LTD

Cover photography: The Rumps by Peter Edwards

southwestcoastpath.org.uk

Welcome

Welcome to the Complete Guide to the South West Coast Path. Whatever your reason for taking a step onto the Coast Path, this is the start of a journey of a lifetime. You won't be disappointed. Where else can you enjoy 630 miles of such superb coastline which make up the longest National Trail in the UK? The heritage, wildlife, geology, scenery and people that you will meet along the way are truly inspirational and every day will bring with it stunning new experiences.

Whether you're looking for an afternoon stroll to take you to a beautiful view, or for a challenge like no other in hiking the entire 630 miles from Somerset's Minehead around to the shores of Poole Harbour in Dorset, you've come to the right place to start your adventure.

This Guide is produced by the South West Coast Path Association, the voice and heart of the Path. Our aim is to promote and protect the Path and we need a huge range of supporters to help us to deliver our promises and look after the Path, conserving it for future generations and promoting it for the enjoyment of everyone.

We have a membership base of well over 6,000 dedicated South West Coast Path lovers, a handful of these members have been supporting us since the very beginning in 1973. Some are individual members and some joint, we also have a number who live overseas and want to enable us to continue the good work from afar. Whatever the reason for being a member, we always welcome new supporters to join us.

We also have some wonderful business supporters, one of which is South West Water who have been contributing to the Coast Path since 2014. Other business supporters include Cotswold Outdoors and Shearings Holidays.

In addition, a range of local businesses support us through our business membership scheme which offers advertising for businesses and support for them to promote themselves to visitors of the Path. Latest figures show that South West Coast Path walkers spent £487 million, mostly in local businesses, which supports the equivalent of over 10,000 full-time jobs.

All the places to eat, stay and do listed in this Guide are Business Members, to ensure that they continue to support the Path and advertise with us, please support them and in turn help support the Path!

> Thank you! It costs at least £1,000 every year to look after each mile of Coast Path, with the help of our members we are able to protect and promote it for future generations.

CONTENTS

Photographs courtesy of:
Colin J Broadbent, Artur Szczesze, Kerry Roberts, James Styles, Steve Luck, Piotr Piasecki, Richard F Taylor, Brian Bradshaw, Rosie Spooner, Kyle Harman, Barry Lockwood, Deena Drees, Kingsley Scott, Wing Yin Chan, Andrew Ray, David Carvey, Jen Rogers, Mike Chadwick, Jennifer Rowlandson, Ted Forman, Terry Hawkes, Trevor Taylor, Gary Holpin, Stephen Emerson, Bogdan Zarkowski, Malcolm Stone, Valentina Scarpa Bandelloni, Neil Burnell, Andy Emmett, Simon Hodgkiss, Samuel Hunt, Katharina Renner, Fiona French, Audrey Rowlatt, Graham Woollven, Rob Kendall, Vicky Williams, Louise Scott, Andrew Ray, Bob Small, Christopher Small, Chris Parker, Jen Rogers, Martin Streathe, Rosie Spooner, Martin Dolan, Jon Speed, Daryl Hutchinson, Tim Barker, Aaron Brett, Frank Leavesle, Andrew Wheatley.

Important – Please Note

Information included or available through the Association is given in good faith and is believed to be accurate and correct at the time of going to print – however it cannot be guaranteed not to include inaccuracies or typographical errors.

Advice received via the the Association should not be relied upon for personal decisions and you should take into account the weather and your own capabilities before following the walks set out in this Guide. It is for the individual concerned to weigh up the risks of each of the walks described in this book.

The Association makes no representations about the suitability of walks to any one person and will accept no liability for any loss or damage suffered as a result of relying on this book; it should be used for guidance only.

In no event shall the Association be liable for any personal injury or any loss suffered as a result of using this publication.

The South West Coast Path is a 630 mile (just over 1,000 kilometres) adventure along the coast line of England's south west peninsula, starting at Minehead in Somerset and travelling all the way round to Poole Harbour in Dorset. You can join it anywhere, simply arrive at the coast turn left or right and follow the acorn mark for your next walking or running adventure. The South West Coast Path is a National Trail, which means it receives a high standard of care and travels through some of our finest landscape. Almost 70% of the Path travels through a protected landscape and some of our finest heritage assets can be seen from the Path both ancient and more 'modern' such as our mining history.

The sheer variety of the South West Coast Path means that there are plenty of gentle stretches as well as dramatic headlands and steep coastal valleys where the going can be strenuous and demanding. We hope you find this Guide helpful in planning your walking. We have included the amount of ascent involved in each of the Sections - anyone completing all 630 miles will have climbed a total of 115,000 feet (35,024 metres), just a little short of climbing Mount Everest four times! Whether you are a challenge seeker, contemplator, walker and talker or pub seeker you will also find inspiration on our website **www.southwestcoastpath.org.uk** as well as all the practical information you need to start or continue your adventure.

The South West Coast Path Association – Protecting and Promoting the Path

The Association is a registered charity working to protect and conserve the Coast Path to give us all the opportunity to improve our health in the great outdoors. We work to ensure the Path is one of the best walks in the world and protect it for all to enjoy. The Association is a volunteer led organisation governed by Trustees, that works closely with Natural England, the Local Authorities and the National Trust to achieve the best possible Coast Path. As part of this role the Association is a member of the South West Coast Path Trail Partnership, the body whose role is to take collective responsibility for providing a high quality trail meeting National Quality Standards.

We try to ensure as many people as possible know about, and have information to enjoy, the Coast Path, including producing this Guide, other publications and maintaining our website with over one million visits. We also fund vital improvement projects to protect the Path for future generations - you can see lots of these projects at **www.southwestcoastpath.org.uk/projects** Every one of the 630 miles from Somerset's Minehead around to the shores of Poole Harbour in Dorset costs at least £1,000 every year for each mile to keep it open, in good shape and clearly signed.

Funding for the Coast Path has traditionally come from Natural England, the Government body responsible for the National Trails, and from the Local Highway Authorities. However, substantial budget reductions for these bodies have meant consequent reductions in spending on the Coast Path. As a result, the Association has taken on the role of raising funds to try and plug these gaps, something which, as a charity whose focus is on the Coast Path, it is uniquely well placed to do.

Whether you plan to walk all 630 miles, have already done so, are happy to stroll along the coast on a sunny afternoon or spend a couple of days a year when on holiday, and even if you are no longer able to enjoy the Path, if you love the Coast Path Association, membership is for you. The South West Coast Path holds a special place in many people's hearts as walking and visiting it creates priceless memories. Donations and legacies towards Path improvements can provide a lovely tribute to special people or to commemorate special occasions. Each year we organise a series of events you may wish to take part in, many of these are focussed around our annual Challenge month in October. For more information on forthcoming events visit our website at **www.southwestcoastpath.org.uk/events** If you have a business you may wish to become a business member or sponsor. Details of ways to support us can be found on **www.southwestcoastpath.org.uk** and where you can sign up to our free monthly e-newsletter.

Membership

You're possibly already a member but if not please join us or encourage a friend to sign up. Supporting the charity and adding a voice as a member helps us to improve the Path and keep the way open to beautiful coastal places. As a member you give us a voice. With more members we have a stronger voice which helps us to gain more funding for the Path.

Our members are great supporters of the Path, if you would like to join us prices for 2018 are:

Individual Membership	**£22**
Joint Membership	**£29**
International Membership	**£29**

You can join at **www.southwestcoastpath.org.uk** or by calling us on **01752 896237**

Funding Path Improvements

- £25 buys one oak step board
- £100 buys a stone step
- £250 - £350 covers the cost of buying and installing an oak fingerpost
- £400 enables us to fund the purchase and installation of an oak gate

Follow the Acorn

The South West Coast Path is one of the "family" of National Trails. It is generally well signposted and waymarked, using the National Trail symbol of the acorn. In some parts of the Coast Path waymarking relates to the local environment, for example the use of granite waymarks in parts of West Cornwall and Purbeck stone signs in Dorset. Be sure when walking the route to follow any such directions on the ground rather than relying on literature – things change over time, even including the route of the South West Coast Path, literature can become out of date.

Those who set out to walk all or any of this beautiful trail should remember that much of it is a cliff top Path – in places a very high cliff top. Those who manage the Coast Path want to keep it as safe as possible, but walkers should be reminded that it is unwise to leave the Path at any point on the seaward side. Sometimes the edges of cliff tops away from the Path can be unstable and unsafe.

Now and again the descriptions suggest an alternative path away from the officially designated route. Please feel free to use these alternatives that follow rights of way or, occasionally, "permitted routes" maintained by the landowner for use by the public.

History of the South West Coast Path Association

The Association was originally formed on 5th May 1973. The motivation of principal founding members Philip and Mary Carter was to make the Coast Path at least as enjoyable as the Peninne Way, which the Carter family had walked the year before. They felt that the Coast Path did not meet those standards. They intended the Charity to promote the Path as well as lobby for its completion, which finally occurred in 1978. Though officially complete in 1978, the South West Way Association (as we were first known) had a long list of improvements which they wanted to see happen. Slowly, over the last forty years, most of these have been achieved. The Path today is a huge improvement on that 1970's route and in no small way due to the efforts of Philip, Mary and the many others who came after them volunteering for the Charity. You can read more about our history on our website at **www.southwestcoastpath.org.uk/love-the-coast-path/about-us/our-history**

Planning Your Walk

You might be planning to walk the whole 630 miles or just taking to the Path for a few hours, half a day or perhaps just a picnic! In any event you are likely to know your capabilities and not need detailed advice. However, it is worth remembering that some lengths of the Coast Path can be quite arduous, with frequent repeated climbs and descents or occasional awkward terrain, and it is not always possible to calculate the time or effort to be taken for a length purely on the distance. The degree of difficulty has to be considered so check in this Guide for the grading – easy, moderate, strenuous or severe – of any length you're looking to walk for an idea of what to expect. For example, the time and effort required for a 'severe' length can be twice that for the same distance of an 'easy' section.

Long Distance Walking

If you are looking for advice on a walk along the Coast Path spanning more than a day, there are some helpful points below to ensure you have a safe and memorable time.

Newcomers to the Coast Path

A great way of getting an idea of what coastal walking is about is to take a day walk first. Perhaps start with a length graded 'easy' or 'moderate' in the Guide – start at one end and turn back when still feeling quite fresh to avoid fighting fatigue at the end. Alternatively, walk a section shown as having convenient public transport. If doing this, try to use the public transport at the start and walk back to your base. This avoids having to race the clock to catch a bus at the end of the walk.

While there is little need for special kit on the 'easy' sections – good shoes and a rainproof jacket will probably be enough – once you progress further decent boots and a rucksack for food and drink and other bits and pieces will be needed. And although it is unlikely you will get lost many walkers like to have the appropriate map to keep track of where they are, what is around them, etc.

Long Distance Coast Path Walking

If you have not undertaken walking for more than a day at a time, bear in mind that you will not be able to keep up the same distance day after day as you do in a one-off day walk. The first reason for this is that you will probably be carrying more gear than usual. This may include a change of clothes and overnight kit, all in a bigger rucksack than usual. However, it is possible to overcome this by using a kit transfer company – see page 10 of this Guide or check the website.

Secondly, there is the 'wear' factor – for the first few days especially it is simply more tiring having to walk each day. And finally, there is the 'interest' factor – the walk is likely to take you through new places and new scenery; there is more to see and you will need more time to look round.

These factors will influence your planning. It is very important not to be too optimistic about what you can achieve each day, especially if booking accommodation ahead. Booking ahead does have the advantage of knowing you have a bed for the night, which can be important in the south west in the summer. On the other hand, it does mean that even if you are tired, have developed blisters and the weather is awful, you have to keep going. Be sure to check the grading in the Guide for the length you will be walking – remember the time and effort for a 'severe' length will be much more than that for the same distance on an 'easy' section.

Some Practical Details

While you will have to carry more gear than usual, think long and hard about every item you think you will need and travel as light as possible. Also remember that rucksacks are very rarely waterproof. A plastic liner, used as an additional inner layer, will prevent arriving at your accommodation after a day in the rain to find that your change of clothes is wet. Another practical point to be aware of is the availability of refreshments. You are recommended to carry water whenever out walking on the coast. Nevertheless, during the summer season, refreshments are quite widely available except for the relatively few remote lengths which are highlighted in the Guide. However, out of the holiday season refreshments can be quite far apart on long stretches of coast and you should take your own food supplies as well as water.

Walking Alone

The most important thing to remember if walking alone is to make sure someone knows your destination and estimated time of arrival. You are most unlikely to get into trouble but it is comforting to know that you will be missed if you don't arrive and that anyone searching for you knows roughly where to look.

Also, make sure you take a mobile phone. It is true that signal coverage is patchy along the coast but it's still worth having one.

And if you have a smart phone, there are apps available that enable you to share your progress with family or friends, and so can give a further indication of where you are if you haven't arrived where and when you were expected.

At the Association we have a scheme that enables female members who are a little nervous about walking alone to team up with other female members.

Contact **hello@southwestcoastpath.org.uk** for details.

Finding your way - just follow the acorn

Over the 630 miles of the South West Coast Path you'll pass thousands of signs and waymarks to help you find your way. All of these will have the acorn logo on them, which is the symbol used by all the UK's National Trails.

The acorn is used alongside coloured arrows or the words 'footpath', 'bridleway' or 'byway' to indicate who can use that particular stretch of Path.

- ▷ Yellow arrows indicates that it is a 'Public Footpath' that can only be used by walkers.

- ▶ Blue arrows are used on 'Public Bridleways' which can be used by walkers, horseriders and also cyclists.

- ▶ A red or black arrow indicates that the track is a 'Public Byway' which can be used by walkers, horseriders, cyclists and carriage driver and motorised vehicles.

At some Path junctions you will find a waymark posts with multiple arrows. The arrow at the top nearest the acorn indicates the direction of the Coast Path. Below that, separated by a black line you may find other arrows which indicate the direction of the side routes and their status. Alternatively the side routes may be marked with arrows on the sides of the post that don't have acorns on.

In most cases the direction indicated by the arrow is obvious, but if unsure they are designed to be read when you are standing looking straight at the arrow.

Report a Problem

Be our Eyes, Ears as well as Feet on the ground!

If you spot a problem on the Path please let us know. Council and National Trust Rangers and Wardens work really hard to keep the Path well looked after and it really helps to have problems reported promptly. So if you find a broken signpost, or one that's missing, stiles or gates in need of repair or have any real difficulties with the Path surface, please use the Report a Problem form on the website, contact us on **01752 876237** or email us at **hello@southwestcoastpath.org.uk** and we'll make sure your report gets to the right person.

Walking Guides

These Walking Guides provide detailed instructions for short sections of the Path, laid out in both directions. They include maps and photos as well as offering interesting facts, history, wildlife and geological information. These are available to buy through our online shop, or by telephoning the office on **01752 896237**. They are an excellent addition to this Guide.

Walk No.	Section Name	Distance (miles)	Distance (km)
1	Minehead to Porlock Weir	8.9	14.3
2	Porlock Weir to Lynton	12.1	19.5
3	Lynton to Combe Martin	13.7	22.0
4	Combe Martin to Ilfracombe	5.4	8.7
5	Ilfracombe to Woolacombe	8.5	13.7
6	Woolacombe to Croyde Bay	5.2	8.4
7	Croyde Bay to Braunton	9.8	15.8
8	Braunton to Barnstaple	5.4	8.7
9	Barnstaple to Bideford	10.7	17.2
10	Bideford to Westward Ho!	8	12.9
11	Westward Ho! to Clovelly	11.1	17.9
12	Clovelly to Hartland Quay	10.3	16.6
13	Hartland Quay to Bude	15.2	24.5
14	Bude to Crackington Haven	9.8	15.8
15	Crackington Haven to Boscastle	6.7	10.8
16	Boscastle to Tintagel	4.7	7.6
17	Tintagel to Port Isaac	9.1	14.6
18	Port Isaac to Padstow	11.7	18.8
19	Padstow to Harlyn Bay	6.5	10.5
20	Harlyn Bay to Porthcothan	6.7	10.8
21	Porthcothan to Newquay	10.3	16.6
22	Newquay to Holywell Bay	8.1	13.0
23	Holywell Bay to Perranporth	4.5	7.2
24	Perranporth to Portreath	12.4	20.0
25	Portreath to Hayle	11.7	18.8
26	Hayle to St Ives	6.1	9.8
27	St Ives to Pendeen	13.7	22.0
28	Pendeen to Sennen Cove	9.1	14.6
29	Sennen Cove to Porthcurno	6.3	10.1
30	Porthcurno to Lamorna	5.4	8.7
31	Lamorna to Marazion	9.2	14.8
32	Marazion to Porthleven	10.8	17.4
33	Porthleven to Poldhu Cove	5.2	8.4
34	Poldhu Cove to The Lizard	8.2	13.2
35	The Lizard to Coverack	10.4	16.7
36	Coverack to Helford	12.9	20.8
37	Helford to Falmouth	10.3	16.6
38	Falmouth to Portscatho	6.2	10.0

The Reverse Guide

A useful guide providing directions of the whole 630 miles of Coast Path from Poole (Dorset) to Minehead (Somerset). Price £5.50 from **http://shop.southwestcoastpath.org.uk/**

Maps

The Coast Path is very well signposted. However we do understand that many people like to walk with a map – finding out what else is around you, peace of mind and of course access to the Coast Path.

A-Z Adventure Maps

The A-Z Map Company has now mapped the entire 630 miles of the South West Coast Path and covered the entire route in five convenient Adventure Maps.

The maps use 1:25 000 scale and are in a booklet format making them very user friendly – as you walk along to Coast Path you can simply turn the page. There are QR barcodes providing up to date details on public transport, the weather, tides and other tourist information.

39	Porthscatho to Portloe	7.4	11.9
40	Portloe to Mevagissey	12.2	19.6
41	Mevagissey to Par	10.7	17.2
42	Par to Fowey	6.8	10.9
43	Fowey to Polperro	7.1	11.4
44	Polperro to Looe	5	8.0
45	Looe to Portwrinkle	7.7	12.4
46	Portwrinkle to Plymouth	13.2	21.2
47	Plymouth (Admiral's Hard) to Mount Batten	7.5	12.1
48	Mount Batten to Wembury (ferry)	7.5	12.1
49	Wembury to River Erme	10.3	16.6
50	River Erme to Hope Cove	9.3	15.0
51	Hope Cove to Salcombe	8.1	13.0
52	Salcombe to Torcross	12.6	20.3
53	Torcross to Dartmouth	10.3	16.6
54	Dartmouth to Brixham	10.9	17.5
55	Brixham to Babbacombe	13.2	21.2
56	Babbacombe to Teignmouth	6.4	10.3
57	Teignmouth to Exmouth	8	12.9
58	Exmouth to Budleigh Salterton	5.4	8.7
59	Budleigh Salterton to Sidmouth	7.1	11.4
60	Sidmouth to Seaton	10.3	16.6
61	Seaton (Devon) to Lyme Regis	7.1	11.4
62	Lyme Regis to West Bay	10	16.1
63	West Bay to Abbotsbury	9.3	15.0
64	Abbotsbury to Ferry Bridge (Weymouth)	10.9	17.5
65	Ferrybridge around Isle of Portland	13	20.9
66	Ferrybridge (Weymouth) to Lulworth Cove	14.4	23.2
67	Lulworth Cove to Kimmeridge Bay	7.1	11.4
68	Kimmeridge Bay to Worth Matravers (Winspit)	7.1	11.4
69	Worth Matravers (Winspit) to Swanage	6.5	10.5
70	Swanage to South Haven Point	7.5	12.1
71	Alternative route between West Bexington and Osmington Mills along the South Dorset Ridgeway	17.1	

Map 1 North Devon & Somerset

Map 2 North Cornwall

Map 3 South Cornwall

Map 4 South Devon

Map 5 Dorset

Maps cost £9.50 including p&p and are available from
http://shop.southwestcoastpath.org.uk/

Other Map Resources

Harvey Maps cover the Path using a scale of 1:40:000.

Ordnance Survey Maps include the Landranger series using a scale of 1:50:000 as well as the Explorer & Outdoor Leisure Maps with a scale of 1:25:000.

Circular Walk Books

A series of colour books providing circular walks along the Path using aerial photography to map each route with walk descriptions giving an estimated walking time and grading. Also details interesting facts about the past from the landscape and heritage of today - including wildlife, geology and revealing fascinating stories. Each book costs £6.50 including p&p and is available from
http://shop.southwestcoastpath.org.uk/

Kit Transfer

Walking is even more enjoyable when all you have to carry is a light day pack, so why not take advantage of a kit transfer service? Packing becomes much easier when you're not worrying about the weight and your overnight bags will be ready and waiting when you arrive at the place you're staying.

Several companies offer this service, moving your bags between overnight stops. All you need to do is arrange on the morning of your departure to leave them with the proprietor of your hotel, B&B or campsite and they will organise for it to be delivered to your next night's accommodation.

There are two luggage transfer companies that proudly support the South West Coast Path Association; Luggage Transfers and WD Transfers. Details of both can be found on our website under 'Baggage Transfers'.

 Luggage Transfers are the only luggage transfer specialist covering the whole 630 miles of the South West Coast Path from Minehead to Poole. Coming up to their 9th year and with over 50 local drivers, they continue to support the South West Coast Path Association through voluntary donations from their private walkers. Delivering around 10,000 bags each month for walkers they pride ourselves on reliability and excellent customer service. They are happy to pick up and collect from anywhere you are staying. Next day bookings welcome!
🌐 www.luggagetransfers.co.uk

 WD Transfers operate across the West Cornwall section of the South West Coast Path between Padstow and Falmouth. We have over 10 years combined experience transporting luggage for walkers around Cornwall and are the only luggage transfer company solely focussed on this region. We provide point to point baggage transfers for walkers and walking holiday companies alike and are confident that we cannot be beaten for price, reliability and customer service.
🌐 www.cornwallluggagetransfer.co.uk

Package holidays

Need some help planning your holiday? We recommend contacting one of the walking holiday companies listed in this section who provide complete walking holiday packages along parts of the South West Coast Path. These include guided and self-guided options depending on how you prefer to travel, as well as themed walks from food foraging to wildlife watching.

For those of you who are keen to walk long sections of the Coast Path, companies can book accommodation along your chosen route and move your bags each day to the next place you will be staying. Alternatively, if you don't fancy packing your bags each morning, you can ask to stay in the same hotel or guest house and arrange to be transported to do a different walk each day.

Walking Holiday Companies

Absolute Escapes offers self-guided walking holidays on the South West Coast Path. They provide packages that include carefully selected accommodation, door-to-door bag transfers, and comprehensive Information Pack with guidebook, map, route notes and recommendations for lunch and dinner each day. They are a leading specialist in walking holidays and offer packages on many long distance trails in the UK & Ireland.
🌐 www.absoluteescapes.com

Contours Walking Holidays are the specialists in self-guided walking holidays in Scotland, England, Wales and Ireland. Their packages cover the whole of the South West Coast Path, as well as The Saints Way, Two Moors Way, Dartmoor Way and Tarka Trail. With hand-picked accommodation, maps, guidebooks, daily luggage transportation and a choice of itineraries, every detail is taken care of. You'll be fully free to enjoy the sights and sounds of the Coast Path.
🌐 www.contours.co.uk

Encounter Walking Holidays provide walking holidays and short breaks on every section of the Coast Path. They specialise in helping with the requests that others struggle with or don't want to take on - whether you are a small group looking for the best prices, walking with your dogs, have an unusual itinerary idea or are just arriving from overseas and are new to UK Walking Routes. They provide detailed quotes for walkers with no commitment to book so get in touch with your ideas and questions!
🌐 www.encounterwalkingholidays.com

Explore in Cornwall provides guided multiday, day and half day walks on the South West Coast Path throughout the Cornwall sections of the Trail. All walks are guided by Steve Crummay who has over 30 years' experience of working in Cornwall's amazing coast and countryside. They provide the very best bespoke walking on the Cornish Coast Path and show you the amazing places, wildlife and fascinating heritage that can be encountered on Britain's longest National Trail.
⊕ www.exploreincornwall.co.uk

Footscape provide walking holidays and short breaks along the famous World Heritage Jurassic Coast. We provide flexibility of choice: where and how much to walk each day, where to stay and precise, foolproof directions. Based in Dorset we constantly update the trails and provide interesting information, bringing the coast to life. Get in touch for a no commitment quote.
⊕ www.footscape.co.uk

Footpath Holidays is a family owned walking holiday company founded in 1983. Self guided holidays along the South West Coast; single centre and 'moving on' with accommodation and baggage transfer. Guided group holidays in Devon, Cornwall and Dorset.
⊕ www.footpath-holidays.com

Jurassic Coast Walking offer bespoke walking holidays for individuals, couples or small groups on the beautiful Isle of Purbeck. Walks can be guided or self-guided and guided walks are led by local writer and photographer Robert Westwood, author of a number of books on the Jurassic Coast, including walking guides for the Jurassic Coast Trust. Robert trained as a geologist and will help you enjoy and appreciate the wonderful history of this beautiful stretch of coastline.
⊕ www.jurassiccoastwalking.co.uk

Nearwater Holidays specialise in single base, inn to inn trips and bespoke walking holidays along sections of the Coast Path in Cornwall. The walks have been developed with the benefit of their local knowledge to ensure the visiting walker has the chance to see a few extra special places that they would otherwise overlook.
⊕ www.nearwaterwalkingholidays.co.uk

Sherpa Expeditions, founded in 1973, is a specialist in self-guided and guided walking & cycling holidays throughout Europe. With a dedicated team, they've been working on detailed route notes, which help walkers and cyclists explore the many paths all over Europe. The company pioneered the trips in their Walkers' Britain collection, including the Coast-to-Coast Trail & Cornish Coast Path.
⊕ www.sherpaexpeditions.co.uk

Walk Kernow Nordic Walking in Cornwall is a fantastic pastime. Not only will you be exercising your whole body with the use of poles, you will also have a few advantages over other walkers on the path such as remaining more upright as you walk and finding it easier to move through the mud. The poles also make it easier to walk up hills, so your walks become more enjoyable. Walk Kernow provides Beginners Workshops, weekly Nordic Walks and Nordic Walking weekend breaks.
⊕ www.walkkernow.co.uk

Walk the Trail offer self-guided walking holidays throughout the South West including the South West Coast Path, The Two Moors Way, and The Saints Way along with many other routes across the UK. All holidays include a personalised holiday pack complete with luggage transfers, accommodation location information, maps and guidebooks. Their unique Holiday Finder Tool allows you to choose your start and end locations, giving you greater flexibility to enjoy the Coast Path at a pace to suit you.
⊕ www.walkthetrail.co.uk
☏ +44 (0)1326 567252

Westcountry Walking Holidays specialise in delivering flexible and great value self-guided walking holidays and short breaks on the South West Coast Path. They design your holiday itinerary around your requirements. Accommodation is secured within two weeks of booking, which they let you approve before it is confirmed. Their standard package is comprehensive including B&B accommodation, baggage transfer, maps and guides.
⊕ www.westcountry-walking-holidays.com

Western Discoveries are the local experts for walking holidays in Cornwall. They are based in West Cornwall and specialise in providing self-led walking holidays along the Cornwall section of the stunning South West Coast Path. Accommodation, luggage transfers, maps, their own detailed route notes and arrival/departure transfers from local transport terminals are all provided with an unparalleled attention to detail.
⊕ www.westcornwallwalks.co.uk

southwestcoastpath.org.uk

Wild Rambling Guided walking adventures in St Ives and West Penwith. Experience the stunning views and fascinating history of the coast and countryside of this beautiful area with your own private guide. Fascinating mining and industrial heritage Beautiful and inspiring coastline, with stunning beaches and lofty cliffs Cornwall's ancient history - sacred wells, Iron Age settlements, hill forts, burial sites, stone circles. Your walk will be tailored personally to your own requirements and interests. You can specify any distance, level of difficulty and length of time (from an hour or two, half day or full day).
🌐 wildrambling.com/explore-cornwall.html

Kit list for walking the South West Coast Path

Planning a walking trip along the Coast Path? Take a look at our suggested kit list to make sure you pack the essentials:

Base Layer

A base layer is a good place to start most walking outfits. Merino wool is ideal for colder weather as it will keep the heat in, whilst wicking away your sweat.

Spare Insulating Layer

It's always worth having a spare insulation layer, but the conditions you choose to walk in dictate what level of insulation you will need. A light fleece is fine for summer, but British winters demand a down or synthetic insulated jacket.

Waterproof Top and Bottoms

Waterproof layers are vital when exploring the Coast Path to ensure you don't get caught out and end up walking in damp clothes. Your waterproofs should be breathable, with ventilation to allow sweat vapour to escape.

Sturdy Footwear

You will need some sturdy walking trainers or boots to take on the sometimes-uneven terrain of the Coast Path in comfort. For personal advice on picking out the right footwear you can visit your local Cotswold Outdoor store, and use your 15% members discount. They will get to know your feet, any previous injuries and then measure you up to find the right shoe for your walk.

First Aid Kit, Whistle and Torch

Whilst you are unlikely to be find yourself in danger when walking sensibly on the Coast Path, it never hurts to be prepared. Carry a first aid kit and make sure you know how to use everything in it. Take a torch in case you get caught out after dark, and a whistle is a lightweight way to help attract attention in an emergency.

Food and water

Keeping hydrated is essential for an enjoyable day on the trail. Aim for at least 2 litres per day, but remember the amount you need to drink is entirely dependent on the length of time you plan to be walking and the temperature. Even if you have planned a lunch stop into your walk, we recommend always keeping a snack with you to keep your energy levels up.

Eye Protection and Sun Cream

When it is sunny you'll want to block out the bright light with sunglasses so you can fully enjoy the spectacular sea views. Walking when it's warm is great, but it's important to be sun safe, even on overcast days, so pack some sun cream and apply it accordingly.

Map and Compass

Even though the Coast Path is exceptionally well signed, taking a map and compass, and knowing how to use them, is essential on any longer walk. You never know when you might have to change route due to unforeseen circumstances, and a quick look at a map can give you a safe alternative.

Walking poles

Whilst not essential, walking poles can help you move more confidently over difficult terrain and even come in handy should you need to cross a stream or muddy area of the Path.

Mobile phone

You cannot rely on it, as signal is very patchy along many parts of the Coast Path, but it is handy to have a mobile phone with you. To help with any navigation issues, the route of the Coast Path outside of towns is shown on Google Maps, but be aware that using GPS will drain your battery, so it's worth taking a USB power bank as backup.

Access to the start of the Path

Access to the start of the Path can be made locally and from outside the region, with a bus service linking Minehead to the mainline railway station at Taunton.

Railways

Few people have the time to complete the entire Path in one go, instead they split it over a number of holidays. The easiest way to arrange this is to start and finish your trip at one of the towns along the Path with a train station, as this saves having to get back to your starting point to retrieve your car.

Please go to the map inside front cover to see the main rail links and also have a look at our Suggested Itineraries on pages 29 and 30.

Throughout the year there is a regular service linking London Paddington with Taunton, Exeter St. David's, Newton Abbot, Plymouth and Cornwall. There are also regular services linking Birmingham, the North West, North East and Scotland with Taunton, Exeter St. David's, Plymouth, Cornwall and Bournemouth.

There is also an overnight sleeper service between Paddington and Penzance.

There is a half hourly South West Trains service linking London Waterloo, Woking, Basingstoke and Southampton with Bournemouth, Poole, Wareham (for Swanage), Dorchester (for Bridport and Lyme Regis) and Weymouth for those intending to walk the Dorset end of the Coast Path.

East Devon is also served by South West Trains with an hourly service from London Waterloo to Exeter St David's calling at Woking, Basingstoke and Salisbury to Axminster (for Lyme Regis & Seaton), Honiton (for Sidmouth).

The cost of rail tickets varies considerably depending on when you buy them and what time you travel. For the best deals, avoid travelling at peak times and book in advance. If you need to travel during peak time it can often work out cheaper to buy separate tickets for the same train, splitting them between the peak and off-peak part of your journey.

In addition, with a bit of planning you can make your journey even more special by using one of the heritage steam railways that go to the coast.

To book your tickets to the South West, you can visit:

- ⊕ **www.thetrainline.com**
- 🕔 **0871 244 1545 / 0333 202 2222 8am to 10pm**

- ⊕ **www.nationalrail.co.uk**
- 🕔 **03457 484950**

- ⊕ **www.traveline.info**

Bus Services

For information on buses to the South West, visit
- ⊕ **www.travelinesw.com**
or to buy tickets go to
- ⊕ **www.nationalexpress.com**
- **0871 781 8181** or **uk.megabus.com**
For Megabus timetable enquiries call
- 🕔 **+44 141 352 4444** open 24 hours a day or
- 🕔 **+44 900 1600 900** for booking a ticket from 7am to 10pm.

Tourist Information Centres (TICs) can be very helpful with bus enquiries. For details of all coastal TICs see page 197.

Dawlish railway

southwestcoastpath.org.uk

Airports

There are airports in or near towns close to the Coast Path. In Path order, they are:

Newquay Airport

Daily flights from London Gatwick and year round flights from Manchester and Isles of Scilly. Many more seasonal destinations. St Mawgan, Newquay, TR8 4RQ
- **01637 860600**
- info@cornwallairportnewquay.com
- www.newquaycornwallairport.com

Land's End

For flights to the Isles of Scilly: Information from Isles of Scilly Travel, Steamship House, Quay Street, Penzance, TR18 4BZ
- **+44 (0) 1736 334220**
- sales@islesofscilly-travel.co.uk
- www.islesofscilly-travel.co.uk

Exeter

Exeter International Airport, Exeter, EX5 2BD
- **01392 354 988**
- www.exeter-airport.co.uk

Bournemouth

Bournemouth Airport Ltd., Christchurch, Bournemouth BH23 6SE
- **01202 364000**
- www.bournemouthairport.com

Sea Transport

Brittany Ferries provide a ferry link as follows to the South West Coast Path: Plymouth/Roscoff; Poole/Cherbourg (Not Dec - Feb); Plymouth/Santander.

- **0330 159 7000**
- reservations@brittanyferries.com
- www.brittany-ferries.co.uk or contact by mail to Brittany Ferries, Millbay, Plymouth, Devon, PL1 3EW

· ·

The Trip Planning page of our website offers suggestions for how the Path can be completed as a series of day walks, using public transport www.southwestcoastpath.org.uk/walk-coast-path/trip-planning

Bus Information

Listed below, in Path order, are details of services and information available from County Councils and local bus operators; it is intended for guidance use only. All information provided is correct at the time of going to print; responsibility for any inaccuracies or changes cannot be accepted by County Councils or bus operators. For up to date bus service information, telephone the relevant numbers given in the following paragraphs.

Somerset

For service 28 from Taunton to Minehead. From Taunton you can get a bus to Lyme Regis or Weymouth changing at Exeter and Axminster. Use Traveline (details at top of page)
- www.firstgroup.com
- **0871 200 2233**

Somerset County Council can send you a free paper copy of the timetables
- **0300 123 2224**
- transport@somerset.gov.uk
- www.somerset.gov.uk

North Devon

The North Devon coast has a range of bus services which may be of use to coastal walkers. The greatest choice of coastal destinations is provided from Barnstaple.

Devon & Cornwall's First Buses are useful for those walking between North Devon and North Cornwall.

For timetable enquiries telephone
- Traveline **0871 200 2233** or go online at
- www.travelinesw.org.uk

Alternatively the Devon County Council web site has a variety of options. There is an interactive bus map to look at and also Area Bus Timetable Booklets to download:
- www.journeydevon.info

They do advise that previously printed timetables will vary from these digital guides, but that the digital guides are the most up to date.

If you find yourself at a bus stop and want to know when the next bus is coming along, find the eight letter reference number on the stop and text it to 84268. You will receive a reply with the times of the next three buses to come past that stop.

Cornwall

Cornwall Council have an informative website at **www.cornwallpublictransport.info** with up to date and full timetables and frequency guides for all the different operators.
There are weekday, evening and weekend timetables. On the site there is an Interactive Cornwall County Map, which shows all the bus lines and their numbers. All the main towns have bus routes to and from them but do check the times especially out of the main holiday times. We have not listed as much detail here as in previous years simply due to the changing nature of the timetables and technology making the information more readily available to people.

📞 Traveline: **0871 200 2233**
🌐 **www.travelinesw.com**

Also local bus operator First:
www.firstgroup.com Their information is included on the Cornwall Council site too.

Stagecoach run service 6A from Exeter to Bude, if you are coming to the South West by train this may be useful.

South Devon

The coastline between Plymouth and Exeter is accessible by bus from many inland towns. As for North Devon, the Devon County Council web site has a variety of options. There is an interactive bus map to look at and also Area Bus Timetable Booklets to download:
🌐 **www.journeydevon.info**

Also as for North Devon, when you are at a bus stop, use the 8 letter reference number on the bus stop and text it to 84268. You will receive a reply with the times of the next three buses to come past that stop.

For more timetable enquiries telephone
📞 Traveline **0871 200 2233** or go online at
🌐 **www.travelinesw.com**

The main operators are Stagecoach, First Group and Tally Ho.
🌐 **www.tallyhocoaches.co.uk**

For Plymouth Citybus map and services go to
🌐 **www.plymouth.gov.uk** and follow links for the transport section.

East Devon

The East Devon coastline is accessible by bus from Exeter, Ottery St. Mary, Honiton and Axminster. Trains are also available from London Waterloo stop at Axminster, Honiton and Exeter or the quicker train from London Paddington stops at Exeter as do trains coming from Bristol. Please note, as previously, that the summer and winter timetables do vary a lot.

Dorset

The Dorset Coast is accessible by bus from various inland points with train connections for the distant traveller. For a complete and up to date list of bus routes, timetables and bus numbers go to **www.dorsetforyou.com** and follow the links for Transport. There is a useful journey planner as well as individual timetables.

The sea tractor taking visitors to Burgh Island

southwestcoastpath.org.uk

15

COTSWOLD
outdoor

Let's Go Somewhere

Exclusive **15% discount*** for
South West Coast Path Association
members in-store and online.

Proud to support

South West
Coast Path
Association

Stores nationwide | cotswoldoutdoor.com

Ferries & River Crossings

The nature of the Coast Path means that many ferries must be used to cross estuaries along the length of the Path. It is recommended the ferry operator be contacted direct for the service to be used. Please do this especially when a fairly late timing is expected and it is necessary to confirm the time of the last run. Also do this when using outside the main tourist season or if use by a party of walkers is planned.

All information correct at time of going to print. Ferries can be subject to change due to weather conditions and tides.

We have attempted to list those directly necessary. The ferry crossings encountered, in Path order, are: River Torridge (Instow/Appledore) (optional); River Camel (Rock/Padstow); River Gannel (Newquay/Crantock); Helford River (Helford/Helford Passage); Fal Estuary (Falmouth/St Mawes and St Mawes/Place); River Fowey (Fowey/Polruan); River Tamar (Cremyll/Plymouth); River Yealm (Wembury/Noss Mayo); River Avon (Bigbury-on-Sea/Bantham); River Dart (Dartmouth/Kingswear); River Teign (Shaldon/Teignmouth); River Exe (Starcross/Exmouth, Turf/Topsham); Weymouth Harbour.

Instow/Appledore (River Torridge)

⊕ www.appledoreinstowferry.com
⊖ contact@appledoreinstowferry.com

This service is an optional means of crossing the Torridge without passing through Bideford. Since the ferry is bound by tides, operating times vary daily so walkers are urged to check the website for operating times, but it generally runs for 2 hours either side of high tide.

The ferry will operate from early April until October.

Padstow/Rock (River Camel)

☎ 01841 532239
⊕ www.padstow-harbour.co.uk
⊖ padstowharbour@btconnect.com

The ferry will depart from one of two points in Padstow depending on tides. On big spring tides ferry may disembark at Daymer Bay over the extreme low water period.

Ferry runs every 20 minutes from Padstow starting at 08:00am. November to 31 March the last ferry from Padstow: 4.50pm and from Rock: 4.30pm. April to 31 May the last ferry from Padstow: 5.50pm and from Rock: 5.30pm. June to mid July and first two weeks in September last ferry from Padstow: 6.50pm and from Rock: 6.30pm. Mid July to 31 August the last ferry from Padstow: 7.50pm and from Rock: 7.30pm. 1st to mid Sept last ferry from Padstow 6.50pm and 6.30pm from Rock. Mid Sept to end Oct 5.50pm from Padstow and 5.30 from Rock.

Water taxi

An evening water taxi service operates between Rock and Padstow between 19:00 and midnight from Easter to end October apart from mid-July to the end of August when we start at 19.31, weather and tides permitting.

☎ 01208 862815 (9am to 5pm)
⊕ www.rock-watertaxi.co.uk
⊖ info@rock-watertaxi.co.uk
Or contact the boat direct on 07778 105297.

Newquay/Crantock (River Gannel)

Fern Pit Ferry, Fern Pit, Riverside Crescent, Newquay, Cornwall TR7 1PJ

☎ 01637 873181
⊕ www.fernpit.co.uk
⊖ mail@fernpit.co.uk

Ferry operates as follows: End May to mid September continuous, 7 days a week, 10:00-18:00. Weather dependent.

Gillan Creek

Sailaway St. Anthony Ltd

☎ 01326 231357
⊕ www.sailawaystanthony.co.uk
⊖ info@stanthony.co.uk

Ferry operates April 1st to October 31st on demand during normal office hours. It runs approx 3 hours either side of high tide when the stepping stones are submerged. Alternatively, Telstar Taxis can take walkers around the river. **Tel: 01326 221007**

Helford River

River Boats, Helford Passage, Falmouth, Cornwall TR1 5HP

☎ 01326 250770
⊕ www.helford-river-boats.co.uk
⊖ ian@helford-river-boats.co.uk

Ferry operates Good Friday to 31st October 09:30 to 17:00 daily on demand. July & August ferry may run into the evening. It is possible to use local taxi services if the ferry is not operating. Alternatively, Telstar Taxis can take walkers around the river. **Tel: 01326 221007**

Falmouth to St Mawes (River Fal)

Cornwall Ferries

☎ 01326 741194
⊕ www.falriver.co.uk

Ferry operates all year. June-October 3 ferries per hour, fewer at other times. Ferries run from either Prince of Wales Pier or Custom House Quay so please check before setting off.

St Mawes - Place Ferry across Percuil River
Cornwall Ferries (see overleaf)
- 📞 01326 741194
- 🌐 www.falriver.co.uk
- ✉ info@falriver.co.uk

In March, April May, October and November the ferry runs on demand. From 1st June to 30th September it runs every half hour. If needed, it is advisable to telephone 2-3 days in advance in the Summer.
- 📞 07522 446659
- 🌐 www.falmouthwatertaxi.co.uk

St Mawes Kayaks also offer a water taxi service: Telephone 07971 846786 or visit www.stmaweskayaks.co.uk

Fowey/Polruan (River Fowey)
- 📞 01726 870232
- 🌐 www.ctomsandson.co.uk
- ✉ enquiries@ctomsandson.co.uk

Polruan Ferry Co Ltd, Toms Yard, East Street Polruan-by-Fowey, Cornwall PL23 1PB
Ferry operates all year at 10-15 min intervals.
07:00 to 23:00 1st May-30th September
(Saturdays 07:30 start, Sundays 09:00 start)
07:00 to 19:00 1st October-30th April (Saturdays 07:30 start, Sundays 10:00 to 17:00).
During winter months and summer evenings, ferry runs to Town Quay (centre of Fowey). During summer months, daytime service runs to Whitehouse slipway (situated on the Esplanade).

Cremyll/Plymouth
Cremyll Ferry, Cremyll Quay, Cremyll, Torpoint, Cornwall PL10 1HX
- 📞 01752 822105
- 🌐 www.cremyll-ferry.co.uk

The ferry operates depending on weather, tides and other circumstances permitting.
All year round at 30 minute intervals.
Summer Service from 1st April to 30th September.
From Mt Edgcumbe:
Weekdays 06:45 to 20:30, Saturdays 08:00 to 21:30, Sundays 09:00 to 21:00.
From Plymouth:
Weekdays 07:15 to 20:45. Saturdays 08:15 to 21:45, Sundays 09:15 to 21:15.
Winter Service from 1st October to 31st March.
From Mt Edgcumbe: Weekdays 06:45 to 18:30.
Saturdays 08:00 to 18:30. Sundays 09:00 to 18:00.
From Plymouth: Weekdays 07:15 to 18:45.
Saturdays 08:15 to 18:45. Sundays 09:15 to 18:15.
Closed Christmas, Boxing & New Year's Days
We urge you to contact the ferry operator direct if you are relying on this service, particularly if you are anticipating a fairly late finish and need to confirm the time of its last run.

Sutton Harbour/Mount Batten
Mount Batten Ferry
- 📞 07930 838614
- 🌐 www.mountbattenferry.co.uk
- ✉ mountbattenferry@gmail.com

All year round, every ½ hour.
Summer weekdays 07:45 to 23:00, Saturday 08:45 to 22:30 and Sunday 08:45 – 18:15
Winter weekdays 07:45 – 18:15, Saturday 08:45 - 23:00 and Sunday 08:45 – 18:15
We urge you to contact the ferry operator direct if you are relying on this service, particularly if you are anticipating a fairly late finish and need to confirm the time of its last run.

Wembury (Warren Point)/Noss Mayo (River Yealm)
- 📞 **Bill Gregor: 07817 132757**

Ferry operates 26 March until 30 September, 10:00 to 16:00. In quieter times ie poor weather, service may be restricted to the core hours of 10:00 to 12:00 & 15:00 to 16:00.
Use the signal board to attract the ferryman's attention.

Eco-Taxi based in Kingsbridge will carry walkers between Plymouth and Dartmouth and from all estuaries in South Devon.
- 📞 07811 385275.

Alternatively, **Ivy Cabs** may also carry walkers round the South Hams estuaries.
- 📞 01752 696969

Mothecombe/Wonwell (River Erme)
There is no ferry at the River Erme - please refer to page 20. Alternatively, Wembury Cars will carry walkers.
- 📞 01752 863710

Bigbury/Bantham (River Avon)
Marsh Dawes, The Boathouse, Bantham, Kingsbridge, Devon
- 📞 01548 561196
- 📞 07837 361306

Ferry operates May to September daily except Sundays, 10:00 to 11:00 and 15:00 to 16:00.
Eco-Taxi based in Kingsbridge will carry walkers between Plymouth and Dartmouth and from all estuaries in South Devon 07811 385275
Alternatively, **Ivy Cabs** may also carry walkers round the South Hams estuaries 01752 696969

Salcombe to East Portlemouth Ferry
The Salcombe Ferry, Simon Shortman
☎ 01548 842061/07769 319375

Ferry operates all year: November – March every half hour and continuously April – October. Please note that the ferry point is Jubilee Pier in summer & Whitestrand Pontoon in winter. We urge you to contact the ferry operator direct if you are relying on this service, particularly if you are anticipating a fairly late finish and need to confirm the time of its last run.

Dartmouth/Kingswear (River Dart)
Sat Nav Codes – Kingswear TQ6 0AA
Dartmouth TQ6 9AP
☎ 01803 752342
⊕ www.southhams.gov.uk
DartmouthLowerFerry
Email: clare.thomas@southhams.gov.uk

Ferry operates all year on a continuous service 07:00 to 22:45, Sundays 08:00 to 22:45

Dartmouth Passenger Ferry
(River Dart)
Dartmouth Steam Railway & River Boat Co.
5 Lower Street, Dartmouth TQ6 9AJ
☎ 01803 555872
⊕ www.dartmouthrailriver.co.uk

Ferry operates all year on a continuous service 07:30 to 23:10, Sundays 09:00 to 23:10. Check web for specific times.

Shaldon/Teignmouth
Ferry operated by Greg Allen
☎ 07896 711822 / 07940503314
⊕ www.teignmouthshaldonferry.co.uk

April – End July	08:00 to 18:00
End July – End Aug	08:00 to dusk
September – October	08:00 to 18:00
November – January	08:00 to 16:30
February – March	08:00 to 17:00
Winter Weekends	Starts at 10:00
Summer Weekends	Starts at 09:00

Service operates between Teignmouth back beach, near the Lifeboat House and Shaldon Beach running daily, with restricted service in winter. Ferry runs on demand and approximately every 10-15 minutes in busy periods. We do not run on Christmas Day or New Year's Day.

Starcross/Exmouth (River Exe)
Exe to Sea Cruises, Mr Mark Rackley
☎ 01626 774770 / 07974 022536

Ferry operates mid-April – end October, hourly, 7 days a week. From Starcross,on the hour from 10:10 until 16:10, until 17:10 (mid-May to mid September). From Exmouth, on the half hour from 10:40 until 16:40 (Easter and October), until 17:40 (mid-May and June-mid September).

Turf/Topsham (River Exe)
Steve Garrett Tel: 07778 370582
⊕ www.topshamtoturfferry.co.uk
✉ seadreamferry@gmail.com

Ferry operates weekends Easter - end May. Daily June – August. Weekends in September, from Turf 11:45 to 15:00 and from Topsham 11:30 to 14:15. In peak season ferry runs until 16:00 from Turf and 15:15 from Topsham.

Topsham Ferry (River Exe)
(between Topsham Quay riverside and Topsham Lock canalside)
Exeter City Council, Canals and Rivers Department
☎ 01392 274306 (office)
☎ 07801 203338 (ferryman).

This service is tide dependent - please check tide times. Ferry operates Easter-September 09:30-17:00 daily except Tuesdays (tide dependent but may also be available outside these times weather and tide permitting). October-March ferry operates 11:00-17:00 or sunset on weekends and Bank Holidays (tide dependent). Wave or phone ferryman for service (on above number).

Weymouth Harbour
Weymouth and Portland Borough Council, Harbour Master's Office,
13 Custom House Quay, Weymouth DT4 8BG
☎ 01305 838423
⊕ www.weymouth-harbour.co.uk

From April, Ferries operate (rowing boats), but are weather dependant.

South Haven Point to Sandbanks, Poole
Shell Bay/Sandbanks (Mouth of Poole Harbour)
Bournemouth - Swanage Motor Road & Ferry Company, Shell Bay, Studland BH19 3BA
☎ 01929 450203   Fax: 01929 450498
⊕ www.sandbanksferry.co.uk

All year round. Daily every 20 mins.
Sandbanks 07:00 to 23:00 hrs
Shell Bay 07:10 to 23:10 hrs
Christmas Day every half hour.

If you are relying on a ferry service we urge you to contact the ferry operator direct, particularly if you anticipate a fairly late finish and need to confirm the time of its last run.

Tide Times

The tide times included in this edition refer to the times of low water at Devonport. These tables act as a guide only for those wishing to paddle across the Gannel (Newquay) or the Erme. Please be sure to read the warnings given under the relevant section in the Guide. Walkers of the Coast Path are advised not to wade across any of the other estuaries around the route. Walkers should consult the local tide times.

Those crossing the Gannel or Erme should note that there can be considerable differences in height between spring and neap tides; and the information below should be used for general timing guidance only. Again, details are available in tide tables locally.

- Newquay (The Gannel) deduct 30 minutes
- River Erme as at Devonport

TIDE TIMES FOR 2018

JANUARY		LOW TIDE Morning		LOW TIDE Afternoon	
		Time	Height	Time	Height
1	Monday	1104	0.9	2328	0.8
2	Tuesday	1156	0.7		
3	Wednesday	0019	0.7	1247	0.5
4	Thursday	0107	0.6	1335	0.5
5	Friday	0153	0.7	1421	0.6
6	Saturday	0238	0.8	1505	0.8
7	Sunday	0320	1.1	1549	1.1
8	Monday	0404	1.4	1633	1.5
9	Tuesday	0450	1.7	1723	1.8
10	Wednesday	0544	2.0	1821	2.0
11	Thursday	0650	2.2	1932	2.1
12	Friday	0806	2.1	2043	2.0
13	Saturday	0914	2.0	2142	1.8
14	Sunday	1009	1.7	2230	1.6
15	Monday	1054	1.5	2312	1.4
16	Tuesday	1135	1.3	2350	1.3
17	Wednesday			1211	1.2
18	Thursday	0024	1.2	1245	1.2
19	Friday	0056	1.2	1317	1.2
20	Saturday	0126	1.2	1348	1.2
21	Sunday	0156	1.3	1419	1.3
22	Monday	0227	1.4	1451	1.4
23	Tuesday	0302	1.5	1529	1.5
24	Wednesday	0343	1.6	1614	1.7
25	Thursday	0434	1.8	1713	1.9
26	Friday	0544	2.0	1832	2.0
27	Saturday	0715	2.0	1959	1.8
28	Sunday	0840	1.8	2115	1.6
29	Monday	0951	1.4	2220	1.2
30	Tuesday	1052	1.0	2317	0.9
31	Wednesday	1146	0.7		

FEBRUARY		LOW TIDE Morning		LOW TIDE Afternoon	
		Time	Height	Time	Height
1	Thursday	0008	0.6	1237	0.4
2	Friday	0056	0.4	1323	0.3
3	Saturday	0140	0.4	1406	0.3
4	Sunday	0221	0.5	1446	0.5
5	Monday	0259	0.8	1523	0.9
6	Tuesday	0336	1.1	1559	1.3
7	Wednesday	0413	1.5	1638	1.7
8	Thursday	0456	1.9	1724	2.0
9	Friday	0551	2.2	1824	2.3
10	Saturday	0701	2.3	1939	2.3
11	Sunday	0824	2.2	2100	2.1
12	Monday	0938	1.9	2202	1.8
13	Tuesday	1030	1.6	2249	1.5
14	Wednesday	1113	1.4	2329	1.3
15	Thursday	1152	1.1		
16	Friday	0005	1.1	1228	1.0
17	Saturday	0040	1.0	1301	0.9
18	Sunday	0112	1.0	1333	0.9
19	Monday	0143	1.0	1404	1.0
20	Tuesday	0214	1.0	1435	1.1
21	Wednesday	0246	1.1	1509	1.2
22	Thursday	0323	1.3	1549	1.5
23	Friday	0409	1.6	1641	1.7
24	Saturday	0511	1.9	1754	2.0
25	Sunday	0642	2.0	1933	2.0
26	Monday	0823	1.9	2101	1.7
27	Tuesday	0941	1.4	2210	1.3
28	Wednesday	1042	1.0	2306	0.9

MARCH

		LOW TIDE Morning		LOW TIDE Afternoon	
		Time	Height	Time	Height
1	Thursday	1134	0.6	2355	0.5
2	Friday			1221	0.3
3	Saturday	0040	0.3	1305	0.2
4	Sunday	0122	0.3	1345	0.2
5	Monday	0200	0.4	1421	0.4
6	Tuesday	0234	0.6	1454	0.8
7	Wednesday	0306	1.0	1525	1.2
8	Thursday	0337	1.4	1556	1.6
9	Friday	0413	1.8	1634	2.0
10	Saturday	0502	2.1	1731	2.3
11	Sunday	0612	2.4	1846	2.4
12	Monday	0731	2.3	2007	2.3
13	Tuesday	0854	2.1	2123	2.0
14	Wednesday	0957	1.7	2217	1.6
15	Thursday	1043	1.3	2301	1.3
16	Friday	1124	1.1	2340	1.0
17	Saturday			1202	0.9
18	Sunday	0017	0.9	1238	0.7
19	Monday	0052	0.8	1313	0.7
20	Tuesday	0126	0.7	1346	0.7
21	Wednesday	0158	0.8	1419	0.8
22	Thursday	0232	0.9	1453	1.1
23	Friday	0309	1.2	1533	1.4
24	Saturday	0354	1.5	1623	1.7
25	Sunday	0456	1.8	1735	2.0
26	Monday	0627	2.0	1917	2.1
27	Tuesday	0814	1.8	2050	1.8
28	Wednesday	0929	1.4	2156	1.3
29	Thursday	1027	0.9	2249	0.9
30	Friday	1116	0.5	2336	0.5
31	Saturday			1201	0.3

APRIL

		LOW TIDE Morning		LOW TIDE Afternoon	
		Time	Height	Time	Height
1	Sunday	0019	0.3	1242	0.2
2	Monday	0059	0.3	1320	0.3
3	Tuesday	0134	0.4	1354	0.5
4	Wednesday	0207	0.7	1424	0.9
5	Thursday	0236	1.0	1451	1.2
6	Friday	0305	1.4	1518	1.6
7	Saturday	0335	1.7	1548	2.0
8	Sunday	0417	2.1	1639	2.3
9	Monday	0528	2.3	1802	2.5
10	Tuesday	0647	2.3	1920	2.4
11	Wednesday	0803	2.1	2033	2.1
12	Thursday	0909	1.7	2134	1.7
13	Friday	1002	1.4	2224	1.3
14	Saturday	1048	1.1	2308	1.0
15	Sunday	1131	0.8	2350	0.8
16	Monday			1211	0.7
17	Tuesday	0029	0.7	1250	0.6
18	Wednesday	0107	0.6	1327	0.6
19	Thursday	0144	0.6	1404	0.8
20	Friday	0221	0.8	1442	1.0
21	Saturday	0302	1.1	1525	1.3
22	Sunday	0350	1.4	1617	1.7
23	Monday	0453	1.7	1729	2.0
24	Tuesday	0621	1.9	1903	2.0
25	Wednesday	0757	1.7	2030	1.8
26	Thursday	0908	1.4	2133	1.4
27	Friday	1004	1.0	2225	1.0
28	Saturday	1052	0.7	2312	0.7
29	Sunday	1135	0.5	2354	0.6
30	Monday			1216	0.5

MAY

		LOW TIDE Morning		LOW TIDE Afternoon	
		Time	Height	Time	Height
1	Tuesday	0032	0.5	1253	0.6
2	Wednesday	0108	0.6	1326	0.8
3	Thursday	0140	0.8	1355	1.0
4	Friday	0209	1.1	1421	1.3
5	Saturday	0236	1.4	1447	1.6
6	Sunday	0305	1.7	1514	1.9
7	Monday	0342	2.0	1556	2.2
8	Tuesday	0444	2.2	1713	2.4
9	Wednesday	0603	2.2	1835	2.3
10	Thursday	0715	2.1	1945	2.1
11	Friday	0820	1.8	2048	1.8
12	Saturday	0918	1.4	2143	1.4
13	Sunday	1010	1.1	2233	1.1
14	Monday	1058	0.9	2321	0.8
15	Tuesday	1144	0.7		
16	Wednesday	0005	0.7	1228	0.6
17	Thursday	0049	0.6	1311	0.6
18	Friday	0132	0.6	1353	0.7
19	Saturday	0215	0.7	1436	0.9
20	Sunday	0300	1.0	1522	1.2
21	Monday	0351	1.3	1616	1.6
22	Tuesday	0451	1.5	1720	1.8
23	Wednesday	0605	1.7	1838	1.9
24	Thursday	0726	1.7	1956	1.8
25	Friday	0836	1.5	2101	1.5
26	Saturday	0933	1.2	2156	1.2
27	Sunday	1023	1.0	2244	1.0
28	Monday	1108	0.9	2327	0.9
29	Tuesday	1149	0.8		
30	Wednesday	0007	0.9	1226	0.9
31	Thursday	0043	0.9	1259	1.0

JUNE

		LOW TIDE Morning		LOW TIDE Afternoon	
		Time	Height	Time	Height
1	Friday	0115	1.0	1329	1.2
2	Saturday	0145	1.2	1357	1.4
3	Sunday	0214	1.4	1424	1.6
4	Monday	0244	1.6	1453	1.8
5	Tuesday	0318	1.8	1531	2.0
6	Wednesday	0405	1.9	1625	2.1
7	Thursday	0511	2.0	1740	2.2
8	Friday	0625	2.0	1855	2.1
9	Saturday	0733	1.8	2002	1.9
10	Sunday	0835	1.5	2104	1.5
11	Monday	0933	1.3	2201	1.2
12	Tuesday	1028	1.0	2254	0.9
13	Wednesday	1119	0.8	2345	0.7
14	Thursday			1209	0.7
15	Friday	0034	0.6	1257	0.6
16	Saturday	0122	0.5	1344	0.7
17	Sunday	0210	0.6	1431	0.8
18	Monday	0257	0.8	1518	1.0
19	Tuesday	0346	1.0	1607	1.3
20	Wednesday	0439	1.3	1701	1.6
21	Thursday	0537	1.5	1803	1.8
22	Friday	0644	1.7	1912	1.8
23	Saturday	0754	1.7	2021	1.8
24	Sunday	0857	1.6	2122	1.6
25	Monday	0952	1.4	2215	1.4
26	Tuesday	1040	1.3	2301	1.2
27	Wednesday	1123	1.2	2343	1.1
28	Thursday			1202	1.1
29	Friday	0021	1.1	1237	1.2
30	Saturday	0055	1.1	1309	1.2

JULY

		LOW TIDE Morning		LOW TIDE Afternoon	
		Time	Height	Time	Height
1	Sunday	0127	1.2	1338	1.3
2	Monday	0156	1.3	1407	1.5
3	Tuesday	0226	1.4	1436	1.6
4	Wednesday	0258	1.5	1509	1.7
5	Thursday	0335	1.7	1550	1.8
6	Friday	0423	1.8	1645	2.0
7	Saturday	0526	1.9	1757	2.0
8	Sunday	0642	1.8	1916	1.9
9	Monday	0755	1.7	2028	1.7
10	Tuesday	0902	1.4	2133	1.4
11	Wednesday	1003	1.2	2233	1.1
12	Thursday	1101	0.9	2330	0.8
13	Friday	1155	0.7		
14	Saturday	0022	0.5	1246	0.6
15	Sunday	0113	0.4	1335	0.5
16	Monday	0201	0.4	1421	0.6
17	Tuesday	0247	0.5	1505	0.8
18	Wednesday	0331	0.8	1548	1.0
19	Thursday	0415	1.1	1633	1.4
20	Friday	0502	1.4	1723	1.7
21	Saturday	0556	1.7	1822	1.9
22	Sunday	0700	1.9	1932	2.0
23	Monday	0813	1.9	2045	1.9
24	Tuesday	0920	1.8	2147	1.7
25	Wednesday	1014	1.6	2238	1.5
26	Thursday	1100	1.4	2322	1.3
27	Friday	1141	1.3		
28	Saturday	0001	1.2	1218	1.2
29	Sunday	0037	1.1	1250	1.2
30	Monday	0109	1.1	1320	1.2
31	Tuesday	0138	1.2	1349	1.3

AUGUST

		LOW TIDE Morning		LOW TIDE Afternoon	
		Time	Height	Time	Height
1	Wednesday	0207	1.2	1417	1.4
2	Thursday	0236	1.3	1447	1.5
3	Friday	0309	1.4	1523	1.6
4	Saturday	0348	1.6	1607	1.8
5	Sunday	0439	1.8	1707	1.9
6	Monday	0549	1.9	1832	2.0
7	Tuesday	0718	1.9	2000	1.9
8	Wednesday	0838	1.7	2115	1.5
9	Thursday	0947	1.4	2220	1.1
10	Friday	1048	1.0	2318	0.8
11	Saturday	1143	0.7		
12	Sunday	0011	0.5	1234	0.5
13	Monday	0100	0.3	1320	0.4
14	Tuesday	0145	0.2	1404	0.4
15	Wednesday	0227	0.4	1444	0.6
16	Thursday	0307	0.7	1522	0.9
17	Friday	0345	1.0	1600	1.3
18	Saturday	0423	1.5	1642	1.7
19	Sunday	0507	1.9	1733	2.1
20	Monday	0604	2.2	1840	2.3
21	Tuesday	0719	2.3	2003	2.3
22	Wednesday	0845	2.2	2121	2.0
23	Thursday	0949	1.9	2216	1.7
24	Friday	1037	1.6	2300	1.4
25	Saturday	1118	1.3	2339	1.2
26	Sunday	1155	1.2		
27	Monday	0014	1.1	1229	1.1
28	Tuesday	0046	1.0	1259	1.1
29	Wednesday	0116	1.0	1328	1.1
30	Thursday	0145	1.0	1357	1.2
31	Friday	0214	1.1	1426	1.3

SEPTEMBER

		LOW TIDE Morning		LOW TIDE Afternoon	
		Time	Height	Time	Height
1	Saturday	0245	1.3	1459	1.4
2	Sunday	0321	1.5	1540	1.7
3	Monday	0407	1.8	1635	1.9
4	Tuesday	0512	2.0	1800	2.1
5	Wednesday	0652	2.1	1944	2.0
6	Thursday	0825	1.9	2106	1.6
7	Friday	0937	1.5	2210	1.2
8	Saturday	1037	1.0	2306	0.7
9	Sunday	1129	0.7	2355	0.4
10	Monday			1216	0.4
11	Tuesday	0041	0.2	1300	0.3
12	Wednesday	0123	0.2	1341	0.4
13	Thursday	0202	0.4	1418	0.6
14	Friday	0238	0.7	1452	0.9
15	Saturday	0310	1.1	1526	1.4
16	Sunday	0343	1.6	1602	1.8
17	Monday	0421	2.0	1649	2.2
18	Tuesday	0515	2.4	1755	2.5
19	Wednesday	0630	2.5	1918	2.5
20	Thursday	0800	2.4	2048	2.2
21	Friday	0918	2.1	2147	1.8
22	Saturday	1008	1.7	2230	1.5
23	Sunday	1049	1.4	2309	1.2
24	Monday	1126	1.2	2344	1.0
25	Tuesday			1201	1.0
26	Wednesday	0018	0.9	1234	1.0
27	Thursday	0051	0.9	1306	1.0
28	Friday	0122	0.9	1336	1.0
29	Saturday	0153	1.0	1408	1.1
30	Sunday	0225	1.2	1442	1.3

OCTOBER

		LOW TIDE Morning		LOW TIDE Afternoon	
		Time	Height	Time	Height
1	Monday	0301	1.5	1523	1.6
2	Tuesday	0347	1.8	1619	2.0
3	Wednesday	0453	2.2	1746	2.2
4	Thursday	0638	2.3	1936	2.1
5	Friday	0816	2.0	2056	1.6
6	Saturday	0925	1.5	2156	1.1
7	Sunday	1021	1.1	2248	0.7
8	Monday	1110	0.7	2334	0.5
9	Tuesday	1155	0.5		
10	Wednesday	0017	0.3	1237	0.4
11	Thursday	0058	0.4	1315	0.5
12	Friday	0134	0.6	1350	0.7
13	Saturday	0207	0.9	1422	1.1
14	Sunday	0236	1.3	1453	1.5
15	Monday	0305	1.7	1526	1.9
16	Tuesday	0336	2.1	1608	2.2
17	Wednesday	0424	2.5	1713	2.5
18	Thursday	0544	2.7	1833	2.6
19	Friday	0708	2.6	1954	2.3
20	Saturday	0827	2.3	2100	2.0
21	Sunday	0924	1.9	2149	1.6
22	Monday	1010	1.5	2231	1.3
23	Tuesday	1051	1.3	2310	1.1
24	Wednesday	1130	1.1	2348	0.9
25	Thursday			1207	0.9
26	Friday	0025	0.9	1244	0.9
27	Saturday	0101	0.9	1319	0.9
28	Sunday	0136	1.0	1355	1.1
29	Monday	0212	1.2	1433	1.3
30	Tuesday	0251	1.5	1518	1.6
31	Wednesday	0340	1.9	1617	1.9

NOVEMBER		LOW TIDE Morning		LOW TIDE Afternoon	
		Time	Height	Time	Height
1	Thursday	0448	2.2	1741	2.1
2	Friday	0624	2.3	1920	2.0
3	Saturday	0757	2.0	2036	1.6
4	Sunday	0904	1.6	2135	1.2
5	Monday	0958	1.2	2225	0.9
6	Tuesday	1046	0.9	2310	0.7
7	Wednesday	1131	0.7	2352	0.6
8	Thursday			1211	0.7
9	Friday	0031	0.7	1249	0.8
10	Saturday	0106	0.9	1324	0.9
11	Sunday	0138	1.1	1356	1.2
12	Monday	0207	1.4	1426	1.5
13	Tuesday	0234	1.7	1457	1.8
14	Wednesday	0302	2.1	1533	2.1
15	Thursday	0340	2.3	1629	2.4
16	Friday	0450	2.6	1744	2.5
17	Saturday	0615	2.6	1859	2.4
18	Sunday	0729	2.4	2004	2.1
19	Monday	0832	2.1	2101	1.7
20	Tuesday	0926	1.7	2150	1.4
21	Wednesday	1014	1.4	2236	1.2
22	Thursday	1059	1.2	2320	1.0
23	Friday	1142	1.0		
24	Saturday	0002	0.9	1225	0.9
25	Sunday	0043	0.9	1306	0.9
26	Monday	0124	1.0	1348	1.0
27	Tuesday	0206	1.1	1432	1.2
28	Wednesday	0250	1.4	1521	1.4
29	Thursday	0341	1.7	1618	1.7
30	Friday	0443	1.9	1728	1.9

DECEMBER		LOW TIDE Morning		LOW TIDE Afternoon	
		Time	Height	Time	Height
1	Saturday	0600	2.1	1850	1.9
2	Sunday	0723	2.0	2004	1.7
3	Monday	0833	1.8	2106	1.5
4	Tuesday	0931	1.5	2158	1.2
5	Wednesday	1021	1.2	2245	1.1
6	Thursday	1107	1.1	2328	1.0
7	Friday	1148	1.0		
8	Saturday	0007	1.0	1227	1.0
9	Sunday	0043	1.1	1303	1.1
10	Monday	0115	1.2	1335	1.3
11	Tuesday	0145	1.4	1406	1.5
12	Wednesday	0213	1.6	1436	1.7
13	Thursday	0241	1.9	1509	1.9
14	Friday	0313	2.1	1548	2.1
15	Saturday	0358	2.3	1644	2.2
16	Sunday	0505	2.4	1757	2.3
17	Monday	0626	2.4	1908	2.2
18	Tuesday	0738	2.2	2012	1.9
19	Wednesday	0841	1.9	2110	1.6
20	Thursday	0938	1.6	2204	1.3
21	Friday	1031	1.3	2254	1.1
22	Saturday	1121	1.0	2343	0.9
23	Sunday			1210	0.8
24	Monday	0030	0.8	1258	0.8
25	Tuesday	0117	0.8	1345	0.8
26	Wednesday	0203	0.9	1432	0.9
27	Thursday	0249	1.1	1519	1.1
28	Friday	0336	1.3	1609	1.3
29	Saturday	0427	1.6	1703	1.6
30	Sunday	0525	1.8	1806	1.8
31	Monday	0634	2.0	1918	1.9

TIDE TIMES FOR 2019

JANUARY		LOW TIDE Morning		LOW TIDE Afternoon	
		Time	Height	Time	Height
1	Thursday	07 50	2.0	20 29	1.8
2	Wednesday	08 59	1.8	21 29	1.6
3	Thursday	09 56	1.6	22 21	1.5
4	Friday	10 45	1.4	23 07	1.3
5	Saturday	11 30	1.3	23 48	1.2
6	Sunday			12 10	1.2
7	Monday	00 25	1.2	12 47	1.2
8	Tuesday	00 59	1.2	13 20	1.2
9	Wednesday	01 29	1.3	13 50	1.3
10	Thursday	01 57	1.4	14 19	1.5
11	Friday	02 24	1.6	14 47	1.6
12	Saturday	02 52	1.7	15 18	1.7
13	Sunday	03 26	1.9	15 56	1.9
14	Monday	04 10	2.0	16 47	2.0
15	Tuesday	05 11	2.2	17 59	2.1
16	Wednesday	06 34	2.2	19 20	2.0
17	Thursday	07 57	2.0	20 32	1.8
18	Friday	09 06	1.7	21 36	1.5
19	Saturday	10 09	1.4	22 35	1.2
20	Sunday	11 06	1.0	23 30	0.9
21	Monday	11 59	0.7		
22	Tuesday	00 21	0.7	12 50	0.5
23	Wednesday	01 10	0.6	13 38	0.4
24	Thursday	01 56	0.5	14 23	0.5
25	Friday	02 40	0.7	15 07	0.6
26	Saturday	03 22	0.9	15 49	0.9
27	Sunday	04 04	1.2	16 33	1.3
28	Monday	04 50	1.6	17 21	1.7
29	Tuesday	05 44	1.9	18 21	2.0
30	Wednesday	06 54	2.1	19 38	2.1
31	Thursday	08 20	2.1	20 59	2.0

FEBRUARY		LOW TIDE Morning		LOW TIDE Afternoon	
		Time	Height	Time	Height
1	Friday	09 33	1.9	22 00	1.8
2	Saturday	10 28	1.6	22 50	1.5
3	Sunday	11 14	1.4	23 32	1.3
4	Monday	11 55	1.2		
5	Tuesday	00 10	1.2	12 32	1.1
6	Wednesday	00 44	1.1	13 05	1.1
7	Thursday	01 14	1.1	13 33	1.1
8	Friday	01 40	1.2	13 59	1.2
9	Saturday	02 05	1.3	14 25	1.3
10	Sunday	02 31	1.4	14 52	1.4
11	Monday	03 01	1.5	15 24	1.5
12	Tuesday	03 37	1.7	16 05	1.7
13	Wednesday	04 25	1.9	17 01	2.0
14	Thursday	05 35	2.1	18 25	2.1
15	Friday	07 14	2.1	19 59	2.0
16	Saturday	08 41	1.8	21 16	1.7
17	Sunday	09 53	1.4	22 21	1.3
18	Monday	10 54	1.0	23 18	0.8
19	Tuesday	11 48	0.6		
20	Wednesday	00 10	0.5	12 38	0.3
21	Thursday	00 57	0.3	13 24	0.1
22	Friday	01 41	0.2	14 06	0.2
23	Saturday	02 22	0.3	14 46	0.4
24	Sunday	03 00	0.6	15 24	0.7
25	Monday	03 38	1.0	16 01	1.2
26	Tuesday	04 16	1.4	16 40	1.6
27	Wednesday	05 02	1.8	17 30	2.1
28	Thursday	06 03	2.2	18 39	2.3

southwestcoastpath.org.uk

TIDE TIMES 2019

MARCH		LOW TIDE Morning		LOW TIDE Afternoon	
		Time	Height	Time	Height
1	Friday	07 27	2.3	20 18	2.3
2	Saturday	09 10	2.1	21 39	2.0
3	Sunday	10 10	1.7	22 30	1.6
4	Monday	10 55	1.4	23 12	1.3
5	Tuesday	11 35	1.1	23 50	1.1
6	Wednesday			12 11	1.0
7	Thursday	00 23	1.0	12 42	0.9
8	Friday	00 53	1.0	13 10	0.9
9	Saturday	01 19	1.0	13 36	1.0
10	Sunday	01 44	1.0	14 02	1.0
11	Monday	02 10	1.1	14 29	1.2
12	Tuesday	02 39	1.2	14 59	1.3
13	Wednesday	03 13	1.4	15 37	1.6
14	Thursday	03 58	1.7	16 28	1.9
15	Friday	05 03	2.0	17 48	2.1
16	Saturday	06 46	2.1	19 35	2.1
17	Sunday	08 25	1.8	21 01	1.7
18	Monday	09 40	1.3	22 08	1.2
19	Tuesday	10 40	0.8	23 03	0.8
20	Wednesday	11 32	0.4	23 53	0.4
21	Thursday			12 19	0.1
22	Friday	00 38	0.2	13 03	0.0
23	Saturday	01 21	0.1	13 44	0.1
24	Sunday	01 59	0.2	14 21	0.4
25	Monday	02 36	0.5	14 56	0.7
26	Tuesday	03 10	0.9	15 29	1.2
27	Wednesday	03 46	1.4	16 05	1.7
28	Thursday	04 28	1.8	16 51	2.1
29	Friday	05 25	2.2	17 55	2.4
30	Saturday	06 41	2.4	19 20	2.4
31	Sunday	08 29	2.2	21 02	2.2

APRIL		LOW TIDE Morning		LOW TIDE Afternoon	
		Time	Height	Time	Height
1	Monday	09 39	1.8	2158	1.8
2	Tuesday	10 24	1.5	2241	1.4
3	Wednesday	11 03	1.2	2319	1.2
4	Thursday	11 39	1.0	2353	1.0
5	Friday			1211	0.9
6	Saturday	00 24	0.9	12 42	0.8
7	Sunday	00 54	0.9	13 11	0.9
8	Monday	01 23	0.9	13 40	0.9
9	Tuesday	01 52	1.0	14 09	1.1
10	Wednesday	02 23	1.1	14 41	1.3
11	Thursday	02 59	1.3	15 21	1.5
12	Friday	03 45	1.6	16 14	1.9
13	Saturday	04 53	1.9	17 34	2.1
14	Sunday	06 33	2.0	19 19	2.1
15	Monday	08 10	1.7	20 43	1.7
16	Tuesday	90 22	1.3	21 48	1.2
17	Wednesday	10 20	0.8	22 43	0.8
18	Thursday	11 10	0.4	23 31	0.5
19	Friday	11 56	0.2		
20	Saturday	00 15	0.3	12 39	5.6
21	Sunday	00 57	0.2	13 19	0.3
22	Monday	01 37	0.4	13 55	0.5
23	Tuesday	02 10	0.7	14 28	0.9
24	Wednesday	02 44	1.0	15 01	1.3
25	Thursday	03 19	1.4	15 35	1.7
26	Friday	04 00	1.8	22 03	4.5
27	Saturday	04 53	2.2	23 06	4.2
28	Sunday	06 02	2.3	18 34	2.4
29	Monday	07 21	2.2	19 53	2.3
30	Tuesday	08 39	1.9	21 03	1.9

MAY		LOW TIDE Morning		LOW TIDE Afternoon	
		Time	Height	Time	Height
1	Wednesday	09 34	1.6	21 54	1.6
2	Thursday	10 18	1.3	22 37	1.3
3	Friday	10 58	1.1	23 16	1.1
4	Saturday	11 36	0.9	23 53	1.0
5	Sunday			1211	0.9
6	Monday	00 28	0.9	12 47	0.8
7	Tuesday	01 03	0.9	13 21	0.9
8	Wednesday	01 38	0.9	13 56	1.0
9	Thursday	02 14	1.1	14 33	1.2
10	Friday	02 55	1.3	15 17	1.5
11	Saturday	03 46	1.5	16 14	1.8
12	Sunday	04 54	1.8	17 29	2.0
13	Monday	06 21	1.8	18 59	1.9
14	Tuesday	07 47	1.6	20 18	1.7
15	Wednesday	08 56	1.3	21 22	1.3
16	Thursday	09 54	0.9	22 17	1.0
17	Friday	10 45	0.7	23 06	0.7
18	Saturday	11 31	0.5	23 51	0.6
19	Sunday			12 14	0.5
20	Monday	00 33	0.5	12 54	0.6
21	Tuesday	01 12	0.7	13 30	0.8
22	Wednesday	01 48	0.9	14 04	1.1
23	Thursday	02 22	1.1	14 37	1.4
24	Friday	02 57	1.5	15 11	1.7
25	Saturday	03 35	1.8	15 50	2.0
26	Sunday	04 22	2.0	16 42	2.2
27	Monday	05 22	2.2	17 47	2.3
28	Tuesday	06 28	2.2	18 56	2.3
29	Wednesday	07 34	2.0	20 01	2.1
30	Thursday	08 34	1.8	21 00	1.8
31	Friday	09 27	1.5	21 51	1.5

JUNE		LOW TIDE Morning		LOW TIDE Afternoon	
		Time	Height	Time	Height
1	Saturday	10 15	1.3	22 38	1.3
2	Sunday	11 00	1.1	23 22	1.0
3	Monday	11 43	0.9		
4	Tuesday	00 05	0.9	12 26	0.9
5	Wednesday	00 47	0.8	13 07	0.9
6	Thursday	01 29	0.8	13 49	1.0
7	Friday	02 13	0.9	14 33	1.1
8	Saturday	02 59	1.1	15 20	1.3
9	Sunday	03 51	1.3	16 14	1.5
10	Monday	04 50	1.5	17 18	1.7
11	Tuesday	06 00	1.6	18 30	1.8
12	Wednesday	07 15	1.6	19 45	1.7
13	Thursday	08 24	1.4	20 52	1.5
14	Friday	09 25	1.2	21 50	1.3
15	Saturday	10 19	1.1	22 42	1.1
16	Sunday	11 07	0.9	2329	0.9
17	Monday	11 51	0.9		
18	Tuesday	00 12	0.9	12 32	0.9
19	Wednesday	00 52	0.9	13 10	1.0
20	Thursday	01 29	1.0	13 44	1.2
21	Friday	02 04	1.1	14 17	1.4
22	Saturday	02 37	1.4	14 48	1.6
23	Sunday	03 11	1.6	15 22	1.8
24	Monday	03 48	1.8	16 01	2.0
25	Tuesday	04 33	2.0	16 52	2.1
26	Wednesday	05 31	2.0	17 57	2.2
27	Thursday	06 36	2.0	19 06	2.1
28	Friday	07 40	1.9	20 10	1.9
29	Saturday	08 41	1.7	21 09	1.7
30	Sunday	09 37	1.4	22 04	1.4

JULY

		LOW TIDE Morning		LOW TIDE Afternoon	
		Time	Height	Time	Height
1	Monday	10 30	1.2	22 57	1.1
2	Tuesday	11 20	1.0	23 47	0.9
3	Wednesday			12 09	0.9
4	Thursday	00 35	0.8	12 58	0.8
5	Friday	01 24	0.7	13 44	0.8
6	Saturday	02 11	0.7	14 30	0.9
7	Sunday	02 57	0.8	15 17	1.0
8	Monday	03 45	1.0	16 04	1.2
9	Tuesday	04 35	1.2	16 56	1.5
10	Wednesday	05 31	1.4	17 56	1.7
11	Thursday	06 35	1.6	19 05	1.8
12	Friday	07 47	1.7	20 18	1.8
13	Saturday	08 56	1.6	21 24	1.6
14	Sunday	09 55	1.5	22 21	1.4
15	Monday	10 47	1.3	23 11	1.2
16	Tuesday	11 33	1.2	23 56	1.1
17	Wednesday			12 15	1.1
18	Thursday	00 36	1.0	12 53	1.1
19	Friday	01 13	1.1	13 27	1.2
20	Saturday	01 46	1.2	13 57	1.3
21	Sunday	02 16	1.3	14 25	1.4
22	Monday	02 44	1.4	14 52	1.6
23	Tuesday	03 12	1.6	15 20	1.7
24	Wednesday	03 43	1.7	15 56	1.9
25	Thursday	04 25	1.9	16 46	2.1
26	Friday	05 26	2.0	18 00	2.2
27	Saturday	06 45	2.0	19 23	2.1
28	Sunday	08 00	1.9	20 35	1.9
29	Monday	09 06	1.6	21 39	1.5
30	Tuesday	10 07	1.4	22 38	1.2
31	Wednesday	11 04	1.1	23 33	0.9

AUGUST

		LOW TIDE Morning		LOW TIDE Afternoon	
		Time	Height	Time	Height
1	Thursday	11 57	0.8		
2	Friday	00 25	0.6	12 47	0.6
3	Saturday	01 14	0.4	13 35	0.5
4	Sunday	02 01	0.4	14 19	0.5
5	Monday	02 45	0.5	15 02	0.7
6	Tuesday	03 27	0.7	15 44	1.0
7	Wednesday	04 10	1.1	16 28	1.3
8	Thursday	04 56	1.4	17 19	1.7
9	Friday	05 52	1.8	18 22	2.0
10	Saturday	07 03	2.0	19 43	2.1
11	Sunday	08 28	2.0	21 05	1.9
12	Monday	09 38	1.8	22 07	1.7
13	Tuesday	10 32	1.6	22 57	1.4
14	Wednesday	11 18	1.3	23 41	1.2
15	Thursday	11 59	1.2		
16	Friday	00 20	1.1	12 36	1.1
17	Saturday	00 55	1.0	13 08	1.1
18	Sunday	01 25	1.0	13 35	1.2
19	Monday	01 51	1.1	13 59	1.3
20	Tuesday	02 14	1.3	14 22	1.4
21	Wednesday	02 38	1.4	14 47	1.5
22	Thursday	03 05	1.5	15 18	1.7
23	Friday	03 40	1.7	15 59	1.9
24	Saturday	04 28	2.0	16 59	2.2
25	Sunday	05 44	2.2	18 39	2.2
26	Monday	07 26	2.1	20 09	2.0
27	Tuesday	08 44	1.8	21 21	1.6
28	Wednesday	09 51	1.4	22 24	1.2
29	Thursday	10 50	1.0	23 20	0.7
30	Friday	11 43	0.7		
31	Saturday	00 10	0.4	12 32	0.4

SEPTEMBER

		LOW TIDE Morning		LOW TIDE Afternoon	
		Time	Height	Time	Height
1	Sunday	00 58	0.2	13 18	0.3
2	Monday	01 42	0.2	14 00	0.3
3	Tuesday	02 23	0.3	14 40	0.5
4	Wednesday	03 02	0.7	15 19	0.9
5	Thursday	03 40	1.1	15 58	1.3
6	Friday	04 20	1.6	16 43	1.8
7	Saturday	05 09	2.0	17 42	2.2
8	Sunday	06 17	2.3	19 07	2.4
9	Monday	08 02	2.4	20 50	2.2
10	Tuesday	09 22	2.1	21 52	1.8
11	Wednesday	10 14	1.7	2238	1.5
12	Thursday	10 57	1.4	2319	1.2
13	Friday	11 36	1.2	2356	1.0
14	Saturday			12 11	1.1
15	Sunday	00 28	1.2	12 42	1.0
16	Monday	00 57	1.0	13 08	1.1
17	Tuesday	01 21	1.1	13 31	1.2
18	Wednesday	01 45	1.2	13 54	1.3
19	Thursday	02 08	1.3	14 19	1.4
20	Friday	02 35	1.5	14 50	1.6
21	Saturday	03 09	1.7	15 29	1.9
22	Sunday	03 54	2.0	16 26	2.2
23	Monday	05 04	2.3	18 07	2.3
24	Tuesday	07 01	2.3	19 52	2.1
25	Wednesday	08 29	2.0	21 07	1.6
26	Thursday	09 37	1.5	22 09	1.1
27	Friday	10 34	1.0	23 02	0.7
28	Saturday	11 25	0.6	23 51	0.3
29	Sunday			12 12	0.4
30	Monday	00 36	0.2	12 56	0.3

OCTOBER

		LOW TIDE Morning		LOW TIDE Afternoon	
		Time	Height	Time	Height
1	Tuesday	01 19	0.2	13 37	0.3
2	Wednesday	01 58	0.4	14 15	0.6
3	Thursday	02 35	0.8	14 52	1.0
4	Friday	03 10	1.2	15 29	1.4
5	Saturday	03 47	1.7	16 12	1.9
6	Sunday	04 32	2.2	17 08	2.3
7	Monday	05 38	2.5	18 28	2.5
8	Tuesday	07 17	2.6	20 23	2.3
9	Wednesday	08 54	2.3	21 24	1.9
10	Thursday	09 45	1.9	22 09	1.6
11	Friday	10 27	1.5	22 48	1.3
12	Saturday	11 05	1.3	23 23	1.1
13	Sunday	11 39	1.1	23 55	1.0
14	Monday			12 10	1.1
15	Tuesday	00 24	1.0	12 38	1.1
16	Wednesday	00 51	1.1	13 05	1.1
17	Thursday	01 18	1.1	13 31	1.2
18	Friday	01 45	1.3	13 59	1.4
19	Saturday	02 14	1.5	14 32	1.6
20	Sunday	02 49	1.7	15 13	1.8
21	Monday	03 36	2.0	16 12	2.1
22	Tuesday	04 48	2.3	17 52	2.3
23	Wednesday	06 41	2.4	19 35	2.1
24	Thursday	80 11	2.0	20 49	1.6
25	Friday	09 17	1.5	21 48	1.1
26	Saturday	10 13	1.1	22 40	0.7
27	Sunday	11 03	0.7	23 28	0.5
28	Monday	11 49	0.5		
29	Tuesday	00 12	0.4	12 32	0.4
30	Wednesday	00 54	0.4	13 13	0.5
31	Thursday	01 32	0.6	13 51	0.8

NOVEMBER		LOW TIDE Morning		LOW TIDE Afternoon	
		Time	Height	Time	Height
1	Friday	02 08	1.0	14 27	1.1
2	Saturday	02 42	1.4	15 04	1.5
3	Sunday	03 18	1.8	15 45	2.0
4	Monday	04 01	2.3	16 38	2.3
5	Tuesday	05 01	2.6	17 47	2.5
6	Wednesday	06 19	2.7	19 14	2.4
7	Thursday	07 52	2.5	20 34	2.1
8	Friday	08 58	2.1	21 24	1.8
9	Saturday	09 45	1.8	22 05	1.5
10	Sunday	10 25	1.5	22 43	1.3
11	Monday	11 02	1.3	23 18	1.2
12	Tuesday	11 36	1.2	23 52	1.1
13	Wednesday			12 10	1.1
14	Thursday	00 24	1.1	12 43	1.1
15	Friday	00 57	1.1	13 15	1.2
16	Saturday	01 29	1.3	13 49	1.3
17	Sunday	02 04	1.4	14 27	1.5
18	Monday	02 44	1.7	15 13	1.7
19	Tuesday	03 34	2.0	16 14	2.0
20	Wednesday	04 44	2.2	17 38	2.1
21	Thursday	06 17	2.2	19 09	2.0
22	Friday	07 43	2.0	20 22	1.6
23	Saturday	08 51	1.6	21 23	1.3
24	Sunday	09 48	1.2	22 16	1.0
25	Monday	10 39	0.9	23 04	0.8
26	Tuesday	11 26	0.8	23 48	0.7
27	Wednesday			12 10	0.7
28	Thursday	00 30	0.7	12 52	0.8
29	Friday	01 10	0.9	13 31	1.0
30	Saturday	01 46	1.2	14 08	1.2

DECEMBER		LOW TIDE Morning		LOW TIDE Afternoon	
		Time	Height	Time	Height
1	Sunday	02 21	1.5	14 45	1.5
2	Monday	02 56	1.8	15 23	1.8
3	Tuesday	03 34	2.1	16 08	2.1
4	Wednesday	04 23	2.4	17 04	2.3
5	Thursday	05 25	2.5	18 09	2.4
6	Friday	06 37	2.5	19 17	2.3
7	Saturday	07 47	2.3	20 20	2.0
8	Sunday	08 47	2.1	21 13	1.8
9	Monday	09 38	1.8	21 59	1.5
10	Tuesday	10 23	1.5	22 42	1.3
11	Wednesday	11 05	1.3	23 23	1.2
12	Thursday	11 46	1.2		
13	Friday	00 03	1.1	12 27	1.1
14	Saturday	00 43	1.1	13 07	1.1
15	Sunday	01 23	1.2	13 48	1.2
16	Monday	02 04	1.3	14 31	1.3
17	Tuesday	02 48	1.4	15 19	1.4
18	Wednesday	03 37	1.6	16 13	1.6
19	Thursday	04 35	1.8	17 17	1.8
20	Friday	05 45	2.0	18 31	1.8
21	Saturday	07 03	2.0	19 46	1.7
22	Sunday	08 17	1.8	2053	1.5
23	Monday	09 21	1.5	2151	1.3
24	Tuesday	10 17	1.3	22 43	1.1
25	Wednesday	11 07	1.1	23 29	1.0
26	Thursday	11 53	1.0		
27	Friday	00 13	1.0	12 36	1.0
28	Saturday	00 53	1.1	13 16	1.0
29	Sunday	01 30	1.2	13 53	1.2
30	Monday	02 05	1.4	14 28	1.4
31	Tuesday	02 37	1.6	15 02	1.6

St Michael's Mount near Marazion

Coast Path Safety Advice

Please remember that your safety is your responsibility – look after yourself and other members of your group. Keep to the Path and stay away from cliff edges – please follow advisory signs and waymarks. Supervise children and dogs at all times. Be prepared and well equipped – wear suitable clothing and footwear and be ready for possible changes in the weather.

Stay within your capabilities – some sections of the Coast Path can be strenuous and/or remote. In an emergency dial 999 and ask for the coastguard.

Weather

The South West Coast Path is more exposed to wind than any other long distance trail, so please pay attention to gale forecasts as well as rain. Along some sections, strong winds can be dangerous, especially when rounding exposed headlands and crossing bridges; a high backpack can act like a sail.

Always use sun protection especially on bright cloudy or breezy days when the risk of sunburn seems lower.

Military Ranges

Two lengths of the Coast Path may be affected by the use of military ranges. The use of one, at Tregantle in south east Cornwall, only means that a more inland and less pleasant route must be used for a length of some 1.25 miles/2km in Section 46, Portwrinkle-Cremyll (Plymouth Ferry). However, if there is military use of the other, east of Lulworth Cove in Dorset, this means the whole of Section 67 between Lulworth Cove and Kimmeridge Bay will be impossible. Generally, the Lulworth ranges are closed to walkers Monday to Friday during school term time and also up to six times a year at weekends. Try to arrange your walk so as not to miss this superb but tough section.

Information and details for the ranges are included in the relevant Section descriptions and online.

Route Changes

The coast would not look so beautiful and dramatic if it wasn't for cliff and beach erosion. The downside is that sometimes cliff falls or landslips close sections of the Coast Path resulting in temporary inland diversions, which can occasionally be quite lengthy, being needed. In these instances, always follow signing and information on the ground.

We are also constantly looking for opportunities to improve the route in the few places where it is not as good as it could be. The Government's plans to create a Coast Path around the entire coast of England by 2020 will help with this, and over the next few years we are expecting the route to be changed in many places.

Whilst any route changes and diversions are signed, they may make your walk longer so it's worth checking the route changes pages of our website before you set out.

Photography

As you can see from the many photos in this guide, you're going to be walking through beautiful coastal scenery, so a camera is a great way of recording your journey. We'd also love to see your photos, and each year we run a photo competition, with the best pictures winning some great prizes and are used in a South West Coast Path calendar. See **www.southwestcoastpath.org.uk/photo-competition** for tips on how to improve your photography and how to enter the competition.

Telephones

Mobile phones will not work in some remote places and it's reassuring to see a public telephone box just when you need it. However, many of these remote telephones have recently been converted to only take debit cards. You can use the following cards in these boxes - Switch; Maestro; Delta; Solo; Visa Debit but not Electron. There are still some telephone boxes which will accept BT Phonecards and all boxes will accept BT Chargecards (these are only available to BT landline customers). Mobile phones are always useful to have whilst on the Coast Path. However, do not rely on them as coverage is not always good in the South West. You may also have difficulty in obtaining top-up in some areas.

Banks

There are small Post Offices in some villages. Overseas visitors will probably find their cashpoint cards very useful. ATM machines are widely available along the Coast Path and can be sourced at www.link.co.uk/atmlocator. Please note, there are some smaller accommodation providers who are not equipped to take payment via credit/debit card and you may need cash to settle your bill.

Dogs

Beaches

Most district councils and unitary authorities have dog bans on beaches generally from 1st May to 31st October. The Association and most of the general public regard this as a sensible measure.

There are several sections of the South West Coast Path that cross beaches and are officially marked as such. These beaches are Croyde Bay in Devon, Harlyn Bay, Constantine, Treyarnon, Perranporth and Penberth slipway in Cornwall, and Studland in Dorset. The routing of the Coast Path (with its designation as a National Trail) across these beaches means that they are public rights of way. A public right of way does carry precedence over seasonal regulations banning dogs, and ultimately any walker in the process of walking along, but not stopping on, these sections of the Path may be accompanied by a dog under total control.

However we strongly recommend the following:

❧ If an alternative route is provided and signposted, that you use it

❧ That residents near to dog ban beaches use other walks and do not use the beach Path during the ban period

❧ Total control means that the dog should be on a short (not extendable) lead

❧ That your progress should be as unobtrusive as possible to other beach users. To aid this, close attention should be paid to the actual route marked on the map

❧ Lastly, but most importantly, all dog mess MUST be removed from the beach

The Association shop has handy poo bag dispensers that attach to a backpack or lead and these can be bought online or by calling 01752 896237.

Along the Coast Path

Many walk the Coast Path with their dogs and all have an enjoyable time and we receive many reports of dogs completing the whole Path. However we do urge caution because the Coast Path is very high along many sections and it takes only an excited dog to go chasing after a rabbit to cause much grief if it goes over the edge. If your dog is well trained and you can trust it, then please enjoy your Coast Path walk with your four legged friend. If it is not and you cannot, then do take care particularly on the many sections along the South West Coast Path that have farm livestock grazing.

It is also extremely important that you clean up after your dog. Bag it and bin it wherever you are otherwise you give all dog owners a bad name and can pass on diseases to people and farm animals.

The Pinnacles, Handfast Point

Below and throughout the Guide, we've split the path into 52 day lengths. Each of these allows time for breaks and covers what we think is a comfortable day's walking, whilst finishing at places where you can find accommodation. If you think you'd like to go slower or faster than this, you can find alternative itinerary suggestions on our website

Week 1 (Seven days)

Day	Distance		From - to
1	10mi	15km	**Minehead – Porlock Weir**
			Take National Rail main line to Taunton; bus Taunton - Minehead; or National Express coach to Minehead
2	12mi	20km	**Porlock Weir – Lynton**
3	13mi	21km	**Lynton – Combe Martin**
4	13mi	20km	**Combe Martin – Woolacombe**
5	16mi	27km	**Woolacombe – Braunton**
6	12mi	20km	**Braunton – Instow**
7	11mi	18km	**Instow – Westward Ho!**
Total	87mi	141km	*Take bus Westward Ho! - Barnstaple; train Barnstaple - Exeter; National Rail main line from Exeter; or National Express coach from Westward Ho!*

Week 2 (Seven days)

Day	Distance		From - to
1	11mi	18km	**Westward Ho! – Clovelly**
			National Rail main line to Exeter; train Exeter - Barnstaple; bus Barnstaple - Westward Ho!; or National Express coach to Westward Ho!
2	10mi	16km	**Clovelly – Hartland Quay**
3	15mi	25km	**Hartland Quay – Bude**
4	10mi	16km	**Bude – Crackington Haven**
5	11mi	18km	**Crackington Haven – Tintagel**
6	9mi	15km	**Tintagel – Port Isaac**
7	12mi	19km	**Port Isaac - Padstow**
Total	78mi	127km	*Bus to Bodmin Parkway; National Rail main line from Bodmin Parkway*

Week 3 (Six days)

Day	Distance		From - to
1	14mi	22km	**Padstow – Porthcothan**
			National Rail main line to Bodmin Parkway; bus Bodmin Parkway - Padstow
2	11mi	18km	**Porthcothan – Newquay**
3	11mi	18km	**Newquay – Perranporth**
4	12mi	20km	**Perranporth – Portreath**
5	12mi	20km	**Portreath – Hayle**
6	6mi	9km	**Hayle – St Ives**
Total	66mi	107km	*Train St Ives-St Erth; National Rail main line from St Erth; or National Express coach from St Ives.*

Week 4 (Six days)

Day	Distance		From - to
1	14mi	22km	**St Ives – Pendeen Watch**
			National Rail main line to St Erth; train St Erth - St Ives; or National Express coach to St Ives
2	9mi	15km	**Pendeen Watch – Sennen Cove**
3	12mi	19km	**Sennen Cove – Lamorna Cove**
4	9mi	15km	**Lamorna Cove – Marazion**
5	11mi	17km	**Marazion – Porthleven**
6	13mi	22km	**Porthleven – Lizard**
Total	68mi	110km	*Bus Lizard Town - Helston; bus Helston - Redruth; National Rail main line from Redruth*

Week 5 (Six days)

Day	Distance		From - to
1	11mi	17km	**Lizard – Coverack** *National Rail main line to Redruth; bus Redruth-Helston; bus Helston - Lizard Town*
2	13mi	21km	**Coverack – Helford**
3	10mi	16km	**Helford – Falmouth**
4	14mi	22km	**Falmouth – Portloe**
5	12mi	20km	**Portloe – Mevagissey**
6	12mi	19km	**Mevagissey – Par**
Total	72mi	115km	*National Rail main line from Par*

Week 6 (Seven days)

Day	Distance		From - to
1	13mi	21km	**Par – Polperro** *National Rail main line to Par*
2	12mi	20km	**Polperro – Portwrinkle**
3	13mi	21km	**Portwrinkle – Plymouth**
4	15mi	24km	**Plymouth – Wembury (ferry crossing)**
5	14mi	22km	**Wembury (ferry crossing) – Bigbury on Sea**
6	14mi	22km	**Bigbury on Sea – Salcombe**
7	13mi	21km	**Salcombe – Torcross**
Total	**94mi**	**151km**	*Bus Torcross - Plymouth; National Rail main line or National Express coach from Plymouth*

Week 7 (Six days)

Day	Distance		From - to
1	10mi	16km	**Torcross – Dartmouth** *National rail main line or National Express coach to Plymouth; bus Plymouth - Torcross*
2	11mi	17km	**Dartmouth – Brixham**
3	11mi	17km	**Brixham – Babbacombe**
4	16mi	27km	**Babbacombe – Exmouth**
5	13mi	21km	**Exmouth – Sidmouth**
6	11mi	17km	**Sidmouth – Seaton (Devon)**
Total	**72mi**	**115km**	*Bus Seaton - Exeter; National Rail main line or National Express Coach from Exeter*

Week 8 (Seven days)

Day	Distance		From - to
1	14mi	23km	**Seaton (Devon) – Seatown (Dorset)** *National Rail main line or National Express coach to Exeter; bus Exeter - Seaton.*
2	12mi	19km	**Seatown (Dorset) – Abbotsbury**
3	11mi	17km	**Abbotsbury – Ferry Bridge (Wyke Regis)**
4	13mi	21km	**Isle of Portland**
5	14mi	23km	**Ferry Bridge (Wyke Regis) – Lulworth Cove**
6	14mi	23km	**Lulworth Cove – Worth Matravers**
7	14mi	22km	**Worth Matravers – South Haven Point (Poole Harbour)**
Total	**92**	**148km**	*Ferry South Haven Point-Sandbanks; bus Sandbanks-Poole or Bournemouth; National Rail main line or National Express coach from Poole or Bournemouth.*

South West
Water

Proud to suport the South West Coast Path Association

Transforming our region's bathing waters from polluted seas 25 years ago to some of the finest beaches in Europe today has been our focus for a quarter of a century.

We continue to make improvements to ensure our bathing waters meet stringent standards for bathing water cleanliness.

Nowadays, the region is reaping the benefits of that work: a booming tourist economy where visitors and locals alike enjoy the Coast Path, the beaches, the sea and all the opportunities afforded by our stunning coastline.

The Environment of the South West Coast Path

The South West Coast Path is one of the country's National Trails; it is, indeed, the longest of them at 630 miles/1,105 km. In common with all National Trails, the Coast Path passes through an outstanding environment, and Coast Path walkers will experience the finest coastal landscapes in the country. This range of coastal landscapes includes high cliffs, extensive beaches, wide bays, tiny coves, wooded estuaries and prominent headlands.

This range of outstanding landscapes has been recognised officially by the large number of formal designations, both international and national, around the length of the Coast Path.

International Designations

UNESCO has designated certain world-class environments as Biosphere Reserves. These are areas with a special blend of landscapes and wildlife, a rich cultural heritage and a community that cares about it and wishes to sustain it for the future. The Coast Path passes through the North Devon Biosphere Reserve, which has as its core the dunes of Braunton Burrows (Section 7 of the Trail Descriptions following), but includes as its outer areas the whole Coast Path between Lynton and Marsland Mouth (Sections 3 to 13).

World Heritage Sites (WHSs) are also designated by UNESCO, in this case for their "Outstanding Universal Value". The South West Coast Path passes through two World Heritage Sites. The Cornwall and West Devon Mining Landscape WHS is defined by the mining landscape which was formed by the cultural tradition of non-ferrous hard-rock mining. It contributed to developing the Industrial Revolution in Britain and pioneered its transfer overseas. The designation covers ten distinct areas and includes iconic relic mining landscapes with their old engine houses as well as old harbours. Five of these areas relate to the Coast Path – the St Agnes area (Section 24), the Port of Hayle (Sections 25 and 26), the St Just area (Sections 27 and 28), the area around Rinsey and Trewavas (Section 32) and Charlestown (Section 41).

The Coast Path's second WHS is the Jurassic Coast, England's first such site to be designated for its natural properties. It is designated as it clearly depicts a geological "walk through time" of 185 million years of Earth's history in 95 miles/152 km. geological history, and resulting landscapes, of the Triassic, Jurassic and Cretaceous periods are successively exposed over the length of the WHS, which stretches between Exmouth and Swanage (Sections 58 to 70).

National Designations

The country's finest landscapes are designated nationally as National Parks or Areas of Outstanding Natural Beauty. In landscape terms these designations are regarded as of equal value. Most of the South West Coast Path is covered by such designations.

Exmoor (Sections 1 to 3), with its cliffs and deep wooded valleys, has National Park status. Most of the remainder of the Coast Path is covered by Area of Outstanding Natural Beauty (AONB) status.

The North Devon AONB extends along much of the coast between Exmoor and the Devon/Cornwall border (Sections 4 to 7 and 11 to 13), excluding only Ilfracombe and the area around the Taw-Torridge estuary. The Cornwall AONB covers the vast majority of the Cornish coast (Sections 13 to 25 and 27 to 46), excluding only a few mainly urban lengths. The whole length of coast between Plymouth and Brixham (Sections 47 to 54) falls with the South Devon AONB. East of the River Exe, most of the coast, excluding only the urban areas, as far as the Devon/Dorset border, is covered by the East Devon AONB. And finally, all of the Dorset coast except the largely urban Weymouth and Portland is within the Dorset AONB.

The wealth of landscape and environmental designations outlined above gives some idea of the quality of the landscape through which the South West Coast Path passes. However, this hides the fact that there is a wide range of landscape types to be experienced. For an idea of the more detailed landscape types, a description will be found at the start of each of the seven lengths we have divided the Coast Path into – Exmoor, North Devon, North Cornwall, West Cornwall, South Cornwall, South Devon and the Jurassic Coast.

Based on the Suggested Itinerary on pages 29-30, the South West Coast Path has been divided into 70 Sections. Each Section represents a day's or half-day's walk of the Itinerary. However, it must be emphasised that these Sections should not be confined to use by those walking long stretches of the Coast Path. Each Section is designed to be used on its own as a one-off if so wished, as well as by those planning long walks of several days. The Sections are arranged in anti-clockwise order, from Minehead to Poole, with an additional Section 71 for the alternative inland South Dorset Ridgeway. In a number of coastal locations it is now necessary to pay for the toilet facilities. If so, there is usually a 20p fee so it is prudent to carry a supply of 20p pieces to cater for this. Also be aware that in winter a number of toilets close, or are only opened at weekends, so extra careful planning may be needed.

Each Section entry follows in the following format:

Distance – length of the Section in miles and kilometres;

Cumulative distance – total length of the Coast Path from Minehead to the end of the Section in miles and kilometres;

Ascent – height climbed during the Section in feet and metres;

Cumulative ascent – total height climbed on the Coast Path from Minehead to the end of the Section in feet and metres;

Grading – each Section is graded as Easy, Moderate, Strenuous or Severe. Inevitably, such grading is subjective to an extent, and not all of any Section will be identical throughout, but the grading will give an idea of the effort required;

Timing – this is an estimated fair average for completing the Section. Times will vary depending on weather, number in party, gear carried, number of refreshment or photograph stops. The estimate should be an aide in planning;

OS Maps – the reference numbers of the OS Maps needed to walk the Section are given. Both Landranger (1:50,000) and Explorer (1:25,000) maps are given;

Area – for those not geographically acquainted with the South West, the Coast Path has been sub-divided into 7 areas for ease of identification. These can be seen on the map on the inside cover of the Guide and at the start of each section throughout the Guide;

Walking Guides – the Association has published a series of Walking Guide booklets which give detailed walking directions as well as pointing out items of interest along the route; see page 8. The relevant Walking Guide booklet title for the Section is given.

There is then an overview of each Section. This covers the landscape, its general character and some of its highlights.

Next, there is a short description of how the Section can be undertaken as a day or part-day walk with public transport or a local circular walk. For more details about local public transport see pages 14-15.

Finally, the main body of the Section description contains simplified instructions for walking in a Minehead – Poole direction, generally only highlighting those locations where it is possible to go astray.

At the end of each section are places to Sleep, places to Eat & Drink and things to Do in that area. Please support these businesses as they are all members and supporters of the Path, you can identify them by looking for the blue South West Coast Path Association window sticker.

Remember, as a National Trail, the South West Coast Path is usually well signed and waymarked throughout its length, using the National Trail acorn symbol. Bear in mind that things change over the years, including the actual route of the Coast Path, so using out-of-date literature can be misleading. If in doubt, follow the signs and waymarks on the ground.

The various areas are identified by using a colour coding system as shown on the map on the inside cover and set out in the Contents page 3. The colour code is used on the top bar of the Walk Sections, the title information and the page numbers.

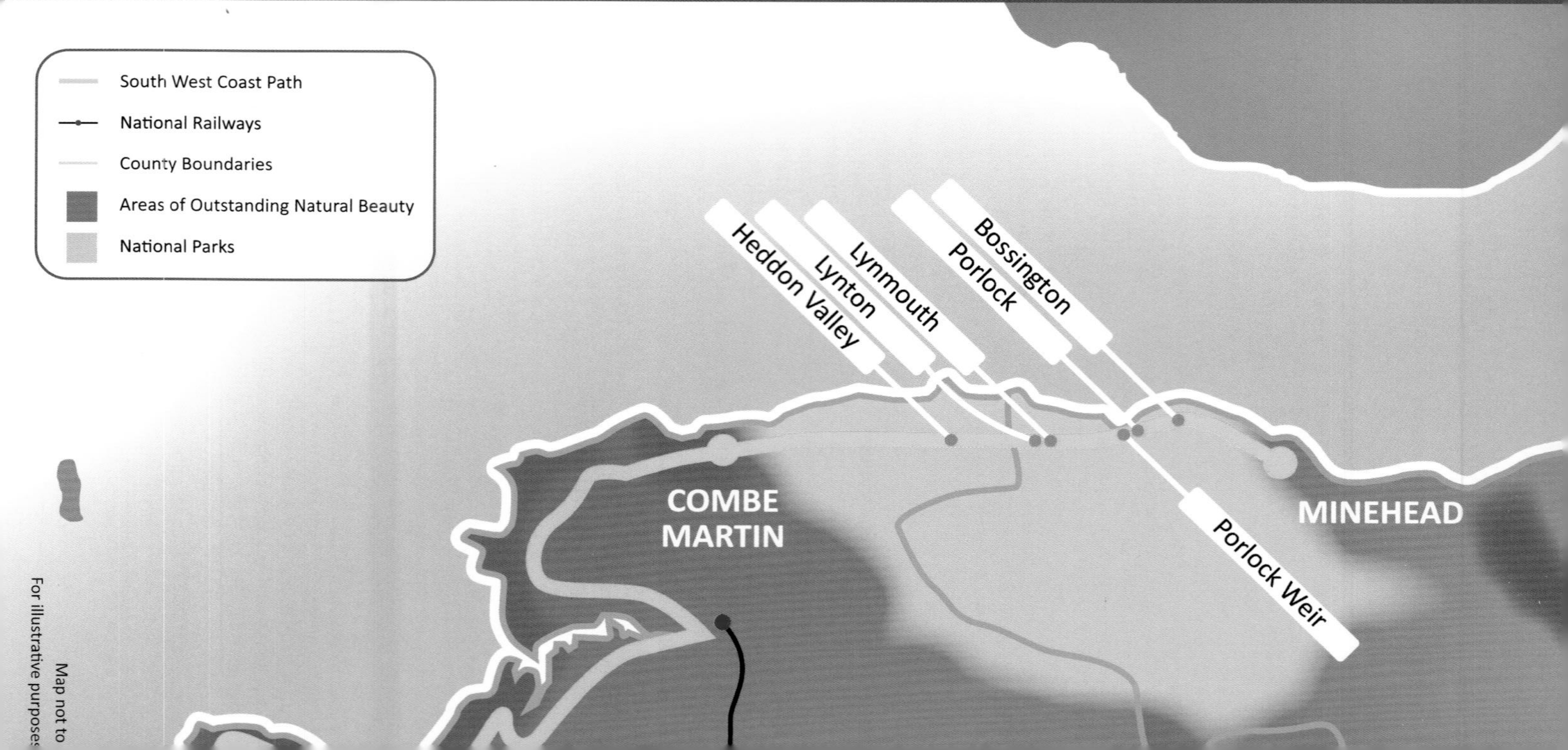

MINEHEAD

Porlock Weir

Bossington
Porlock

Lynmouth
Lynton
Heddon Valley

COMBE
MARTIN

South West Coast Path

National Railways

County Boundaries

Areas of Outstanding Natural Beauty

National Parks

Map not to
For illustrative purposes

Exmoor
Minehead to Combe Martin

(Sections 1-3)

The Exmoor coast is characterised by two main landscape types. The first is the meeting of the rolling expanse of high moorland and the sea. The coastline itself is one of high cliffs, some of them among the highest sea cliffs in England, but this height is sometimes disguised by the cliffs' convex shape, usually referred to as "hog's back". Views are often extensive inland, over the undulating moorland, while seaward in good visibility the coast of Wales may be seen across the Bristol Channel. Contrasting with this landscape is the Vale of Porlock, a flat-floored break in the cliffs crossed by the South West Coast Path over marshland at its mouth. In contrast, some lengths of the Exmoor coast comprise deep and steep valleys cutting across the high land. These valleys, locally known as "combes", are typically wooded, often with ancient oak woodland. Often this woodland spreads along the adjacent cliff faces, also convex in shape. Views from the Coast Path here are inevitably less extensive, and sometimes quite limited by the woodland, but the nature of the ancient woodland makes for an environment of considerable ecological interest. The combes and the height of the cliffs in the Exmoor length result in some notable gradients for walkers in places.

Exmoor

OS Maps: Landranger 181; Explorer OL9

	This Walk	Cumulative	This Walk	Cumulative	Grading	Timing
Ascent	1,824ft	1,824ft	556m	556m	Official: Moderate Alternative: Strenuous	4.5 hours
Distance	8.9mi	8.9mi	14.3km	14.3km		

For detailed directions see our Walking Guide no. 1, Minehead to Porlock Weir.

This is a classic example of where moorland meets the sea. Inland, the high expanse of Exmoor rolls away, broken by deep wooded valleys; where it meets the Bristol Channel there are high, convex cliffs, cut by deep and narrow "coombes". This is a lonely, remote length, away from main roads and settlements, with often the only evidence of modern life being development far away on the opposite shore of the Bristol Channel on the South Wales coast. At the western end is the contrasting landscape of Porlock Vale, a flat-floored area of farmland and marshland behind its shingle ridge, quite different in character from the rest of this Section.

Directions

Regular buses run between Minehead and Porlock Weir.

The South West Coast Path starts from the celebratory marker on the sea front. The current route, which may not be shown on older maps, proceeds along the sea front, past the quay. Just before Greenaleigh Farm it turns left on ascending zigzags to North Hill.

At the summit of North Hill follow the acorn sign towards Selworthy and Bossington. At the next Coast Path sign there is a fork, the route to the right being marked "Rugged Cliff Top Path", and either option can be taken. Do not be put off by the description of the seaward path as "rugged" – it is a splendid alternative and not difficult, and gives much better sea views than the inland "official" path. It is well waymarked, and dogs are permitted but must be under very close control. There is likely to be cattle grazing.

On the "rugged" path, at the stile, take the left fork towards a bench, then continue downhill to take the lower path by a "Rugged Path" signpost. From Grexy Combe (GR 937 481) take the well-defined diagonal path up the hill to a wall, which is then followed first towards the sea then parallel to it to Western Brockholes. Here it turns inland to re-join the inland "official" path behind Hurlstone Point. (This seaward path will add about an hour to the estimated time.)

The inland route, meanwhile, follows good tracks parallel to the sea. Joining the "rugged" path on Bossington Hill, the now-combined route descends Hurlstone Combe. There is an optional diversion out to Hurlstone Point which gives a superb view. From Hurlstone, take care not to follow the obvious path to the left which contours round Bossington Hill.

The Path descends and goes inland to Bossington village and then just past the car park out towards the sea again. The route now crosses the marsh to Porlock Weir, easy to follow the whole way. At high spring tides it can become impassable, and signs to Porlock village should be followed. (For tidal information contact Minehead Tourist Information Centre (TIC) - see page 197.) If the diversion via Porlock village is taken, leave the village on the Toll Road then bear right on a footpath that goes behind West Porlock to Porlock Weir.

OS Maps: Landranger 181 (eastern half); Landranger 180 (western half); Explorer OL9

	This Walk	Cumulative	This Walk	Cumulative	Grading	Timing
Ascent	3,156ft	4,980ft	962m	1,518m	Moderate, strenuous in parts	5.5 hours
Distance	12.1mi	21.0mi	19.5km	33.8km		

For detailed directions see our Walking Guide no. 2, Porlock Weir to Lynmouth.

This is a Section of two halves. In the east, approximately between Porlock Weir and the Devon/Somerset border, Exmoor meets the sea at a run of high, convex but well-wooded cliffs. The Coast Path here is a woodland walk with frequent glimpses of the sea, quiet and remote in character. To the west the cliffs become more open and steeper and the area around The Foreland and Countisbury is a spectacular viewpoint with panoramas over the double-decker towns of Lynton and Lynmouth.

Directions

The bus service which linked Porlock Weir and Lynton ended in September 2014 after the bus company which operated it ceased trading. At the time of writing, it is not yet known if another company will fill this gap in bus provision. For up to date details, it is recommended you visit www.travelinesw.com, or telephone 0871 200 2233.

The official route is signposted left of the Hotel at Porlock Weir but it is possible to go in front of the hotel, past the shops then left signposted to Culbone.

Reaching Culbone turn right to visit the charming tiny church, which is recommended. From the church retrace steps and turn right uphill on the Coast Path. After about 300 yards/275m bear right into Culbone, Embelle and Yenworthy Woods. This route may not be shown on some older maps. Unfortunately, recent land slippages towards the end of Yenworthy Wood have forced an inland diversion via Yenworthy Combe.

Continue to Sister's Fountain, where the access path to the bus route at County Gate on the A39 leaves the Coast Path. Go uphill through a pair of wild boar head gateposts, then take care not to miss the narrow signposted path 300 yards/275m past the cottage as the drive bears left. An alternative waymarked route may be taken between Culbone and Yenworthy Wood. Although slightly more inland, it offers better views than the mainly woodland more coastal route.

At Coddow Combe, the route is signposted left off the lighthouse track "Countisbury 1.5 miles". From Countisbury the now spectacular Path continues down the seaward side of the A39 road. Lower down it joins the road for a short way before descending on zigzags to the foreshore. Walk into Lynmouth, crossing the footbridge, then turn right to the sea front. Lynton is vertically above Lynmouth and is reached by turning left up the steps before the cliff railway (which can be taken as an interesting alternative). A new route is also available past the Esplanade car park at the end of the sea front, where a pleasant path, signposted to Lynton, goes left up the steep wooded hillside to emerge on the Coast Path west of Lynton. Both Lynmouth and Lynton have all facilities.

It is interesting to know that from Lynmouth it is possible to walk Devon's Coast to Coast route using the Two Moors Way and its southern extension to the south coast at Wembury. Guide books are available from Lynton Tourist Information Centre (TIC).

OS Maps: Landranger 180; Explorer OL9

	This Walk	Cumulative	This Walk	Cumulative	Grading	Timing
Ascent	3,766ft	8,746ft	1,148m	2,666m	Strenuous	7 hours
Distance	13.7mi	34.7mi	22.0km	55.8km		

For detailed directions see our Walking Guide no. 3, Lynton to Hunter's Inn and Hunter's Inn to Combe Martin.

This generally quiet and remote Section passes through a series of spectacular coastal landscapes: the Valley of Rocks with its rocky crags and pinnacles; the steep wooded cliffs at Woody Bay; the breathtaking scenery of the deep and steep crevice carved through the cliffs at Heddon's Mouth; the wide open spaces of Holdstone Down; and the heights of the Great Hangman, the highest point on the entire Coast Path and one of the highest coastal locations in the country.

Directions

Lynton and Combe Martin are connected by a summer bus service (year-round at weekends). Heddon's Mouth (6.5 miles/10.5km from Lynton) makes a good break in this length (though not on the bus route). It has a selection of refreshment facilities and places to stay and as there is a parallel higher path between here and Woody Bay there is scope for a scenic circular walk.

The Coast Path out of Lynton is on North Walk, and this Path leads to Castle Rock in the Valley of Rocks. The next section follows a minor but sometimes busy road, but a diversion to the right from the turning circle at the end of the Valley avoids its first length. Continue past the Toll House and up the hill. A permissive path on the right to Crock Point then avoids another length, and also gives stunning views.

The Coast Path leaves the road just before the Hotel opposite the Red House. Arriving at another road turn left uphill. Follow the next Coast Path sign ahead. When this superb stretch reaches the dramatic Heddon's Mouth valley follow it down to the valley floor. On reaching the stone bridge over the Heddon River turn right, over the river, and at the next path turn hard left. Continue for 100 yards/91m to the signpost on the right to Combe Martin. (Inland on either side of the river the Path leads to the pub and shop at Hunter's Inn.)

Climb steeply away from the valley floor, keeping right at the top where the Path levels off. Continue round the headland (take care in windy conditions) then the Path heads inland to reach a stone wall; this is followed parallel to the sea. The wall ends and the signed path continues across the heathland of Holdstone Down. At Sherrycombe the route follows the grass track along the top of the combe to the inland end and then down. Ascending Great Hangman from Sherrycombe bear away from the wall on the left and ignore the many paths going to the right, meeting the wall higher up. From Great Hangman the Path is obvious to Little Hangman and beyond to Combe Martin.

If you enjoy sleeping, eating or drinking at any business on the Path please suggest they join us as Business Members so that we can share their brilliance!

The businesses listed here are all supporters of the South West Coast Path Association, they have joined as business members and it would be great if you could show your support for them too. In addition, businesses are listed with more details on our website: www.southwestcoastpath.org.uk Find them through our walk finder or our accommodation finder tools.

KEY:

GR Grid Reference
DP Distance from the Path
NT Nearest Town

🐕 Dogs Welcome
🍴 Evening Meal Available
3 Number Of Rooms

🛒 Grocery Shop On Site
📶 Wifi
🚗 Parking

Bed & Breakfast and Hotels

NAME	OTHER INFO	
Baytree B&B 29 Blenheim Road, Minehead, TA24 5PZ ☎ 01643 703374 ✉ gill.searle@talktalk.net 🌐 www.baytreebandbminehead.co.uk	GR: 969 463 DP: 0.4 miles NT: **MINEHEAD** Offers one night stays **3** 🚗 📶	Other info:
Montrose Guest House 41 Tregonwell Road, Minehead, TA24 5DU ☎ 01643 706473 ✉ montroseminehead@btinternet.com 🌐 www.montroseminehead.co.uk	GR: 972 461 DP: 0.5 miles NT: **MINEHEAD** Offers one night stays **5** 🚗 📶	Other info:
Pardlestone Farm Pardlestone Lane, Kilve, TA5 1SQ ☎ 01278 256629 ✉ annhardy@hotmail.co.uk 🌐	GR: 144 418 DP: NT: **MINEHEAD** Offers one night stays **4** 🚗 📶 🐕	Other info: Self catering cottage available
Yarn Market Hotel High Street, Dunster, Minehead, TA24 6SF ☎ 01643 821425 ✉ enquiries@yarnmarkethotel.co.uk 🌐 www.yarnmarkethotel.co.uk	GR: 991 438 DP: 2 miles NT: **MINEHEAD** Offers one night stays **28** 🚗 📶 🐕 🍴	Other info: Luggage transfers offered to guests
Sunfield B&B 83 Summerland Avenue, Minehead, TA24 5BW ☎ 01643 703565 ✉ stay@sunfieldminehead.co.uk 🌐 www.sunfieldminehead.co.uk	GR: 971 461 DP: 0 miles NT: **MINEHEAD** Offers one night stays **6** 📶 🐕	Other info:
Exmoor Country House Minehead Road, Porlock, TA24 8EY ☎ 01643 863599 ✉ info@exmoor-house.co.uk 🌐 www.exmoor-house.co.uk	GR: 892 467 DP: 1 mile NT: **PORLOCK** Offers one night stays **5** 🚗 📶 🍴	Other info:
Glen Lodge Luxury B&B and Self-Catering Hawkcombe, Porlock, TA24 8LN ☎ 01643 863371 ✉ glenlodge@gmail.com 🌐 www.glenlodge.net	GR: 884 459 DP: 1 mile NT: **PORLOCK** Offers one night stays **5** 🚗 📶 🐕	Other info: Conditions for dogs apply

NAME	OTHER INFO	
Hillside Hillside, High Street, Porlock, TA24 8PY ☎ 07891 774826 ✉ duncanmccanlis@gmail.com ⊕	GR: 884 466 NT: **PORLOCK** Offers one night stays 1 🚗 📶	DP: 1 mile Other info:
Myrtle Cottage High Street, Porlock, TA24 8PU ☎ 01643 862978 ✉ enquiries@myrtleporlock.co.uk ⊕ www.myrtleporlock.co.uk	GR: 884 467 NT: **PORLOCK** Offers one night stays 14 🚗 📶 🐕	DP: 0.25 miles Other info:
Reines House B&B Parsons Street, Porlock, TA24 8QJ ☎ 01643 862446 ✉ info@reineshouse.co.uk ⊕ www.reineshouse.co.uk	GR: 886 466 NT: **PORLOCK** 3 📶	DP: 0.75 miles Other info:
Sea View B&B High Bank, Porlock, TA24 8NP ☎ 01643 853456 ✉ seaview.porlock@btconnect.com ⊕ www.seaviewporlock.co.uk	GR: 884 467 NT: **PORLOCK** 4 🚗 📶	DP: 0.25 miles Other info:
The Cottage B&B High Street, Porlock, TA24 8PU ☎ 01643 862996 ✉ cottageporlock@gmail.com ⊕ www.cottageporlock.co.uk	GR: SS8856846723 NT: **PORLOCK** Offers one night stays 4 🚗 📶	DP: 1 mile Other info:
Ash Farm B&B Ash Farm, Porlock Weir, TA24 8JN ☎ 01643 862414 ✉ jenniferwren@jenniferwren.plus.com ⊕	GR: 842 478 NT: **PORLOCK WEIR** Offers one night stays 3 🚗 📶	DP: 2 miles Other info:
Lorna Doone House 4 Tors Road, Lynmouth, EX35 6ET ☎ 01598 753354 ✉ info@lornadoonehouse.co.uk ⊕ www.lornadoonehouse.co.uk	GR: 726 493 NT: **LYNMOUTH** Offers one night stays 5 🚗 📶 🐕 🍴	DP: 0.25 miles Other info:
Orchard House Hotel 12 Watersmeet Road, Lynmouth, EX35 6ET ☎ 01598 753247 ✉ yvonne.fagan@tesco.net ⊕ www.orchardhousehotel.co.uk	GR: 725 493 NT: **LYNMOUTH** Offers one night stays 6 📶 🐕 🍴	DP: 0 miles Other info: Single occupancy deals offered. Walking parties welcome
The Blue Ball Inn Countisbury, Lynmouth, EX35 6NE ☎ 01598 741 263 ✉ blueballinn@btconnect.com ⊕ www.blueballinn.com	GR: 747 496 NT: **LYNMOUTH** 3 🚗 🐕 🍴	DP: 0.2 miles Other info:
The Old Sea Captains House 1 Tors Road, Lynmouth, EX35 6ET ☎ 01598 753369 ✉ thecaptainshouse@btinternet.com ⊕ www.thecaptainshouseinlynmouth.co.uk	GR: 727 494 NT: **LYNMOUTH** 🐕 📶	DP: 0.3 miles Other info:

NAME	OTHER INFO	
Hillside House B&B 22 Watersmeet Road, Lynmouth, EX35 6EP 01598 753836 hillsidelynmouth@btinternet.com www.hillside-lynmouth.co.uk	GR: 727 494 — DP: 0 miles NT: **LYNMOUTH** Offers one night stays 6 🛜 🐕	Other info:
Bay Valley Of The Rocks Hotel Lee Road, Lynton, EX35 6HS 01598 752349 ⊖ www.shearings.com	GR: 720 494 — DP: 0.3 miles NT: **LYNTON** 68 🛜 🍴	Other info:
Fernleigh Guest House Park Street, Lynton, EX35 6BY 01598 753575 hello@fernleigh.net www.fernleigh.net	GR: 717 493 — DP: 0.5 miles NT: **LYNTON** 5 🛜	Other info:
Gable Lodge Guest House 35 Lee Road, Lynton, EX35 6BS 01598 752367 gablelodge@btconnect.com www.gablelodgelynton.com	GR: SS71720 49408 — DP: 0.25 miles NT: **LYNTON** Offers one night stays 6 🚗 🛜 🍴	Other info:
Sinai House Lynway, Lynton, EX35 6AX 01598 753227 enquiries@sinaihouse.co.uk www.sinaihouse.co.uk	GR: 720 491 — DP: 0.5 miles NT: **LYNTON** 8 🚗 🛜	Other info:
South View Guest House 23 Lee Road, Lynton, EX35 6BP 01598 753728 jubrey@hotmail.co.uk www.southviewguesthouselynton.co.uk	GR: 718 494 — DP: 0.5 miles NT: **LYNTON** Offers one night stays 5 🚗 🛜	Other info: Boot dryer available, packed lunches (if pre ordered)
The Crown Hotel Market Street, Lynton, EX35 6AG 01598 752253 thecrownhotellynton@outlook.com www.thecrownlynton.co.uk	GR: 720 495 — DP: 0.25 miles NT: **LYNTON** 🐕 🍴	Other info:
The Denes Guesthouse 15 Longmead, Lynton, EX35 6DQ 01598 753573 enquiries@thedenes.com www.thedenes.com	GR: 714 493 — DP: 0.5 miles NT: **LYNTON** Offers one night stays 5 🚗 🛜	Other info:
Heddon's Gate Hotel Martinhoe, Parracombe, Barnstaple, EX31 4PZ 01598 763481 stay@heddonsgatehotel.co.uk www.heddonsgatehotel.co.uk	GR: 656 483 — DP: 0.5 miles NT: **HEDDON VALLEY** Offers one night stays 11 🚗 🛜 🐕 🍴	Other info:
The Hunters Inn Parracombe, Barnstaple, EX31 4PY 01598 763230 info@thehuntersinn.net www.thehuntersinnexmoor.co.uk	GR: 654 481 — DP: 0.5 miles NT: **HEDDON VALLEY** 4 🚗 🛜 🐕 🍴	Other info:

Self Catering and Hostels

NAME	OTHER INFO		
Quarry Cottage Hawkcombe, Porlock, Minehead, TA24 8LP ☎ 01643 863351 ✉ sarahlorourke@hotmail.com 🌐 www.quarrycottageporlock.co.uk	GR: 3	DP: 1 mile	
	NT: **MINEHEAD**		
	1 🚗 📶	Other info:	
Rosanda House Holiday Flats 2 Northfield Road, Minehead, TA24 5QQ ☎ 01643 704958 ✉ enquiries@rosanda.co.uk 🌐 www.rosanda.co.uk	GR: 970 466	DP: 0.15 miles	
	NT: **MINEHEAD**		
	3 🚗	Other info:	
Lower House Bossington, Minehead, TA24 8HQ ☎ 345 800 1895 ✉ enquiries@nationaltrust.org.uk 🌐 www.nationaltrust.org.uk/holidays	GR: 896481	DP: 1 miles	
	NT: **BOSSINGTON**		
	5 🚗 🐕	Other info: Open all year	
Martinhoe Cleave Cottages Martinhoe, Parracombe, EX31 4PZ ☎ 01598 753987 ✉ info@exmoorhideaway.co.uk 🌐 www.exmoorhideaway.co.uk	GR: 656 483	DP: 0.75 miles	
	NT: **LYNTON**		
	4 🚗 📶 🐕	Other info:	
Mannacott Farm Martinhoe, Parracombe, Barnstaple, EX31 4QS ☎ 01598 763227 ✉ francesdallyn@gmail.com 🌐 www.southwestcoastpath.org.uk/mannacott-farm-near-hunters-inn	GR: 662 480	DP: 0.5 miles	
	NT: **HEDDON VALLEY**		
	Offers one night stays		
	1 🚗 📶	Other info:	
Heddon Valley Bothy Parracombe, Barnstaple, EX31 4PU ☎ 0350 800 1895 ✉ enquiries@nationaltrust.org.uk 🌐 www.nationaltrust.org.uk/holidays	GR: 655 482	DP: 1 mile	
	NT: **HEDDON VALLEY**		
	Offers one night stays		
	1 🐕	Other info: Open all year	
Foreland Bothy Countisbury, Lynton, EX35 6NE ☎ 353 800 1895 ✉ enquiries@nationaltrust.org.uk 🌐 www.nationaltrust.org.uk/holidays	GR: 756 504	DP: 0 miles	
	NT: **LYNTON**		
	Offers one night stays		
	1 🚗 🐕	Other info: Open all year	

Do

NAME	OTHER INFO		
Exmoor Rambler High Street, Porlock, Minehead, TA24 8PY ☎ 01643 867429 ✉ exmoorrambler@btinternet.com 🌐 www.exmoorrambler.uk	GR: 885 467	DP: 0.25 miles	
	NT: **MINEHEAD**		
	🐕	Other info:	

Campsites and Holiday Parks

NAME	OTHER INFO	
Sparkhayes Farm Campsite Sparkhayes Lane, Porlock, TA24 8NE ☎ 07721 05123 / 01643 862470 ✉ sparkhayes@hotmail.com 🌐 www.sparkhayes.co.uk	GR: 886 468	DP: 0.1 miles
	NT: **MINEHEAD**	
	Offers one night stays	
	🚗🐐	Other info:
Sunny Lyn Holiday Park Lynton, EX35 6NS ☎ 01598 753384 ✉ info@sunnylyn.co.uk 🌐 www.sunnylyn.co.uk	GR: 718 484	DP: 0.8 miles
	NT: **LYNTON**	
	🚗🐐🛒	Other info:

Exmoor pony on Great Hangman, Combe Martin

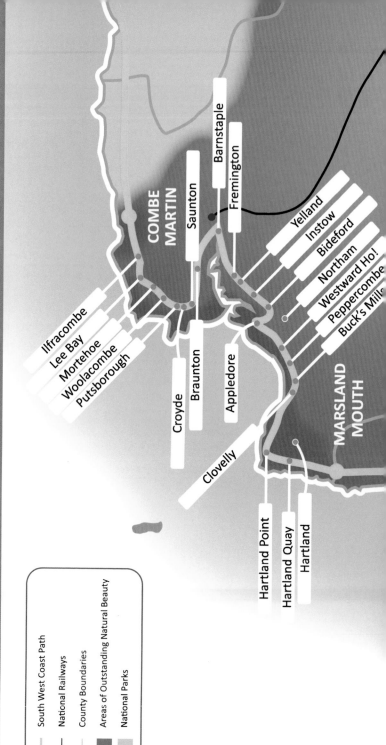

COMBE MARTIN

MARSLAND MOUTH

Barnstaple
Saunton
Fremington
Yelland
Instow
Bideford
Northam
Westward Ho!
Peppercombe
Buck's Mills

Ilfracombe
Lee Bay
Mortehoe
Woolacombe
Putsborough
Croyde
Braunton
Appledore
Clovelly
Hartland Point
Hartland Quay
Hartland

South West Coast Path

National Railways

County Boundaries

Areas of Outstanding Natural Beauty

National Parks

Map not to sc
For illustrative purposes c

North Devon
Combe Martin to Marsland Mouth

(Sections 4-13)

Most of the North Devon coast faces north over the Bristol Channel. Much of this length comprises cliffs of moderate height with, in the east, some prominent headlands like Morte Point and Baggy Point which offer fine coastal vistas. In the centre of the North Devon section is the large joint estuary of the Taw and Torridge Rivers, flanked by areas of sand dunes and marshland. The South West Coast Path partly uses old railway lines around the estuary, crossing the rivers at the towns of Barnstaple and Bideford. Adjacent to the estuary are extensive sandy beaches, popular with surfers and families. The north facing cliffs continue to Hartland Point, one of the Coast Path's major headlands (referred to as the 'Point of Hercules' in a Roman geography). Seascapes typically have the coast of Wales beyond the Bristol Channel as the backdrop; in the west the offshore island of Lundy, at the "mouth" of the Bristol Channel, is the focal point. Hartland Point marks an abrupt change in direction from the east-west of most of North Devon to the north-south beyond. This north-south length is very dramatic, with high cliffs fronted by jagged fingers of rock stretching into the Atlantic. Deep and steep valleys cut the coastline, making for some considerable gradients for walkers, but there are no bays or harbours other than the tiny harbour at Hartland Quay.

Hartland Quay

OS Maps: Landranger 180; Explorer 139 or OL9

	This Walk	Cumulative	This Walk	Cumulative	Grading	Timing
Ascent	1,280ft	10,026ft	390m	3,056m	Moderate, strenuous in parts	2.5 hours
Distance	5.4mi	40.1mi	8.7km	64.5km		

For detailed directions see our Walking Guide no. 4, Combe Martin to Ilfracombe.

This is a Section of rocky inlets, one of which, Watermouth, is spacious enough for boats to be moored. These bays are divided by rugged headlands. The cliffs here are grey and slatey, making for a forbidding looking coastline, notwithstanding the little bays. At the western end the site of a prehistoric hill fort gives a panoramic view over Ilfracombe. This Section is never far from the A399 coast road and various tourist facilities, so despite the impressive cliffs it is not a lonely length.

Directions

Combe Martin and Ilfracombe are linked by a regular bus service, allowing a bus-walk to be easily undertaken on this Section.

The Coast Path leaves the Lime Kiln car park in Combe Martin, passing the Tourist Information Centre (TIC), then forks right to join the A399 road. Turn right (Seaside Hill Road) above the beach. Turn right onto a narrow tarmac lane which climbs steeply to re-join the A399 road. Walk on the slightly raised path along the roadside through two gates. Go along a path beside a field to a flight of steps, then turn left up the slip road back to the main road and on to the brow, passing the bus shelter. Turn right to follow the road down to the old main road, with a bus shelter, now used as an Information Point, over to the right. Here turn left beside the entrance to the Hotel to follow a track towards Watermouth Cove.

At Watermouth it is possible to cross the foreshore for some 110 yards/100m to a flight of steps at most states of the tide; take care, as the rocks can be slippery. However, if the tide is high, use the route running parallel to the main road. (Check the Watermouth tide timings by contacting Ilfracombe or Combe Martin Tourist Information Centres (TICs) - see page 197.)

This roadside path is a great improvement as it avoids the need to walk in the road carriageway. It was completed in late 2013 following the Association's offer of £50,000 from our reserves towards its cost, because of our safety concerns. The offer enabled the remainder of the funding to be secured from the Rural Development Fund for England and Devon County Council, a successful conclusion to a decade of pressure.

The next pleasant section of path passes the western side of Watermouth Cove and on around Widmouth Head and then Rillage Point. There is then a roadside section into Hele. Turn right here then climb some steps on the far left of the beach. The Path zigzags up past Beacon Point to the top of Hillsborough. Follow the waymarks down the hill to Ilfracombe Harbour.

OS Maps: Landranger 180; Explorer 139

	This Walk	Cumulative	This Walk	Cumulative	Grading	Timing
Ascent	2,037ft	12,063ft	621m	3,677m	Easy to moderate; strenuous west of Lee Bay	3.5 hours
Distance	8.5mi	48.6mi	13.7km	78.2km		

For detailed directions see our Walking Guide no. 5, Ilfracombe to Woolacombe.

Most of this Section is characterised by grass-topped cliffs fronting numerous small coves and a foreshore of rock ledges. Half-way along is the focal point of Bull Point lighthouse. At Morte Point the character of the coastline changes abruptly as the enormous beach of Woolacombe Sands in its vast bay comes into view, often dotted with surfers. The dark jagged rocks of Morte Point give this headland a superb brooding atmosphere.

Directions

Ilfracombe and Woolacombe are linked by a regular bus service, allowing a bus-walk to be easily undertaken on this Section.

From Ilfracombe Harbour walk along Capstone Road. After some 170 yards/150m turn right to pass around Capstone Point. At the far end take a flight of steps that goes up behind the back of the Landmark Theatre. Follow this path to the top of the gardens and through a gate by a shelter. Bear right along Granville Road then right again onto an unmetalled road which leads to the Torrs Walk on the right; the Torrs Walk is well waymarked.

At the top of the Torrs Walk bear right and follow the path down the field to the stile in the corner. Continue ahead around the hill to another stile then cross the field to meet the old coach road ahead. Bear right on this track, which later becomes a minor road into Lee Bay.

The next length from Lee Bay is quite strenuous. Proceed up the road from Lee, turning right at the top of the hill through a brick-pillared gate. Two steep valleys are crossed before Bull Point and its lighthouse are reached. The path continues on and out around Morte Point, a spectacular jagged slate ridge like a dinosaur's back emerging from the sea. The path leaves Morte Point and continues beneath the cliffs past small sandy bays to arrive at Woolacombe.

Lee Bay, North Devon

southwestcoastpath.org.uk

OS Maps: Landranger 180; Explorer 139

	This Walk	Cumulative	This Walk	Cumulative	Grading	Timing
Ascent	725ft	12,788ft	221m	3,898m	Moderate	3 hours
Distance	5.2mi	53.8mi	8.4km	86.6km		

For detailed directions see our Walking Guide no. 6, Woolacombe to Croyde Bay.

The main feature of this Section is the vast sandy beach of Woolacombe Sands, backed by a substantial line of dunes. Busy with families and surfers close to the town, it becomes surprisingly empty away from the facilities. Beyond the beach is the superb headland of Baggy Point, a contrast to the beach with its steep cliffs and broad, grassy top. Rounding the headland another, smaller sandy bay comes into view, Croyde Bay, with the wider vista of Bideford Bay beyond.

Directions

Croyde Bay is an excellent centre for a circular walk using the Coast Path, around Baggy Point to Putsborough, giving views over Woolacombe Sands while experiencing the superb character of the headland.

At Woolacombe the Coast Path runs parallel to the Esplanade road, then turns up Challacombe Road. It leaves this road on the right at approximately the National Trust sign – there may be no waymark here. The Path continues through the enormous dunes of Woolacombe Warren – the waymarking means that going astray is unlikely. An alternative is to follow Marine Drive and the track beyond, which gives better views. If the tide is low many walk the length of Woolacombe Sands but this should not be attempted on a high or rising tide.

The official path leaves the Warren by a set of steep steps, joining the extension to Marine Drive and the alternative route. It continues along the track then a road, leaving it to the right after the caravan site. As an alternative, take the earlier path on the right to the car park at Putsborough, where there are seasonal refreshments and toilets (the beach route joins here). Go left of the caravan site to a stile and up the cliff slope to re-join the official path.

The excellent high level path continues to the end of Baggy Point, giving superb views. At the end of the headland, bear right to join the lower path towards Croyde. Follow the road, partly on a parallel path. Do not leave the road at the first slipway. The official path leaves the road a little further on to cross the beach, but many will continue on to visit Croyde and its facilities.

Woolacombe

OS Maps: Landranger 181 (eastern half); Landranger 180 (western half); Explorer OL9

	This Walk	Cumulative	This Walk	Cumulative	Grading	Timing
Ascent	506ft	13,294ft	154m	4,052m	Easy	3.25 hours
Distance	9.8mi	63.6mi	15.8km	102.4km		

For detailed directions see our Walking Guide no. 7, Croyde Bay to Braunton.

The length immediately adjacent to Croyde Bay follows a low cliff and gives stunning views over the truly enormous length of Saunton Sands with the dune complex of Braunton Burrows behind. Beyond is the sweep of Bideford Bay, with the possibility of seeing as far as Hartland Point lighthouse, many miles away. Offshore on the horizon is the isle of Lundy. The remainder of this Section is low and level, through a huge range of dunes (the official route) or along the seemingly endless Saunton Sands. Then comes the twin estuary of the Rivers Taw and Torridge, with mudbanks and reclaimed marshes making for a birdwatcher's delight. This is a length displaying a relatively rare aspect of the South West coast.

Directions

Croyde Bay and Braunton are linked by a regular year-round bus service, making this a good bus-walk possibility.

The Coast Path leaves Croyde Bay via the beach (no dogs May-September) and on to the low cliffs at Down End. Turn left at the old coastguard lookout to the B3231 road. Cross the road with care here, turn left then climb some stone steps. The Path now contours round Saunton Down, parallel to and above the road. This ends opposite the large white building of the Hotel.

From here there are optional routes. The first option is to cross the road and pass around the hotel to the Saunton Sands car park, where there are toilets and seasonal refreshments. Leave the car park by the entrance road and after 55 yards/50m bear right along a stony lane to the B3231. Continue carefully along the road for some 400 yards/365m, past the Golf Club driveway, turning right at a red brick partially rendered house.

If there is no need for the toilets or refreshments, a better option is to turn left uphill opposite the hotel, away from the road. Follow the Path as it bears round to the right until it arrives at the B3231 opposite the red brick house described above. Cross the road to continue on the same route as above.

This route now enters the Braunton Burrows nature reserve, designated a UNESCO Biosphere Reserve for its nature conservation importance. The route through the Burrows is well waymarked; first follow a clear track through patchy woodland along the edge of the golf course with the military training area on the right. After the Sandy Lane car park follow the signing for nearly two miles along a rough, traffic-free, military dirt road known as the American Road to arrive at Broad Sands car park by the estuary of the Taw and Torridge rivers. Follow another dirt road, approximately eastwards, to arrive at the White House, a well-known local landmark.

Many walkers prefer to miss the Burrows and walk from Saunton Sands car park the length of the beach, for some 3.5 miles/5.5km. Near the end of the beach, just after a wooden groyne, look out for a slatted wooden catwalk entering the dunes to the left. Follow this to arrive at the Broad Sands car park. This beach route keeps the sea in sight, not the case with the Burrows route.

From the White House follow the estuary side on top of the Great Sea Bank. This is followed, between estuary and reclaimed marshes, to the old quay at Velator on the edge of Braunton. To visit Braunton and its facilities, turn left at Velator along the footpath and cycleway, following the former railway track.

Saunton Sands

OS Maps: Landranger 180; Explorer 139

	This Walk	Cumulative	This Walk	Cumulative	Grading	Timing
Ascent	16ft	13,310ft	5m	4,057m	Easy	2 hours
Distance	5.4mi	69.0mi	8.7km	111.0km		

For detailed directions see our Walking Guide no. 8, Braunton to Barnstaple.

This is a flat, low-level Section, following the line of the former railway track once used by the Atlantic Coast Express. As well as the Coast Path, it is also used by Devon's Coast to Coast Cycle Route. At the Braunton end, the main item of interest is the Royal Marines air base at Chivenor, next to the Path, but further on the Path runs alongside the estuary of the River Taw, with its interplay of water and sand and mud banks. This makes for a pleasant environment; in character, however, this length is semi-urban.

Directions

There is a regular and year-round bus service between Braunton and Barnstaple, which can also be accessed at Chivenor, approximately mid-way along the route, giving various short walks options.

From Braunton's main car park the signed route to Barnstaple leads to the Coast Path at Velator and from here the Path follows the former railway past Chivenor Royal Marines base and then alongside the Taw Estuary all the way to Barnstaple.

The new high level bridge across the River Taw can be used as an alternative to the Coast Path and offers a superb view down the river. However, most will prefer to continue on the riverside path into Barnstaple, an attractive town with many facilities for walkers.

Approaching Barnstaple on the former railway (signed as Tarka Trail), the Path crosses a bridge over the tributary River Yeo and then passes the old railway station to a riverside embankment. Leave this at steps climbing to Barnstaple's historic Long Bridge. Barnstaple, North Devon's major centre, is a pleasant and interesting historic town well worth exploring, as well as offering a range of facilities, including a branch line railway to the main line at Exeter.

Fremington Station

OS Maps: Landranger 180; Explorer 139

	This Walk	Cumulative	This Walk	Cumulative	Grading	Timing
Ascent	40ft	13,350ft	12m	4,069m	Easy	2.5 hours
Distance	10.7mi	79.7mi	17.2km	128.3km		

For detailed directions see our Walking Guide no. 9, Barnstaple to Bideford.

This is a flat, low-level Section, much of it following a former railway line on the south side of the Taw Estuary. It passes through a landscape of marshland and pastures, with the tidal expanses and sand banks of the river never far away. This is an area of great value for birdlife. Approaching Instow the estuary opens out as the Taw's sister river, the Torridge, joins and there are wide areas of sand bars and dunes. This Section, despite its proximity to "civilisation" and the use of the former railway as part of the Devon Coast to Coast Cycle Route, is nevertheless one of much interest and character.

Directions

There is a regular and frequent all-year bus service between Barnstaple and Bideford, which can also be accessed at Fremington and Instow along the route. A variety of short walk options is therefore available.

Cross Barnstaple's historic Long Bridge then keep to the right of the large roundabout, following Tarka Trail signing, then cross a mini-roundabout to a path which curves around to a subway under the approach road for the high-level bridge. A link path to the railway station goes off to the left here. The main path, signed Coast Path and Tarka Trail, then links to the former railway line. The direct Coast Path route across the high-level bridge joins here.

The former railway continues past the delightfully restored Fremington Quay, with its all-year cafe and Information Point. At Yelland look out for the Path leaving the railway to the right which takes the Coast Path behind the site of an old power station. After passing inland of the cricket ground the route then crosses an area of dunes to arrive at the estuary-side road through Instow, which has all facilities. Go through the old railway station and follow the former railway to the restored Bideford station. Leave the station to cross Bideford Long Bridge, then turn right along the bustling quay. Bideford has all facilities.

Bideford Bridge

OS Maps: Landranger 180; Explorer 139

	This Walk	Cumulative	This Walk	Cumulative	Grading	Timing
Ascent	524ft	13,871ft	159m	4,228m	Easy	4.5 hours
Distance	8.0mi	87.7mi	12.9km	141.1km		

For detailed directions see our Walking Guide no. 10, Bideford to Westward Ho!

Much of this Section follows the estuary of the River Torridge, first on its east bank then turning back on its west. The estuary is largely enclosed by green hills, but houses and roads are ever-present and a high-level road bridge over the estuary is a major feature. The Coast Path crosses the river at the charming old port of Bideford. Passing beyond the estuary and through the characterful old fishing town of Appledore, the Path crosses the open spaces of Northam Burrows and its surrounding marshlands and then alongside an enormous pebble ridge as it arrives again at the open sea. As an alternative option, missing out Bideford, a ferry service is now operating from April to October between Instow and Appledore, for details see page 17.

Directions

A regular bus service links Bideford and Westward Ho! and another connects Bideford to Appledore. These services allow for a range of Coast Path-based walk options.

From Bideford Quay keep alongside the river past the car park then next to the rugby club to a lane which passes under the high-level bridge. Follow the waymarked tracks to a riverside lane then, after the old tank traps, fork right to a small woodland area.

Descend to a boardwalk then, if the tide is low, continue on the old sea wall. At high tide a well waymarked route circles the marshy area. Follow the waymarked route round Appledore shipyard and at the road turn right into Appledore via Myrtle Street. Continue along the quay and on into the charming old part of the town, along Irsha Street and past the lifeboat station. Here the route follows a path along the edge of low cliffs and across a field to a slipway, where the route joins a road. Follow the road for approximately 0.3 mile/0.5km to a crossroads and here turn right.

Follow the track ahead alongside the marshes then on the seaward side of the dunes to the pebble ridge. Continue ahead on the landward side of the ridge. On the approach to Westward Ho! leave Northam Burrows by the pedestrian gate to the right of the cattle grid by the toll booth. Proceed up Pebble Ridge Road using the right side pavement to the crossroads. Turn right into Golf Links Road then, after the Tesco Express store, turn right into Westbourne Terrace. Just before the slipway turn left onto the promenade to Westward Ho!

OS Maps: Landranger 180 (eastern half) ; Explorer 139 (eastern half);
Landranger 190 (western half); Explorer 126 (western half)

	This Walk	Cumulative	This Walk	Cumulative	Grading	Timing
Ascent	2,995ft	16,866ft	913m	5,141m	Strenuous	6 hours
Distance	11.1mi	98.8mi	17.9km	159.0km		

For detailed directions see our Walking Guide no. 11, Westward Ho! to Clovelly

This Section is one of cliffs and woods. The eastern half is an area of undulating cliffs, cut in places by substantial valleys, though in the length closest to Westward Ho!, where the line of an old railway is used, the Path is generally level. The western half passes through lengthy wooded stretches, much of it along the old carriage road known as the Hobby Drive. At the western end, Clovelly is probably one of the most picturesque villages in England.

Directions

There is no direct bus route between Westward Ho! and Clovelly. However, there is one between Bideford and Clovelly, as well as a frequent link to Bideford from Westward Ho! Buck's Mills, about two thirds of the way along this length towards Clovelly, is on the Bideford-Clovelly bus route, giving a possible bus-walk at this end.

At Westward Ho! walk along the Path above the beach. After passing the last of the holiday chalets, the Path follows the track of the long-disued Bideford to Westward Ho! railway. This makes a fine easy scenic walk. Where the railway turns inland, the Path continues along the cliffs, rising and falling to cross a short pebble beach before climbing again. At Peppercombe turn inland to cross the stream and then continue through woodland. Note that some old maps may not show the correct route at Worthygate Wood. The Path drops to Buck's Mills, a picturesque little spot, then climbs again into more woods. On leaving Barton Wood, keep to the bottom edge of the field until crossing a bridge to the Hobby Drive at the end of a second field. The Hobby Drive section is nearly 3 miles/5km long, and although very pleasant offers sea glimpses rather than sea views. The Path arrives at Clovelly at the top of the steep village street. Clovelly is very picturesque and has most facilities, though perhaps limited in range.

Westward Ho!

OS Maps: Landranger 190; Explorer 126

	This Walk	Cumulative	This Walk	Cumulative	Grading	Timing
Ascent	2,382ft	19,248ft	726m	5,867m	Moderate to strenuous	5 hours
Distance	10.3mi	109.1mi	16.6km	175.6km		

For detailed directions see our Walking Guide no. 12, Clovelly to Hartland Quay.

There is a great contrast in this Section between east and west. In the east the landscape is one of parkland, the domesticated and partly ornamental landscape of the grounds of Clovelly Court. After leaving the parkland a run of high cliffs culminates at Hartland Point, one of the great defining headlands of the Coast Path. Here the coast turns from east-west to north-south and its character changes into one of the Coast Path's most breathtaking stretches, with dark brooding cliffs behind jagged fingers of rock stretching into the Atlantic Ocean. Experiencing its magnificent scenery is well worth the effort of crossing the spectacular deep valleys which cut the coast. The Section ends at the pub and hotel at Hartland Quay, which has a wonderful remote atmosphere.

Clovelly High Street

Directions

Hartland Quay has no public transport. However, there are numerous walking links from the Coast Path to Hartland village, 2.5 miles/4km inland, which is on the bus route to Clovelly.

If using Clovelly as a base, it is requested that visitors use the main car park. If you're walking on your own, it might be worth paying for a village visit at £7 which includes car parking.

From the main car park walk out of the entrance and turn right down the road for some 220 yards/200m to a black gate on the left. Go through and follow the track first right and through a gap in the wall, then leave the track and follow the marked path down to the right. After a while go through a kissing-gate then follow the fence on the right to another gate into shrubbery. Continue through the shrubbery through more gates. Turn right at a T-junction and right again at the next fork. Soon the Path arrives at an unusual seat known as the "Angel's Wings". At the track, turn hard right – not along the track. After passing a superb viewpoint the Path descends steeply into a valley to another track. Go right here. The signed detour to the viewpoint is well worth the effort.

The Coast Path goes down the valley to Mouth Mill. Turn left before reaching the shore on to a substantial track. Turn right to cross the new steel and timber bridge.

Turn right after the bridge then left to climb the valley side. Half-way up, follow the steps to the right. On reaching the top pass through fields to a stile on the right leading to some descending zigzags. Cross the bridge at the bottom, turn left then take the first right.

After the prehistoric earthwork of Windbury Castle the Path continues on the cliff-top to Shipload Bay and then on to Hartland Point, where there are seasonal refreshments. The Coast Path turns sharp left off the lighthouse track towards the coastguard lookout before the lighthouse gate. A short diversion gives a good view of a wreck on the rocks below.

From Hartland Point the Path descends into an unusual valley, almost parallel to the coast, at Smoothlands, before climbing again. Descending then to the valley at the Abbey River the Path goes inland to cross at a stone bridge. At the next cliff top, past an old folly tower, the Path arrives at a road by the old Rocket House. Bear right to follow the Path downhill to Hartland Quay, a lonely outpost with car park, toilets and refreshments, as well as a hotel.

Hartland Quay

OS Maps: Landranger 190; Explorer 126 (most of length); Explorer 111 (Bude)

	This Walk	Cumulative	This Walk	Cumulative	Grading	Timing
Ascent	4,170ft	23,418ft	1,271m	7,138m	Severe	8.5 hours
Distance	15.2mi	124.3mi	24.5km	200.0km		

For detailed directions see our Walking Guide no. 13, Hartland Quay to Morwenstow and Morwenstow to Bude.

This is an awe-inspiring and dramatic coastline. Great jagged ridges of rock stretch out into the Atlantic Ocean, backed by high, surf-fringed cliffs. The coast is punctuated by jutting headlands and tiny, often inaccessible beaches. In the south, towards Bude, the coast softens a little and, at low tide, long sandy beaches appear. This is a spectacular Section.

Directions

Hartland Quay has no public transport connections. There is, however, an infrequent bus service between Bude and Morwenstow, half-way along, which could be used for a bus-walk on the southern half of this Section.

Note that this is probably the most arduous of all the days in the suggested itinerary. It is necessary to cross ten river valleys to complete the length, all of them steep and deep. Because of this, many may prefer to split the length at Morwenstow.

From Hartland Quay a track then a grassy path passes behind St Catherine's Tor. There is a climb then the cliff path reaches the dramatic waterfall at Speke's Mill Mouth. Keep to the eastern side of the stream here for some 150 yards/135m then cross by the wooden footbridge. Follow the signs up the valley inland of Swansford Hill. Take care at Sandhole Cliff, after joining the metalled road, to look out for the signpost after about 0.3 mile/0.5km indicating the turn right back to the coast. (It is hoped this length of road may be eliminated in the near future.) After Welcombe Mouth, Marsland Mouth marks the Cornish border, indicated by a wooden sign. The ascents and descents continue, and a diversion to Morwenstow might be worth considering. The church is picturesque and interesting and there are seasonal refreshments nearby. At the radio dishes do not miss the sign directing right towards the cliff edge. Descending to Duckpool, cross the stream by a footbridge. There are toilets here. Continue on to Sandy Mouth where there are more toilets and seasonal refreshments. The going now eases at last and after passing over the open cliffs at Maer Down the Path arrives at Crooklets Beach at Bude. Follow the Path along the low cliffs behind the beaches into the town, which has all facilities.

> If you enjoy sleeping, eating or drinking at any business on the Path please suggest they join us as Business Members so that we can share their brilliance!

The businesses listed here are all supporters of the South West Coast Path Association, they have joined as business members and it would be great if you could show your support for them too. In addition, businesses are listed with more details on our website: www.southwestcoastpath.org.uk Find them through our walk finder or our accommodation finder tools.

KEY:

GR Grid Reference
DP Distance from the Path
NT Nearest Town

🐕 Dogs Welcome
🍴 Evening Meal Available
3 Number Of Rooms

🛒 Grocery Shop On Site
📶 Wifi
🚗 Parking

Bed & Breakfasts and Hotels

NAME	OTHER INFO	
Channel Vista Guesthouse 4 The Woodlands, Combe Martin, EX34 0AT ☎ 01271 883514 ✉ info@channelvista.co.uk 🌐 www.channelvista.co.uk	GR: 574 470 — DP: 0.1 miles NT: **COMBE MARTIN** Offers one night stays 7 🚗 📶	Other info:
Newberry Beach Lodge Newberry Road, Combe Martin, EX34 0AP ☎ 01271 883709 ✉ cjg0040@msn.com 🌐 www.newberrybeachlodge.co.uk	GR: 574 471 — DP: 0 miles NT: **COMBE MARTIN** 4 🚗 📶 🐕	Other info:
Blair Lodge Moory Meadow, Combe Martin, EX34 0DG ☎ 01271 882294 ✉ info@blairlodge.co.uk 🌐 www.blairlodge.co.uk	GR: 578 472 — DP: 0 miles **COMBE MARTIN** Offers one night stays 8 🚗 📶 🍴	Other info:
Fontennay B&B Woodlands, Combe Martin, EX34 0AT ☎ 01271 889368 ✉ sarah@visitfontenay.co.uk 🌐 www.visitfontenay.co.uk	GR: 575 470 — DP: 0.1 miles NT: **COMBE MARTIN** Offers one night stays 3 🚗 📶	Other info: Parking only for one car.
Mellstock House B&B Woodlands, Combe Martin, EX34 0AR ☎ 01271 882592 ✉ enquiries@mellstockhouse.co.uk 🌐 www.mellstockhouse.co.uk	GR: 576 473 — DP: 0.1 miles NT: **ILFRACOMBE** Offers one night stays 5 🚗 📶 🍴	Other info: Free pick ups and drop offs.
Avoncourt Lodge 6 Torrs Walk Avenue, Ilfracombe, EX34 8AU ☎ 01271 862543 ✉ stay@avoncourtilfracombe.co.uk 🌐 www.avoncourtilfracombe.co.uk	GR: 512 475 — DP: 0 miles NT: **ILFRACOMBE** Offers one night stays 10 🚗 📶 🐕	Other info:
Brookdales B&B 23 Brookdale Avenue, Ilfracombe, EX34 8DB ☎ 01271 269388 ✉ christine_goodenough@sky.com 🌐 www.brookdales.co.uk	GR: 513 474 — DP: 0 miles NT: **ILFRACOMBE** Offers one night stays 3 📶 🍴	Other info:

NAME	OTHER INFO		
The Olive Branch Guesthouse	GR: 523 477	DP: 0.1 miles	
56 Fore Street, Ilfracombe, EX34 9DJ	NT: **ILFRACOMBE**		
☏ 01271 879005 / 01271 879076			
✉ enquiries@olivebranchguesthouse.co.uk			Other info:
🌐 www.olivebranchguesthouse.co.uk	5 🛜		
Collingdale Guest House	GR: 526 475	DP: 0.3 miles	
13 Larkstone Terrace, Ilfracombe, EX34 9NU	NT: **ILFRACOMBE**		
☏ 01271 863770			
✉ thecollingdale@gmail.com			Other info: Award winning Guest House
🌐 www.thecollingdale.co.uk	9 🛜		
Cranleigh House Wellness Centre	GR: 583 467	DP: 0.25 miles	
High Street, Combe Martin, Ilfracombe, EX34 0EP	NT: **ILFRACOMBE**		
☏ 01271 889325 / 07985928461	Offers one night stays		
✉ cranleighhouse1@btinternet.com			Other info: Vegetarian, vegan, alcohol free B&B
🌐 www.cranleighhouse.org	4 🛜 🐕 🍴		
Marlyn B&B	GR: 567 470	DP: 0.3 miles	
Home Barton Farmhouse, Barton Lane, Berrynarbour, EX34 9SU	NT: **ILFRACOMBE**		
☏ 07952 244874	Offers one night stays		
✉ brandongwendolyn@yahoo.co.uk			Other info:
🌐	3 🚗 🛜 🍴		
Westwell Hall	GR: 510 473	DP: 0.2 miles	
Torrs Park, Ilfracombe, EX34 8AZ	NT: **ILFRACOMBE**		
☏ 01271 268287	Offers one night stays		
✉ bettybutton@icloud.com			Other info:
🌐 www.westwellhall-ilfracombe.uk	9 🚗 🛜 🍴		
The Old Eclectick	GR: 520 477	DP: 0.7 miles	
26 Fore Street, Waterloo Terrace, Ilfracombe, EX34 9DJ	NT: **ILFRACOMBE**		
☏ 01271 867149	Offers one night stays		
✉ sophia@wordtwister.co.uk			Other info: Dogs stay for free
🌐 www.southwestcoastpath.org.uk/old-eclectick-ilfracombe	2 🚗 🛜 🐕 🛒		
Harcourt Hotel	GR: 520 477	DP: 0 miles	
39 Fore Street, Ilfracombe, EX34 9DJ	NT: **WOOLACOMBE**		
☏ 01271 862931	Offers one night stays		
✉ enquiries@harcourthotel.co.uk			Other info: Two night minimum stay at weekends
🌐 www.harcourthotel.co.uk	8 🛜 🐕		
Lundy House	GR: 454 447	DP: 0.5 miles	
Lundy House, Mortehoe, Woolacombe, EX34 7DZ	NT: **WOOLACOMBE**		
☏ 01271 870372	Offers one night stays		
✉ info@lundyhousehotel.co.uk			Other info:
🌐 www.lundyhousehotel.co.uk	8 🐕		
Marine House B&B	GR: 459 436	DP: 0.25 miles	
South Street, Woolacombe, EX34 7BB	NT: **WOOLACOMBE**		
☏ 01271 870972			
✉ info@marinehouse.co.uk			Other info:
🌐 www.marinehouse.co.uk	2		
Woolacombe Bay Hotel	GR:	DP:	
South Street, Woolacombe, EX34 7BN	NT: **WOOLACOMBE**		
☏ 01271870388			
✉ info@woolacombebayhotel.co.uk			Other info:
🌐 www.woolacombebayhotel.co.uk	60 🚗 🛜 🍴		

NAME	OTHER INFO	
Combas Farm Meadow lane, Croyde, EX33 1PH ☎ 01271 890398 ✉ info@combasfarm.co.uk 🌐 www.combasfarm.co.uk	GR: 449 396 DP: 0.5 miles NT: **CROYDE** Offers one night stays [4] 🛜 🍴	Other info:
North Cottage 14 North Street, Braunton, EX33 1AJ ☎ 01271 812703 ✉ north_cottage@hotmail.com 🌐 www.northcottagebraunton.co.uk	GR: 485 367 DP: 0.5 miles NT: **BRAUNTON** Offers one night stays [4] 🚗 🛜 🐕	Other info:
Silver Cottage B&B 14 Silver Street, Braunton, EX33 2EN ☎ 01271 814165 ✉ silvercottage.braunton@gmail.com 🌐 www.silvercottage.braunton.co.uk	GR: 489 372 DP: 1.5 miles NT: **BRAUNTON** Offers one night stays [2] 🛜	Other info: No single occupancy suppliment
Bennings B&B The Firs, Higher Park Road, Braunton, EX33 2LG ☎ 01271 814358 ✉ alisonbenning@btinternet.com 🌐 www.bennings.co.uk	GR: 499 364 DP: 3 miles NT: **BRAUNTON** Offers one night stays [2] 🚗 🛜 🐕	Other info:
Breakers B&B Downend, Croyde, EX33 1QE ☎ 01271 890101 ✉ croydebreaksbookings@gmail.com 🌐 www.croydebreaksindevon.co.uk	GR: 436 386 DP: 0.1 miles NT: **BRAUNTON** Offers one night stays [4] 🚗 🛜	Other info: Laundry on request. Packed lunches if ordered in advance
Trojen Bed & Breakfast Franklyn Avenue, Braunton, EX33 2JY ☎ 01271 814019 / 07890885825 ✉ jennyjcocker@yahoo.co.uk 🌐 www.staybandbnorthdevon.com	GR: 490 365 DP: 0.5 miles NT: **BRAUNTON** Offers one night stays [1] 🚗 🛜	Other info:
No 2 Broadgate House B&B Bellaire, Pilton, Barnstaple, EX31 1QZ ☎ 01271 373229 ✉ no2broadgate@aol.com 🌐 www.no2broadgate.co.uk	GR: 553 442 DP: 0.8 miles NT: **BARNSTAPLE** [3] 🛜	Other info:
The Poplars B&B Rumsam Road, Barnstaple, EX32 9EW ☎ 01271 378773 ✉ info@thepoplarsbarnstaple.co.uk 🌐 www.barnstaplebedandbreakfast.co.uk	GR: 567 319 DP: 0.75 miles NT: **BARNSTAPLE** Offers one night stays [3] 🚗 🛜	Other info:
Herton Guest House Herton, Lake Hill, Barnstaple, EX31 3HS ☎ 01271 323302 ✉ janmanning.herton@gmail.com 🌐 www.herton-guesthouse.co.uk	GR: 553 321 DP: NT: **BARNSTAPLE** Offers one night stays [2] 🚗	Other info: Separate cottage available
Longmead House 9 Longmead, Lynton, EX35 6DQ ☎ 01598 752523 ✉ info@longmeadhouse.co.uk 🌐 www.longmeadhouse.co.uk	GR: DP: 0.1 miles NT: **BARNSTAPLE** Offers one night stays [8] 🚗 🛜 🍴	Other info:

NAME	OTHER INFO		
The Laurels B&B 26 Church Street, Braunton, EX33 2EL ☎ 01271 812872 ✉ info@thelaurelsbraunton.co.uk 🌐 www.thelaurelsbraunton.co.uk	GR:	DP: 0 miles	
	NT: **BARNSTAPLE**		
	Offers one night stays		
	3 🐕	Other info:	
The Whiteleaf Croyde, Braunton, EX33 1PN ☎ 01271 890266 ✉ bookings@thewhiteleaf.co.uk 🌐 www.thewhiteleaf.co.uk	GR: 441 389	DP: 1 mile	
	NT: **BARNSTAPLE**		
	Offers one night stays		
	5 🚗 📶 🍴	Other info: Dinner must be booked in advance	
The Old Vicarage B&B Barbican Terrace, Barnstaple, EX32 9HQ ☎ 01271 328504 ✉ theoldvicaragebarnstaple@gmail.com 🌐 www.oldvicaragebarnstaple.co.uk	GR: 562 328	DP: 0.25 miles	
	NT: **BARNSTAPLE**		
	Offers one night stays		
	2 🚗 📶	Other info:	
Springfield House B&B New Road, Instow, Bideford, EX39 4LN ☎ 01271 860895 ✉ lucinda@springfield-instow.com 🌐 www.springfield-instow.co.uk	GR: 475 301	DP: 0 miles	
	NT: **INSTOW**		
	3 🐕	Other info: Self-catering available	
Gawlish Farm Gawlish Farm, Hartland, Bideford, EX39 6AT ☎ 01237 441320 ✉ gawlish@btconnect.com 🌐 www.southwestcoastpath.org.uk/gawlish-farm-near-hartland	GR: 260 267	DP: 0.25 miles	
	NT: **BIDEFORD**		
	Offers one night stays		
	4 🚗 📶 🍴	Other info:	
Honeysuckle Cottage B&B Westleigh, Bideford, EX39 4NL ☎ 01271 861067 ✉ bedandbreakfast@honeysucklecottagewestleigh.com 🌐 www.honeysucklecottagewestleigh.com	GR: 472 287	DP: 0.25 miles	
	NT: **BIDEFORD**		
	Offers one night stays		
	2 🚗 📶	Other info:	
Southdown Bed & Breakfast 1 Southdown Cottage, Higher Clovelly, Bideford, EX39 5SA ☎ 01237 431504 ✉ maryfmcoll@hotmail.com 🌐 www.southwestcoastpath.org.uk/southdown-bb-clovelly	GR: 299 235	DP: 2.5 miles	
	NT: **BIDEFORD**		
	2 🐕	Other info:	
Hartland Quay Hotel Hartland Quay, Bideford, EX39 6DU ☎ 01237 441218 ✉ info@hartlandquayhotel.com 🌐 www.hartlandquayhotel.co.uk	GR: 222 247	DP: 0 miles	
	NT: **BIDEFORD**		
	Offers one night stays		
	14 🚗 📶 🍴	Other info: The Bar and one hotel room are dog friendly	
Old Keepers Cottage Tennacott Lane, Bideford, EX39 4QD ☎ 01237 479113 ✉ lucygiddy@btinternet.com 🌐 www.oldkeeperscottage.net	GR: 475 247	DP: 2 miles	
	NT: **BIDEFORD**		
	4 🚗	Other info:	
Pillowery Park Burscott, Higher Clovelly, Bideford, EX39 5RR ☎ 01237 431668 ✉ info@clovellyrooms.co.uk 🌐 www.clovellyrooms.co.uk	GR: 313 241	DP: 0.75 miles	
	NT: **BIDEFORD**		
	Offers one night stays		
	3 🚗 📶	Other info: Lifts by arrangement	

NAME	OTHER INFO		
The Old Smithy B&B 147 Slerra Hill, Clovelly, EX39 5ST ☏ 01237 431202 ✉ oldsmithybandb@gmail.com 🌐 www.oldsmithybandbclovelly.co.uk	GR: 310 243 DP: 0.5 miles NT: **BIDEFORD** Offers one night stays 2 🚗 📶		Other info: No Smoking
Culloden House Culloden House, Fosketh Hill, Westward Ho!, EX39 1UL ☏ 01237 479421 ✉ cullodenhouse@gmail.com 🌐 www.culloden-house.co.uk	GR: 430 289 DP: 0.15 miles NT: **WESTWARD HO!** Offers one night stays 8 📶		Other info:
The Old Police House B&B Higher Clovelly, EX39 5RR ☏ 01237 431256 ✉ enquiries@clovellybandb.co.uk 🌐 www.clovellybandb.co.uk	GR: DP: NT: **CLOVELLY** Offers one night stays 🍴		Other info:
Cheristow Lavender Organic B&B Higher Cheristow, Hartland, Bideford, EX39 6DA ☏ 01237 440101 ✉ cheristow@btinternet.com 🌐 www.cheristow.co.uk	GR: 250 254 DP: 1.25 miles NT: **HARTLAND** Offers one night stays 1 🚗 📶 🍴		Other info:
Copps Castle B&B Hartland, Bideford, EX39 6AS ☏ 01237 441733 ✉ coppscastle@gmail.com 🌐 www.bandbhartland.co.uk	GR: SS2654526223 DP: 0.5 miles NT: **HARTLAND** Offers one night stays 3 🚗 📶		Other info:
Elmscott Farm B&B Elmscott, Hartland, Bideford, EX39 6ES ☏ 01237 441276 ✉ john.goa@virgin.net 🌐 www.elmscott.org.uk/bed-and-breakfast.asp	GR: 231 217 DP: 1 mile NT: **HARTLAND** Offers one night stays 3 🚗 🛒		Other info: Lifts available to path & pub. Open Easter-Oct
Two Harton Manor B&B The Square, Hartland, Bideford, EX39 6BL ☏ 01237 441670 ✉ merlyn@twohartonmanor.co.uk 🌐 www.twohartonmanor.co.uk	GR: 258 244 DP: 2.5 miles NT: **HARTLAND** 3 📶 🐾 🍴		Other info:
Clouds Bed & Breakfast Stoke, Hartland, Bideford, EX39 6DU ☏ 01237 440236 ✉ paul-summers1@hotmail.co.uk 🌐 www.cloudsatstoke.com	GR: SS237246 DP: 0 miles NT: **HARTLAND** Offers one night stays 2 🚗 📶		Other info:
West Titchberry Farm West Titchberry, Hartland, Bideford, EX39 6AU ☏ 01237 441287 ✉ 🌐 www.westtitchberryfarm.co.uk	GR: DP: 0.25 miles NT: **HARTLAND POINT** 3 🚗 📶 🍴		Other info:

Campsites and Holiday Parks

NAME	OTHER INFO	
Hele Valley Holiday Park Hele Bay, Ilfracombe, EX34 9RD ☎ 01271 862460 ✉ holidays@helevalley.co.uk 🌐 www.helevalley.co.uk	GR: 533 472	DP: 0.5 miles
	NT: **ILFRACOMBE**	
	🚗 📶 🐕	Other info:
Little Meadow Campsite Watermouth, Ilfracombe, EX34 9SJ ☎ 01271 866862 ✉ sian@lydfordfarm.co.uk 🌐 www.littlemeadow.co.uk	GR: 554 479	DP: 0.1 miles
	NT: **ILFRACOMBE**	
	Offers one night stays	
	🚗 🐕 🛒	Other info:
Lee Meadow Farm Camping Shaftsborough Lane, Lee, Woolacombe, EX34 8FF ☎ 01271 879825 ✉ info@leemeadowcamping.co.uk 🌐 www.leemeadowcamping.co.uk	GR: 488 448	DP: 0.3 miles
	NT: **WOOLACOMBE**	
	Offers one night stays	
	🚗 🐕 🍴 🛒	Other info:
Westacott Farm Camping Westacott Farm Camping, Abbotsham, Bideford, EX39 5BN ☎ 01237 472351 ✉ enquiries@westacottfarm.co.uk 🌐 www.westacottfarm.co.uk	GR: 409 262	DP: 0.5 miles
	NT: **BIDEFORD**	
	🚗 🐕	Other info:
Greencliff Farm Campsite Abbotsham, Bideford, EX39 5BL ☎ 01237 424674 ✉ greencliff.farm@gmail.com 🌐 www.greencliff-farm.co.uk	GR: 410 268	DP: 0.25 miles
	NT: **BIDEFORD**	
	Offers one night stays	
	🚗 🐕	Other info:
Cheristow Lavendar Campsite Higher Cheristow, Hartland, E39 6DA ☎ 01237 440101 ✉ cheristow@btinternet.com 🌐 www.cheristow.co.uk	GR: 250 254	DP: 1.25 miles
	NT: **HARTLAND**	
	Offers one night stays	
	🚗 🐕 🍴	Other info:
Hartland Caravan & Camping Park Harton Cross, Hartland, EX39 6DG ☎ 01237 441876 ✉ info@hartlandcamping.co.uk 🌐 www.hartlandcamping.co.uk	GR: 264 242	DP: 2.5 miles
	NT: **HARTLAND**	
	🐕 🛒	Other info:
Hartland Caravan Holidays South Lane, Hartland, EX39 6DG ☎ 01237 441664 ✉ info@hartlandcaravanholidays.co.uk 🌐 www.hartlandcaravanholidays.co.uk	GR: 263 242	DP: 3 miles
	NT: **HARTLAND**	
	Offers one night stays	
	🚗 🐕	Other info:
Stoke Barton Farm Campsite Stoke, Hartland, EX39 6DU ☎ 01237 441238 ✉ stokebartoncampsite@gmail.com 🌐 www.westcountry-camping.co.uk	GR: 235 246	DP: 0.5 miles
	NT: **HARTLAND**	
	🚗 🐕 🛒	Other info: 2 Pixie Huts available to hire

Self Catering and hostels

NAME	OTHER INFO		
Ocean Backpackers Hotel 29 St James Place, Ilfracombe, EX34 9BJ ☎ 01271 867835 ✉ info@oceanbackpackers.co.uk 🌐 www.oceanbackpackers.co.uk	GR: 522 478 NT: **ILFRACOMBE** Offers one night stays 12 🚗 📶 🐕	DP: 0.3 miles Other info: Self-catering, drying room available	
Gordons Cabin Morthoe, Woolacombe, EX34 7DR ☎ 0350 800 1895 ✉ enquiries@nationaltrust.org.uk 🌐 www.nationaltrust.org.uk/holidays	GR: 460 453 NT: **MORTHOE** 1 🚗 🐕	DP: 1 mile Other info: Open all year	
The Beach House 3 Granville Terrace, 3 West Road, Woolacombe, EX34 7BW ☎ 01271 871727 ✉ hello@thebeachhousedevon.co.uk 🌐 www.thebeachhousedevon.co.uk	GR: 458 437 NT: **WOOLACOMBE** Offers one night stays 6 🚗 📶 🍴	DP: 0 miles Other info: Hostel, bistro and bar	
Pickwell Barton Georgeham, Braunton, EX33 1LA ☎ 01271 890994 ✉ jane@pickwellbarton.co.uk 🌐 www.pickwellbarton.co.uk	GR: 456 410 NT: **BRAUNTON** 6 🚗 📶	DP: 0.5 miles Other info:	
Marsdens Devon Cottages 2 The Square, Braunton, EX33 2JB ☎ 01271 813 777 ✉ c.coad@tocc.co.uk 🌐 www.marsdens.co.uk	GR: 488 366 NT: **BRAUNTON** 🚗 📶 🐕	DP: Other info:	
Pickwell Manor Pickwell, Georgeham, Braunton, EX33 1LA ☎ 01271 890110 ✉ info@pickwellmanor.co.uk 🌐 www.pickwellmanor.co.uk	GR: NT: **BRAUNTON** 🚗 📶	DP: 0.5 miles Other info:	
Hartland Holiday Barns Higher Huddisford, Woolsery, Bideford, EX39 5QX ☎ 01237 432118 ✉ info@hartlandholidaybarns.co.uk 🌐 www.hartlandholidaybarns.co.uk	GR: 197 302 NT: **BIDEFORD** 3 🚗 📶 🐕	DP: 3 miles Other info: Min 2 night. Walkers & Dogs Pick up drop off by arrangement	
Peppercombe Bothy Horns Cross, Bideford, EX39 5EA ☎ 0350 800 1895 ✉ enquiries@nationaltrust.org.uk 🌐 www.nationaltrust.org.uk/holidays	GR: 380 241 NT: **PEPPERCOMBE** Offers one night stays 1 🐕	DP: 0.5 miles Other info: Open all year	
Elmscott Youth Hostel Elmscott, Hartland, EX39 6ES ☎ 01237 441367 ✉ john.goa@virgin.net 🌐 www.elmscott.org.uk	GR: 231 217 NT: **HARTLAND** Offers one night stays 7 🚗 🛒	DP: 1 mile Other info:	
Southole Barns Southole, Hartland, EX39 6HW ☎ 01237 441621 ✉ enquiries@southole.co.uk 🌐 www.southole.co.uk	GR: 219 201 NT: **HARTLAND** 6 🚗 📶	DP: 0.25 miles Other info:	

at and Drink

NAME	OTHER INFO	
ee Meadow Farm Shop	GR: 490 448	DP: 1.5 miles
haftsborough Lane, Lee, Woolacombe, EX34 8FF	NT: **WOOLACOMBE**	
01271 879825		
leemeadowfarm@icloud.com		Other info:
www.leemeadowcamping.co.uk/leemeadowfarmshop		

Woody Bay

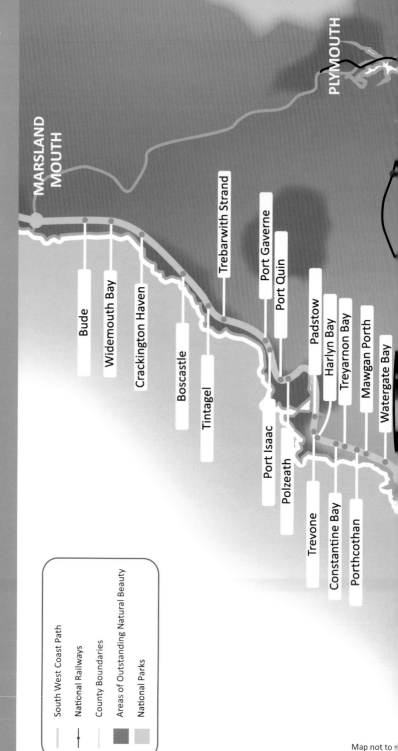

MARSLAND MOUTH

PLYMOUTH

Bude
Widemouth Bay
Crackington Haven
Boscastle
Tintagel
Trebarwith Strand
Port Gaverne
Port Quin
Port Isaac
Polzeath
Padstow
Harlyn Bay
Treyarnon Bay
Mawgan Porth
Watergate Bay
Trevone
Constantine Bay
Porthcothan

South West Coast Path
National Railways
County Boundaries
Areas of Outstanding Natural Beauty
National Parks

Map not to s
For illustrative purposes

North Cornwall
Marsland Mouth to Newquay

This length of coast faces the prevailing Atlantic westerlies, making for a sometimes exposed landscape. This is exacerbated by the fact that much of this length comprises high cliffs, often quite sheer, with prominent headlands giving excellent coastal vistas. In places the feet of these cliffs are fronted by sandy beaches, as around Bude and Newquay. In the centre of this length is the mouth of the Camel Estuary, also flanked by sandy beaches. The uncompromising nature of the cliffs also means there are few ports or harbours; those that do exist tend to be sheltered from the Atlantic winds – Padstow within the Camel Estuary, Newquay behind Towan Head, Boscastle sheltered in its narrow inlet while Bude is a relatively recent development which owes much of its existence to the arrival of a canal here in the early 19th century. North of the Camel this is a length of coast with an untamed atmosphere and including some sometimes challenging gradients for walkers; to the south the extensive beaches are popular among families and surfers alike and the cliffs are kinder to walkers.

Boscastle harbour, North Cornwall

OS Maps: Landranger 190; Explorer 111

	This Walk	Cumulative	This Walk	Cumulative	Grading	Timing
Ascent	2,494ft	25,912ft	760m	7,898m	Easy then strenuous	4.75 hours
Distance	9.8mi	134.1mi	15.8km	215.8km		

For detailed directions see our Walking Guide no. 14, Bude to Crackington Haven.

Low grassy cliffs and surfing beaches south of Bude give way to an ever higher and more rugged coastline fronted by rough rock ledges and cut by deep and steep valleys. There are some superb viewpoints along this later quiet and remote-feeling length which reward the effort. Crackington Haven is a pleasant spot and on the cliffs above, St Gennys Church is a superb spot for contemplation.

Directions

A regular bus service links Bude with Crackington Haven, and also serves Widemouth Bay, about 3 miles/7km from Bude, thus offering a number of bus-walk options.

The Path south from Bude starts at the sea lock on the historic Bude Canal, then climbs to the cliff top at Compass Point and on to Efford Beacon. There are excellent views from here. The Path over Efford Down to Upton and on to Widemouth Bay is easy to follow. Widemouth has toilets and refreshments, the last before Crackington Haven. (There are further refreshment facilities a little inland at Whalesborough, reached by a scenic footpath from Widemouth.)

South of Widemouth the Path follows the low cliff for a short distance then diverts inland slightly at Wanson Mouth to join the coast road in the stream valley. Turn right and follow the road as it climbs steeply to Penhalt Cliff. There are more magnificent views from the cliff-top car park.

From the southern end of the car park the Coast Path crosses a field and descends steeply to Millook Haven. Now follow the steep road uphill for a short distance then turn right onto the cliff top at Raven's Beak. From here the Path climbs steadily past the stunted oak woodland at Dizzard Point and on to Chipman Point. Two further deep and steep valleys are crossed, then a ridge walk leads to Castle Point, which gives tremendous views. Another steep valley crossing leads on to Pencannow Point and views over Crackington Haven. The Path descends easily into the cove, where there are toilets, refreshments, buses and accommodation.

Widemouth Bay

OS Maps: Landranger 190; Explorer 111

	This Walk	Cumulative	This Walk	Cumulative	Grading	Timing
Ascent	2,264ft	28,176ft	690m	8,588m	Strenuous	3.75 hours
Distance	6.7mi	140.8mi	10.8km	226.6km		

For detailed directions see our Walking Guide no. 15, Crackington Haven to Boscastle.

This is a Section of high cliffs, the highest, indeed in Cornwall. Not only are they high, but they also present an appearance of bulk, of being literally massive, and the walker will often feel dwarfed by them, especially on a climb or descent or perhaps on a headland. Much of this Section is also quite lonely, and this combination makes this a coast with an imposing character.

Directions

Crackington Haven and Boscastle are linked by a regular bus service, making this an option for a bus-walk.

There are toilets and seasonal shops, cafes and a pub at Crackington Haven. Leave behind the beach near the toilets and head out for the headland of Cambeak. Rounding the headland, keep away from its high and sheer cliff edges. Beyond Cambeak the Path is relatively level, passing above the landslip zone at Strangles Beach. Ahead looms High Cliff, the appropriately-named highest cliff in Cornwall. There is a steady ascent but the descent on the south side is very steep. The Path then climbs through a landfall at Rusey Cliff, twisting and turning to the top. A cliff top section through fields follows to the sheer black cliff at Buckator. The Path then dips slightly before continuing at high level to Fire Beacon Point. Here the descent is steep, but helped by attractive slate steps. The Path then follows the cliff face into the inlet of Pentargon, with its impressive waterfall. This is best seen from the southern side – do not be tempted to leave the Path for a better view.

The now easy path continues on to Boscastle. Aim for the white mast on Penally Hill, then follow the Path alongside the beautiful harbour inlet into Boscastle, now happily restored after a huge flood washed through the valley in 2014.

Hawker's Hut

OS Maps: Landranger 190 (eastern half); Landranger 200 (western half); Explorer 111

	This Walk	Cumulative	This Walk	Cumulative	Grading	Timing
Ascent	1,230ft	29,406ft	375m	8,963m	Moderate	2.25 hours
Distance	4.7mi	145.5mi	7.6km	234.2km		

For detailed directions see our Walking Guide no. 16, Boscastle to Tintagel.

This fairly short Section is a great local favourite, as it combines all the best of the Coast Path – headlands, sandy bays, historic features and, yes, steep valleys, all in a manageable but picturesque length which is not too taxing. In addition, although popular, it never seems crowded and is, indeed, a "real" walk. With all this and its convenient bus links it is a perfect Coast Path taster.

Directions

Boscastle and Tintagel are linked by a regular bus service. It also serves Rocky Valley, half-way between the two, enabling a variety of bus-walks to be undertaken.

Boscastle has been attractively rebuilt after the floods of 2004, and has all facilities.

The Coast Path leaves the south side of the harbour over the new stone bridge and climbs towards the headland of Willapark, with its prominent white watch tower. The Path cuts across the neck of the headland, but a diversion to the end is worthwhile.

After a steep descent and climb at Grower Gut the Path continues easily, turning seaward of the Manor House at Trevalga. The headland beyond gives views over the rocky offshore islands important for breeding seabirds. The Path continues past Firebeacon Hill – look out for the Ladies Window rock arch in the gully to the right – then passes seaward of a cliff-top caravan and camping site. There is then a descent into the exquisite Rocky Valley. There is a path up the valley to a bus stop on the coast road, passing prehistoric carvings in the cliff wall.

From the footbridge in the valley the Path climbs again, round the edge of the grassy Bossiney Common and above the sandy bay at Bossiney Haven. Another climb then leads to another headland also, confusingly, called Willapark. Again the Coast Path cuts across the neck of the headland and, again, a diversion to the end is worthwhile.

The Path now continues to Barras Nose headland, from where it descends to Tintagel Haven below the castle ruins. Here are toilets, cafe and English Heritage gift shop. A good but steep path leads inland to the village.

Thrift at Boscastle

OS Maps: Landranger 200; Explorer 111 (eastern half); Explorer 106 (western half)

	This Walk	Cumulative	This Walk	Cumulative	Grading	Timing
Ascent	2,589ft	31,995ft	789m	9,752m	Severe	4.75 hours
Distance	9.1mi	154.6mi	14.6km	248.8km		

For detailed directions see our Walking Guide no. 17, Tintagel to Port Isaac.

Both ends of this Section are relatively popular and accessible. At Tintagel the Coast Path passes the remains of the medieval castle perched on its isolated headland then the atmospherically located cliff-top church and the now picturesque evidence of coastal slate quarrying. At the other end is the beautifully quaint village of Port Isaac in its scenic bay. The long central length, though, comprises high cliffs cut by sometimes precipitously steep valleys. It is remote, lonely and often tough, and will be especially appreciated by those who relish an empty, arduous and dramatic coastline.

Directions

It is possible to take a bus between Tintagel and Port Isaac although it is usually necessary to change at Camelford. A bus-walk is therefore possible, particularly using Camelford as a base.

Tintagel has all necessary facilities. Surprisingly, however, little in the village is very old other than the Old Post Office, once a local manor house.

From the village walk down the Path to Tintagel Haven. From here the Coast Path climbs past the entrance to the Castle and gives excellent views over the headland which forms the castle site. A good path continues seaward of the church and on beyond past the Youth Hostel in its former quarry building and round Penhallic Point with its superb views.

The Path drops steeply to Trebarwith Strand, where there are toilets, refreshments and pub, the last facilities before Port Isaac. The next part is particularly tough as it climbs steeply out of the Trebarwith valley then almost immediately drops down to sea level and up again at Backways Cove. There follows a level stretch of about a mile/1.5km to the stream valley behind Tregardock Beach. Descend on the inland side of the detached piece of cliff known as The Mountain, then climb again to Tregardock Cliff. Another level length follows, before the deepest and steepest valley yet at Jacket's Point. At the top yet another deep valley almost immediately follows. Then comes a further valley, at Barrett's Zawn. This is an area of massive rock falls. The next valley follows, this one with exceptionally steep and stony sides.

At last the Path levels out again through cliff-top meadows, with just a small valley to cross at St Illickswell Gug. Eventually, the Path reaches the road at Cartway Cove. Take the Path on the right and round the headland to Port Gaverne, a charming spot. Follow the road uphill to the car park at the edge of Port Isaac. Go through this and follow the well-signed path above the attractive harbour inlet into the village.

Port Isaac is a very picturesque village clustered round the little harbour at the head of a sheltered bay. It has all facilities.

OS Maps: Landranger 200; Explorer 106

	This Walk	Cumulative	This Walk	Cumulative	Grading	Timing
Ascent	2,923ft	34,918ft	891m	10,643m	Strenuous then easy	5.5 hours
Distance	11.7mi	166.3mi	18.8km	267.6km		

For detailed directions see our Walking Guide no. 18, Port Isaac to Padstow.

This Section can be divided into three distinct characters. From Port Isaac to Port Quin is a rollercoaster of a path, closely following the ups and downs and ins and outs of the quiet, scenic but energy-sapping coast. From Port Quin to Polzeath the character becomes rather more open, if still very scenic, including the broad headland of The Rumps and Pentire Point, a wonderful airy lookout. From Polzeath to the Padstow ferry the landscape is tamer, more domesticated, often with housing or tourist development and more estuarine than maritime as it reaches the mouth of the River Camel.

Directions

There is a regular bus service between Port Isaac and Rock, the ferry point for Padstow. This service also passes through Polzeath at the mouth of the Camel estuary, giving several scenic bus-walk options, including an almost level estuary-side one. There is a popular circuit using the Coast Path between Port Isaac and Port Quin and others from Polzeath around Pentire Point.

Port Isaac has all necessary facilities, and is a scenic gem. To leave the village, take the road to the right behind the fish market. Climbing, it bears right and becomes a cliff path, soon dropping into Pine Haven. From here to Port Quin the Path is magnificent and clear, but tough as it follows the cliff edge next to a fence line. There is an optional diversion to the end of Varley Head.

The Path enters the beautiful Port Quin inlet, descending to what was once a busy pilchard port, though there are no facilities here now. Follow the road westbound up the steep hill and a little way up the Coast Path leaves to the right, towards Doyden Point. The Path follows above the cove, keeping seaward of and below the large house. Head to a prominent stone cairn, then continue ahead on a grassy path and past some old mineshafts. From the cairn a diversion to the right goes to the folly of Doyden Castle and to Doyden Point, where there is a superb view back to Port Quin.

There is a sharp descent to Epphaven Cove then the Path passes through a delightful little wooded valley before climbing past the impressive Lundy Hole. The clear cliff path now heads for the Iron Age fortress on The Rumps headland. A detour to the end is well worthwhile.

From The Rumps the Path climbs through a little former quarry area then continues at high level round Pentire Point, giving spectacular views. An easy descent follows into Polzeath all well marked. Polzeath has a great surf beach, and so has all the normal facilities such as café, pubs, accommodation, food and surf shops. The Path follows the road past the beach car park then goes right by the cottages, where the road bends sharp left on the steep hill. It now follows a low cliff to Daymer Bay, where there are toilets and a seasonal cafe, then down steps to the beach. At the far end of the beach it leaves through dunes and over a footbridge below Brea Hill. It is possible to detour to visit the little St Enodoc Church from here.

To continue on the Coast Path follow the Path clinging to the side of Brea Hill, though it is possible to go over the top or, at low tide, along the beach. On the far south side of Brea Hill the well-signed path continues through dunes to arrive at Rock car park. A ferry service operates between Rock and Padstow all year but much less frequently in low season. See page 17 for details.

A water taxi service operates between Rock and Padstow between 7pm and midnight from Easter to 31st October, weather and tides permitting. For further details see page 17.

Note that it is possible to walk Coast to Coast across Cornwall between Padstow and Fowey on the south coast, using the Saints' Way. A guidebook is available from Padstow Tourist Information Centre (TIC).

Padstow sunset

southwestcoastpath.org.uk

OS Maps: Landranger 200: Explorer 106

	This Walk	Cumulative	This Walk	Cumulative	Grading	Timing
Ascent	810ft	35,728ft	247m	10,890m	Easy	2.5 hours
Distance	6.5mi	172.8mi	10.5km	278.1km		

For detailed directions see our Walking Guide no. 19, Padstow to Harlyn Bay.

The length from Padstow to Stepper Point, at the mouth of the Camel, is a scenic length of ever-changing estuarine views with sandy stretches, especially at low tide. Beyond, the coast is an easy but picturesque length of cliffs, which include occasional views right across the headland at the mouth of the estuary and up the Camel as well as west to Trevose Head. The two elements of this Section combine to form a popular local walk.

Directions

A regular bus service links Padstow with Harlyn Bay. This allows for a possible bus-walk. There are also a number of possible circular walks from Padstow using the Coast Path which take in the Stepper Point headland.

Padstow is a charming and bustling little harbour town a short way up the Camel Estuary. If arriving from Rock, notice that normally this arrives in Padstow at the harbour, but at low tide it lands a short distance downstream at St Saviour's Point.

The Coast Path leaves the north end of the harbour past the Tourist Information Centre (TIC) and proceeds on low cliffs alongside the estuary. After passing a wooded little stream valley at St George's Cove the Path heads inland of a marshy area before going back to the cliffs and on to Hawker's Cove. Refreshments are available at Rest a While Tea Rooms at Hawker's Cove. Pass behind the old pilots' houses here then fork right to climb to Stepper Point, with its Daymark tower. From here there are remarkable views, inland to Bodmin Moor as well as along the coast.

The Path is now on the exposed Atlantic coast. Go round the precipitous inlet of Butter Hole Cove, looking out for the small Pepper Hole to the right of the Path just before. An easy length to Gunver Head follows, with excellent sea views. Approaching Trevone the Path skirts the impressive Round Hole collapsed cave – approach this with caution as the sides are sheer. Follow the cliffs round into the bay at Trevone, which has toilets, cafe and pub, as well as a car park. The Path crosses the rear of the beach and leaves behind the little headland on the south-west side of the bay, following the cliff edge to Harlyn Bay, where there are seasonal refreshments and toilets.

OS Maps: Landranger 200; Explorer 106

	This Walk	Cumulative	This Walk	Cumulative	Grading	Timing
Ascent	751ft	36,479ft	229m	11,119m	Easy	3.5 hours
Distance	6.7mi	179.5mi	10.8km	288.9km		

For detailed directions see our Walking Guide no. 20, Harlyn Bay to Porthcothan.

This is a popular Section, never far from a variety of holiday accommodation. It is perhaps most associated with a range of scenic sandy surfing beaches, some of them quite extensive. As a contrast, around the middle of the length is the great landmark of Trevose Head and its lighthouse, visible from great swathes of the North Cornwall coast and an atmospheric location.

Directions

A regular bus service passes Harlyn Bay and links to Porthcothan. The same route serves Constantine Bay, about two-thirds of the way along the coast from Harlyn, giving a potential for a variety of bus-walks.

Harlyn has seasonal refreshments and toilets. From the car park cross the stream on the road bridge then follow the beach below the low cliff for some 330 yards/300m before climbing left onto the cliff and then continuing to the headland at Cataclews Point.

The Path passes inland of Padstow's lifeboat station, accessible by a cul-de-sac path, and then goes on to Trevose Head, passing the lighthouse. On a clear day the coastal views are incredibly extensive, ranging from the satellite dishes north of Bude to the granite hills of West Penwith behind St Ives. This is an atmospheric headland.

After an old quarry the Path passes a Round Hole collapsed cave and descends to the partly rocky Booby's Bay. Continue on to the rear of Constantine Bay, a very attractive and extensive beach at low tide. Walk the length of the beach. There are toilets and seasonal refreshments at the far end and a bus stop a little way inland. Beyond the dunes the Path rounds Treyarnon Head to cross another attractive beach at Treyarnon Bay, with seasonal toilets and refreshments.

An unusually indented coastline follows, with sheer-sided headlands and impressive coves. Near Pepper Cove the ramparts of an Iron Age cliff fort may be seen, and the whole coastline is quite spectacular. The Path then turns into another sandy cove, at Porthcothan Bay, which has toilets and refreshments and also has a pub, the Tredrea Inn, about 500 yards/458m inland up the road.

OS Maps: Landranger 200; Explorer 106

	This Walk	Cumulative	This Walk	Cumulative	Grading	Timing
Ascent	1,447ft	37,926ft	441m	11,560m	Moderate	5 hours
Distance	10.3mi	189.8mi	16.6km	305.5km		

For detailed directions see our Walking Guide no. 21, Porthcothan to Newquay.

This is a relatively well-walked Section, particularly around Newquay. It shows the interplay of high cliffs and sandy beaches particularly well. Almost the whole length is characterised by high, flat-topped cliffs, sometimes with prominent headlands, which for long stretches form the back of extensive attractive sandy beaches, many of them popular with surfers. While never a lonely Section, its cliffs and bays make it one well worth exploring, helped by the relatively easy terrain.

Directions

Porthcothan and Newquay are linked by a regular bus service. This route follows a road parallel and close to the coast, meaning that there are a number of possible links to the Coast Path from this bus, allowing for quite a range of possible bus-walks.

Porthcothan has all facilities that may be needed. The Coast Path leaves past the shop and keeps in front of the houses and on around the headland. After a short steep descent and climb, an easy level walk leads to Park Head, an excellent viewpoint. There have been numerous landslips here so keep to the Path inland of the white posts. The whole headland is worth wandering over and exploring. Ahead now is the National Trust's Carnewas property, with its spectacular beach. The Trust's cafe and Information Centre are open through the summer. On the beach below are the massive stacks forming Bedruthan Steps.

The Bedruthan Steps area can be busy, but the steps to the beach are closed in the winter months. A quieter length follows to Trenance Point and into the sandy bay of Mawgan Porth, where there are toilets, refreshments and a pub as well as a bus stop. Surprisingly, this was once the site of an unfinished canal project.

Cross the stream using the road then leave it to the right on the sharp bend on the hill out of Mawgan Porth. There then follows a long high level length to Watergate Bay on airy flat-topped cliffs, cut by a couple of minor descents. The Path passes Iron Age remains here while inland is the contrast of Newquay Airport. The Path continues on the cliff top behind the magnificent Watergate Beach, much used for surfing and other activities. The Path then descends to the road by the Watergate Bay Hotel, and here there are toilets, refreshments and another bus stop.

Cross the stream at the road then turn right by the car park and climb back to the cliffs, which are now followed to the outskirts of Newquay. The coastal view ahead to the town and its headlands is excellent. The Coast Path leaves the road to pass round the headland of Trevelgue Head, an important prehistoric location. Although the Path bypasses the island at the very end, this can be visited via the footbridge, and is worth the diversion for the views. The Path returns to the road by Porth Beach before leaving it at steps down on the left, to pass underneath the main road and cross the next little headland to emerge above Lusty Glaze beach – look for the information board here relating to the canal previously encountered at Mawgan Porth.

The Path continues into the park at Barrowfields, skirting its seaward side, to reach the main road into Newquay town centre. Follow this just past the railway station then take the old tramway road on the right. Follow the waymarked route along the footpath above Towan Beach.

At the corner go down the steps on the right then from the car park cross Beach Road and follow the tarmac path ahead. At the end follow the steps on the left to pass a bowling green and public toilets to Fore Street. Turn right here as far as the Red Lion and here turn right again to the harbour down North Quay Hill.

As well as all facilities, Newquay has a branch line railway station linking to the main line to Penzance and is the centre of a network of local bus routes.

Perranporth Beach

If you enjoy sleeping, eating or drinking at any business on the Path please suggest they join us as Business Members so that can share their brilliance!

The businesses listed here are all supporters of the South West Coast Path Association, they have joined as business members and it would be great if you could show your support for them too. In addition, businesses are listed with more details on our website: www.southwestcoastpath.org.uk Find them through our walk finder or our accommodation finder tools.

KEY:

GR Grid Reference
DP Distance from the Path
NT Nearest Town

🐕 Dogs Welcome
🍴 Evening Meal Available
3 Number Of Rooms

🛒 Grocery Shop On Site
📶 Wifi
🚗 Parking

Bed & Breakfasts and Hotels

NAME	OTHER INFO		
Breakwater House B&B 3 Breakwater Road, Bude, EX23 8LQ 01288 353137 ptilzey2@gmail.com www.breakwaterhouse.co.uk	GR: 205 062 NT: **BUDE** 🚗📶	DP: 0 miles	Other info: Room only not B&B
Hannahs Cottage Bed & Breakfast Hallagather Farm, Crackington Haven, Bude, EX23 0LA 01840 230955 hannahscottage1@gmail.com www.hannahscottage.com	GR: 147 956 NT: **BUDE** 🚗📶	DP: 0.5 miles	Other info:
Higher Tresmorn Farm St Gennys, Bude, EX23 0NU 01840 230371 tresmorn@btinternet.com www.highertresmorn.co.uk	GR: 161 977 NT: **BUDE** 3 🚗	DP: 0.25 miles	Other info: Self-Catering Cottages also available
Pencarrol Guest House 21 Downs View, Bude, EX23 8RF 01288 352478 pencarrol21@gmail.com www.southwestcoastpath.org.uk/pencarrol-guest-house-bude	GR: 208 070 NT: **BUDE**	DP: 0.25 miles	Other info:
Sea Jade Guesthouse 15 Burn View, Bude, EX23 8BZ 01288 353404 seajadeguesthouse@yahoo.co.uk www.seajadeguesthouse.co.uk	GR: 290 066 NT: **BUDE** Offers one night stays 📶🍴	DP: 0.25 miles	Other info: Will help with travel arrangements. 2 night stays.
Sunrise B&B 6 Burn View, Bude, EX23 8BY 01288 353214 info@sunrise-bude.co.uk www.sunrise-bude.co.uk	GR: 209 067 NT: **BUDE** 🐕	DP: 1 mile	Other info:
Tee-side Guesthouse 2 Burn View, Bude, EX23 8BY 01288 352351 teeside.bude@gmail.com www.tee-side.co.uk	GR: 208 066 NT: **BUDE** Offers one night stays 5 📶	DP: 0.5 miles	Other info:

NAME	OTHER INFO	
The Grosvenor Guest House	GR: 206 066	DP: 0 miles
10 Summerleaze Crescent, Bude, EX23 8HH	NT: **BUDE**	
☎ 01288 352062	Offers one night stays	
✉ enquiries@thegrosvenor-bude.co.uk	[8] [🚗] [📶]	Other info:
🌐 www.thegrosvenorbude.co.uk		
Wyvern Guest House	GR: 209 071	DP: 0.25 miles
7 Downs View, Bude, EX23 8RF	NT: **BUDE**	
☎ 01288 352205		
✉ eileen@wyvernhouse.co.uk		Other info:
🌐 www.wyvernhouse.co.uk		
Lower Meadows House B&B	GR: 100 912	DP: 0.25 miles
Penally Hill, Boscastle, PL35 0HF	NT: **BOSCASTLE**	
☎ 01840 250570		
✉ stay@lowermeadows.co.uk		Other info:
🌐 www.lowermeadows.co.uk		
The Wellington Hotel	GR: 098 912	DP: 0.1 miles
The Harbour, Boscastle, PL35 0AQ	NT: **BOSCASTLE**	
☎ 01840 250202	Offers one night stays	
✉ info@wellingtonhotelboscastle.com	[17] [🚗] [📶] [🐕] [🍴]	Other info:
🌐 www.wellingtonhotelboscastle.com		
Bosayne Guest House	GR: 056 888	DP: 0.25 miles
Atlantic Road, Tintagel, PL34 0DE	NT: **TINTAGEL**	
☎ 01840 770514		
✉ enquiries@bosayne.co.uk	[8] [📶] [🛒]	Other info:
🌐 www.bosayne.co.uk		
Coswarth House	GR: 07907 626084	DP: 0.5 miles
12 Dennis Road, Padstow, PL28 8DD	NT: **PADSTOW**	
☎ 07907 62608	Offers one night stays	
✉ coswarth@cawlimited.co.uk	[4] [🚗] [📶] [🐕]	Other info: Single night supplement of £20 waived for Coast Path Walkers.
🌐 www.coswarthhouse.com		
Ere Tis B&B	GR: 920 749	DP: 0 miles
3 Egerton Road, Padstow, PL28 8DJ	NT: **PADSTOW**	
☎ 01841 532320	Offers one night stays	
✉	[2] [🚗] [🐕]	Other info:
🌐 www.southwestcoastpath.org.uk/ere-tis-bb-padstow		
Penlan B&B	GR: 860 718	DP: 0.12 miles
Penlan, Porthcothan Bay, PL28 8LP	NT: **PADSTOW**	
☎ 01841 520440	Offers one night stays	
✉ mary@idenna.com	[3] [🚗] [📶] [🐕]	Other info:
🌐 www.porthcothanbay.co.uk		
South Quay	GR: 763 938	DP: 0.1 miles
4 Riverside, Padstow, PL28 8BY	NT: **PADSTOW**	
☎ 01841 532383	Offers one night stays	
✉ thepadstowcullinans@gmail.com	[2] [📶] [🐕]	Other info:
🌐 www.southquaybedandbreakfastpadstow.co.uk		
The Slipway	GR: 996 807	DP: 0 miles
Harbour Front, Port Isaac, PL29 3RH	NT: **PADSTOW**	
☎ 01208 880264	Offers one night stays	
✉ slipway@portisaachotel.com	[7] [📶] [🍴]	Other info: Café, B&B, breakfasts, lunches and dinners.
🌐 www.portisaachotel.com		

NAME	OTHER INFO	
Sunny Corner Main Road, Trevone, PL28 8QX ☎ 01841 520476 ✉ mo1884@gmail.com 🌐 www.sunnycorner.info	GR: 892 758 DP: 0.2 miles NT: **TREVONE BAY** Offers one night stays [2] 🚗 📶 🐕	Other info:
Penhalonga Constantine Bay, PL28 8JG ☎ 01841 521122 / 07815833158 ✉ lizkennerley@btinternet.com 🌐 www.southwestcoastpath.org.uk/penhalonga-constantine-bay	GR: DP: NT: **CONSTANTINE BAY** Offers one night stays 🐕	Other info:
Bedruthan Hotel Trenance, Mawgan Porth, Newquay, TR8 4BU ☎ 01637 861 200 ✉ stay@bedruthan.com 🌐 www.bedruthan.com	GR: 851 676 DP: 0.3 miles NT: **MAWGAN PORTH** Offers one night stays [101] 🚗 📶 🍴	Other info:
The Scarlet Hotel Tredragon Road, Mawgan Porth, TR8 4DQ ☎ 01637 861 800 ✉ stay@scarlethotel.co.uk 🌐 www.scarlethotel.co.uk	GR: 850 675 DP: 0.1 miles NT: **MAWGAN PORTH** 📶 🐕 🍴	Other info:
Dalswinton Guest House St Mawgan, Newquay, TR8 4EZ ☎ 01637 860385 ✉ drew@dalswinton.com 🌐 www.dalswinton.com	GR: 874 659 DP: 2.5 miles NT: **NEWQUAY** Offers one night stays [8] 🚗 📶 🐕 🍴	Other info: Close to St Columb Major
The Three Tees Hotel 21 Carminow Way, Newquay, TR7 3AY ☎ 01637 872055 ✉ greg@3tees.co.uk 🌐 www.3tees.co.uk	GR: 824 622 DP: 0.15 miles NT: **NEWQUAY** Offers one night stays [9] 🚗 📶 🐕	Other info:

Campsites and Holiday Parks

NAME	OTHER INFO	
Cerenety Eco Campsite Lynstone Lane, Bude, EX23 0LR ☎ 01288 356778 ✉ cerenetycampsite@hotmail.com 🌐 www.cerenetycampsite.co.uk	GR: 206 050 DP: 0.3 miles NT: **BUDE** Offers one night stays 🚗 📶 🐕 🛒	Other info:
Penhalt Farm Holiday Park Widemouth Bay, Bude, EX23 0DG ☎ 01288 361210 ✉ info@penhaltfarm.co.uk 🌐 www.penhaltfarm.co.uk	GR: 192 000 DP: 0.25 miles NT: **BUDE** 🐕 🛒	Other info:
Wooda Lakes Holiday Park Pancrasweek, Holsworthy, EX22 7JN ☎ 01409 241934 ✉ info@woodalakes.co.uk 🌐 www.woodalakes.co.uk	GR: 306 088 DP: miles NT: **BUDE** [11] 🚗 📶 🐕	Other info: Luxury holiday lodges&course fishing

NAME	OTHER INFO		
Carnevas Holiday Park	GR: 861 726	DP: 0.5 miles	
St Merryn, Padstow, PL28 8PN	NT: **PADSTOW**		
☏ 01841 520230	Offers one night stays		
✉ carnevascampsite@aol.com			Other info: 1 night stays offered for camping only
⊕ www.carnevasholidaypark.com	🚐 🛜 🐕 🍴 🛒		
Dennis Cove Campsite	GR: 921 744	DP: 0.5 miles	
Padstow, PL28 8DR	NT: **PADSTOW**		
☏ 01841 532349	Offers one night stays		
✉ smith.padstow@gmail.com			Other info:
⊕ www.denniscovecampsite.co.uk	🚗 🐕		
Old Macdonalds Farm	GR: 860 711	DP: 0.5 miles	
Porthcothan Bay, Padstow, PL28 8LT	NT: **PADSTOW**		
☏ 01841 540829	Offers one night stays		
✉ info@oldmacdonalds.co.uk			Other info:
⊕ www.oldmacdonalds.co.uk	3 🚗 🛜		

Do

NAME	OTHER INFO		
Bayside Taxis	GR: 206 051	DP: 0.5 miles	
2 The Grange, Lymstone, Bude, EX23 0PR	NT: **BUDE**		
☏ 07769 313654			
✉ baysidetaxis.bude@gmail.com			Other info:
⊕ www.baysidetaxis.co.uk			
Trev's Taxi	GR: 207 071	DP: 0.25 miles	
Flat 2, 33 Downs View, Bude, EX23 8RG	NT: **BUDE**		
☏ 07799 663217			
✉ trevstaxi3217@btinternet.com			Other info:
⊕ www.trevstaxi.co.uk	🛜 🐕		
Newquay Zoo	GR: 820 612	DP: 0.6 miles	
Trenance Gardens, Newquay, TR7 2NL	NT: **NEWQUAY**		
☏ 01803 697500			
✉			Other info: Open 10am daily except Christmas Day
⊕ www.newquayzoo.org.uk	🛜		

Eat and Drink

NAME	OTHER INFO		
Brendon Arms	GR: 206 061	DP: 0 miles	
Falcon Terrace, Bude, EX23 8SD	NT: **BUDE**		
☏ 01288 354542	Offers one night stays		
✉ enquiries@brendonarms.co.uk			Other info:
⊕ www.brendonarms.co.uk	10 🚗 🛜 🍴		
Rectory Farm Tea Rooms	GR: 205 152	DP: 0.25 miles	
Crosstown, Morwenstow, Bude, EX23 9SR	NT: **BUDE**		
☏ 01288 331251			
✉ jill@rectory-tearooms.co.uk			Other info:
⊕ www.rectory-tearooms.co.uk			

Self Catering and hostels

NAME	OTHER INFO	
Little Barton Hartland, Bideford, EX39 6DY 🕿 01237 441259 ✉ enquiries@littlebartonhartland.co.uk 🌐 www.littlebartonhartland.co.uk	GR: 241 237 DP: 3 miles NT: **BUDE** *Offers one night stays* **9** 🚗 📶 🐕	**Other info:** Dogs in the kitchen only. Single nights low season
North Shore Bude Backpackers 57 Killerton Road, Bude, EX23 8EW 🕿 01288 354256 ✉ info@northshorebude.com 🌐 www.northshorebude.com	GR: 213 061 DP: 1 mile NT: **BUDE** **12** 🚗 📶	**Other info:**
Beaver Cottages Tregatta, Tintagel, PL34 0DY 🕿 01840 770378 ✉ beavercottages@outlook.com 🌐 www.beaver-cottages.co.uk	GR: 056 873 DP: NT: **TINTAGEL**	**Other info:**
Martha's Harbour Treknow, Tintagel, PL34 0EN 🕿 01438 714144 ✉ 🌐 www.homeaway.co.uk/p6495058	GR: DP: 0.2 miles NT: **TINTAGEL** 📶	**Other info:**
Carolina Cellar Port Quin, Port Isaac, PL29 3SU 🕿 0349 800 1895 ✉ enquiries@nationaltrust.org.uk 🌐 www.nationaltrust.org.uk/holidays	GR: 972 805 DP: 0 miles NT: **PORT QUIN** **1**	**Other info:** Parking nearby. Open all year
Cornish Horizons 19 New Street, Padstow, PL28 8EA 🕿 01841 533331 ✉ cottages@cornishhorizons.co.uk 🌐 www.cornishhorizons.co.uk	GR: DP: NT: **PADSTOW** 🚗 📶 🐕	**Other info:**
Cornish Traditional Cottages 3 Eddystone Court, Eddystone Road, Wadebridge, PL27 7FH 🕿 01208 895354 ✉ bookings@corncott.com 🌐 www.corncott.com	GR: 989 724 DP: miles NT: **WADEBRIDGE** 📶 🐕	**Other info:**
Mariners Lettings Ltd Rock Road, Rock, Wadebridge, PL27 6JN 🕿 01208 869257 ✉ enquiries@marinerslettings.co.uk 🌐 www.marinerslettings.co.uk	GR: DP: miles NT: **WADEBRIDGE** 🚗 📶	**Other info:**

North Cornwall's coast, Tintagel

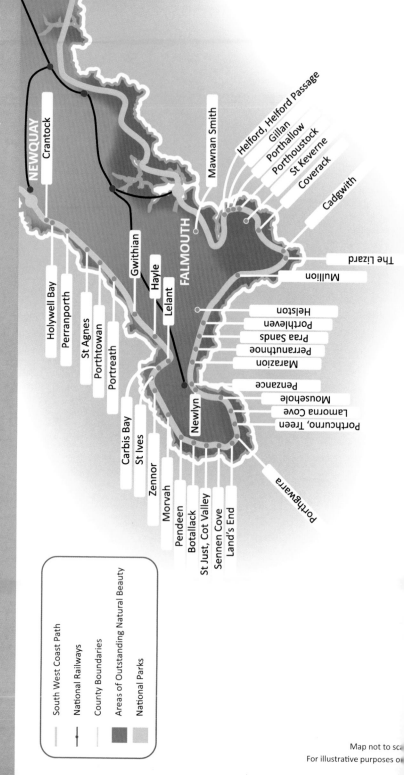

NEWQUAY

Crantock

Holywell Bay

Perranporth

St Agnes

Porthtowan

Portreath

Gwithian

Hayle

Lelant

FALMOUTH

Mawnan Smith

Helford, Helford Passage

Gillan

Porthallow

Porthoustock

St Keverne

Coverack

Cadgwith

The Lizard

Mullion

Helston

Porthleven

Praa Sands

Perranuthnoe

Marazion

Penzance

Mousehole

Lamorna Cove

Porthcurno, Treen

Newlyn

Carbis Bay

St Ives

Zennor

Morvah

Pendeen

Botallack

St Just, Cot Valley

Sennen Cove

Land's End

Porthgwarra

South West Coast Path

National Railways

County Boundaries

Areas of Outstanding Natural Beauty

National Parks

84

Map not to scale

For illustrative purposes only

West Cornwall
Newquay to Falmouth

(Sections 22-37)

The cliffs to the west of Newquay give way to the scenic and sandy St Ives Bay. Beyond St Ives, an old fishing port of medieval origin, the coast encircles two great peninsulas: Penwith, the westernmost part of England, and the Lizard, the southernmost. Both are composed of hard, resistant rocks making for a rugged cliff coastline, but their characters differ. Penwith is largely granite and inland of its impressive cliffs, frequently marked by rock pinnacles and solid jointed slabs, is a rough semi-moorland landscape. Along a length of Penwith's north coast the Coast Path passes a number of old cliff-face tin mines. The Lizard has a much smoother profile, with its inland landscape an unusual flat-topped plateau. The exposed locations of these two peninsulas result in harsh, weather-beaten coastlines with a lack of large-scale tree cover, though both are superbly dramatic. Between these two magnificent peninsulas is the iconic Mount's Bay, site of the fairytale-like setting of St Michael's Mount, surmounted by its castle. The bay is the site of a number of coastal towns; Penzance, the main centre for this far western part of Cornwall, Marazion, with its ancient origins, the fishing port of Newlyn and picturesque Mousehole, once of great importance until burned by the Spanish in the wars of the 16th century. The quiet wooded estuary of the Helford River marks the end of this length.

Porthleven Harbour

OS Maps: Landranger 200; Explorer 104

	This Walk	Cumulative	This Walk	Cumulative	Grading	Timing
Ascent	1,145ft	39,071ft	349m	11,909m	Moderate	3.5 hours
Distance	8.1mi	197.9mi	13.0km	318.5km		

For detailed directions see our Walking Guide no. 22, Newquay (Harbour) to Holywell Bay.

This Section includes some superb viewpoints from headlands in and around Newquay, the panoramas quite unspoiled by the proximity of the large town. Beyond Newquay a range of landscapes is experienced, from wide sandy beaches to exposed cliff tops to small sandy bays to dune systems. In addition, unexpectedly, the wooded estuary valley of the river known as The Gannel is crossed at the edge of Newquay. This variety, and the proximity to a range of facilities and accommodation, make this a popular, well-used length.

Directions

A regular bus service links Newquay with Holywell Bay, and also serves Crantock, between the two. This gives a number of bus-walk possibilities.

Newquay is the biggest town on Cornwall's north coast. Although usually busy, being especially popular with surfers and also with groups of young holidaymakers, it is in a very attractive setting of beaches and headlands. All the facilities are here, and there is a branch railway linking to the main line to Penzance.

From Newquay Harbour the Coast Path climbs past the old Huer's Hut to Towan Head. From Towan Head the Path then follows the back of Fistral Beach. This is probably the country's most popular surfing beach and international competitions are held here. The Path climbs to the cliffs at the southern end and then crosses the road to go along Pentire Crescent which leads into Penmere Drive. The Path then arrives above the Gannel Estuary. However, this misses the major headland of Pentire Point East, which is well worth the diversion to the end. (If following the diversion round the headland, on returning from the end aim for the far bottom of the car park at the neck of the headland. From here head along the suburban road parallel to the Gannel. Follow this to the Fern Pit Cafe.)

There are four options from here for crossing the Gannel, depending on the tide and time of year.

OPTION 1: FERN PIT FERRY (deduct 2 miles/3km from total mileage)

The first option is to use the Fern Pit Ferry from behind the cafe. The cafe is approximately 0.7 mile/1.1km west of Penmere Drive. The ferry operates continuously, 7 days a week, 10.00-18.00 mid May until mid September weather dependent – telephone 01637 873181. For further details see page 17.

OPTION 2: PENPOL CROSSING (official route)

Go along Penmere Drive then turn right into Trevean Way. Follow the waymarks right and go downhill across a grassy area. At the foot of the grass bank turn right along the footpath then take the steps on the left down to the tidal Penpol Footbridge across the Gannel Estuary. This can be used 3-4 hours either side of low water. Cross the Gannel here. (If coming from the headland circuit, continue past the Fern Pit Cafe and on along

Riverside Avenue, then ahead and right. At a junction where there is a footpath to the right keep ahead, ignoring the footpath. Bear right into Penmere Drive, again ignoring another footpath on the right. Go along Penmere Drive and re-join the route detailed on previous page.)

OPTION 3: TRENANCE FOOTBRIDGE (add 3 miles/4.8km to total mileage)

This route is usable at most states of the tide. From the Newquay side of the Penpol crossing continue upstream on the Path parallel to the river until it arrives at the A392 Gannel Road. There is a footbridge on the right just before the junction with the A3058 Trevemper Road. Cross the bridge and continue ahead. Do not follow the creekside path to Penpol but instead take the bridleway on the left towards Trevemper. Turn right just before reaching the tarmac and follow the footpath through Treringey to arrive at the south side of the Penpol tidal footbridge.

OPTION 4: MAIN ROAD ROUTE (add 4.5 miles/7.2km to total mileage)

Continue past the Trenance footbridge and along the A392 Trevemper Road from the roundabout. At the next roundabout turn right and after about 100 yards/90m take the little unsigned lane on the right. This leads to Trevemper, going forward and right as the lane goes left. After the gate turn left on the route described under Option 3 through Treringey.

Options 2, 3 and 4 come together at Penpol. Cross the ford to follow the lane then take the waymarked path on the right above the estuary. After passing the ferry landing for Option 1 this path leads to Crantock Beach car park. Crantock village with its facilities and bus stop is a little way inland. Cross the car park and climb the steps through the gate opposite; bear left at the junction of grassy paths on entering the dune area and follow this inland of the main dune area to re-emerge at a coastal path which leads to the cliffs of Pentire Point West where the Bowgie Inn among others, provide meals and refreshments. The Path goes round Porth Joke (known locally as Polly Joke), then on around Kelsey Head to Holywell Bay, descending across more dunes either into the village or to cross the river on a seaward footbridge. There are facilities, some seasonal here.

Newquay harbour

OS Maps: Landranger 200; Explorer 104

	This Walk	Cumulative	This Walk	Cumulative	Grading	Timing
Ascent	755ft	39,826ft	230m	12,139m	Moderate	2 hours
Distance	4.5mi	202.4mi	7.2km	325.7km		

For detailed directions see our Walking Guide no. 23, Holywell Bay to Perranporth.

The theme of this Section is sand, in the form of both dunes and beaches, although it begins by rounding headlands at Penhale and Ligger Points. However, even at Penhale the inland vista is dominated by dunes, although the adjacent former Army Camp is also prominent. For the bulk of this Section sand is everywhere around, on the seemingly endless length of Perran Beach and the dunes which back it. Both ends, Holywell and Perranporth, are busy holiday settlements but the more remote areas of Perran Beach can be surprisingly quiet.

Directions

Holywell Bay and Perranporth are both served by regular bus services from Newquay, making a bus walk along this length using Newquay as a base an option.

Holywell Bay has all facilities, some seasonal. From Holywell Bay the Path rounds Penhale Point, skirting the seaward edge of the somewhat unattractive former Penhale army camp. It then goes on out to Ligger Point, where there is a panoramic view of the length of Perran Beach. The Path heads towards the dunes then descends behind the cliff quarry to the beach. It now follows the back of the beach for some 1.5 miles/2.5km. This is possible even at high tide, and usually on firm sand. At Cotty's Point the tide often makes it necessary to climb the steps. At the top of the steps turn right following the slate Coast Path waymarks. The Path descends back to the beach on the south side and then crosses the stream by the footbridge when nearly at Perranporth, where there are again all needed facilities.

Millenium Sundial, Perranporth

OS Maps: Landranger 200 (Perranporth); Landranger 203 (remainder); Explorer 104

	This Walk	Cumulative	This Walk	Cumulative	Grading	Timing
Ascent	2,250ft	42,076ft	686m	12,825m	Moderate then strenuous	5.75 hours
Distance	12.4mi	214.8mi	20.0km	345.7km		

For detailed directions see our Walking Guide no. 24, Perranporth to Portreath.

This section is one in which Cornwall's coastal mining heritage is paramount. There is much evidence of former mining activity, this including somewhat stark areas of spoil and sometimes slightly sad building relics, but also some grand and imposing engine houses and chimneys. In some locations, the large-scale level of the activity is difficult to imagine now. Nevertheless, the scale and grandeur of the cliffs, the beaches and the surf mean that nature always re-asserts itself.

Directions

A regular bus service links Perranporth to St Agnes. A skeletal summer service links Perranporth to Portreath, also passing St Agnes and Porthtowan along the way, giving numerous bus-walk options.

Perranporth is a busy holiday centre with all facilities. The Coast Path goes west from the main car park and follows the hill up Cliff Road. Keep left of the castellated building then along Tregundy Lane. Go half left at the entrance to the Youth Hostel and on to the cliffs, the Path clinging to the cliff face out to Cligga Head. Here the Path enters quarry and mine workings, but is well signposted. There is then a level stretch alongside Perranporth Aerodrome before the steep descent to Trevellas Porth, a valley marked by many relics of the mining industry. Go upstream to cross at the road bridge, then back to the cliffs and back down again into Trevaunance Cove, where there are toilets and refreshments. The bus stop at St Agnes is a little way inland.

On reaching the road at Trevaunance Cove go straight across passing the Driftwood Spars car park and a large tall house on the right. Follow the waymarked footpath immediately right along a metalled lane then fork right along a footpath. Soon the Path climbs steeply to the cliff top. A long and scenic high-level Path now goes around St Agnes Head, giving superb views ahead, then past the iconic engine house at Towanroath before descending to Chapel Porth, a small and attractive cove with toilets and seasonal refreshments. The toilets here are only unlocked when the cafe is open. Follow the stream inland for 200 yards/185m then turn right and up to the cliffs, before heading back down again into Porthtowan. Again there are toilets and refreshments and a magnificent beach. There is a bus stop a little inland.

Follow the road inland then turn right up West Beach Road and on to the cliff top. More mine workings are passed, then the Path runs alongside a prominent fence next to MOD land before reaching a road which descends into Portreath. This former industrial harbour town has all facilities.

OS Maps: Landranger 203; Explorer 104 (eastern half); Explorer 102 (western half)

	This Walk	Cumulative	This Walk	Cumulative	Grading	Timing
Ascent	1,362ft	43,438ft	415m	13,240m	Moderate/ easy	5.5 hours
Distance	11.7mi	226.5mi	18.8km	364.5km		

For detailed directions see our Walking Guide no. 25, Portreath to Hayle.

There are two distinct characters to the coast of this Section. Between Portreath and Godrevy it is one of high, level cliffs, the sea far below. In contrast, between Godrevy and Hayle the walk focuses on sand, either dunes or beach, on the focal view of Godrevy lighthouse and on the great colourful sweep of St Ives Bay. This is never a lonely or remote length, but it is a scenic, fascinating and rewarding one.

Directions

A summer bus service links Portreath and Hayle, and also passes Godrevy, half-way between the two. This allows for bus-walk options over the whole Section or over either of the two distinct character lengths.

Portreath has all facilities and a pleasant beach. Leave the town crossing the bridge next to the car park then right, up Battery Hill. Continue ahead, meandering between properties at the end, turning right just beyond them up steps to the top of Western Hill, with its excellent views. After a couple of noticeable valleys the Path then embarks on a long easy cliff-top walk along Reskajeague Downs, eventually arriving at Hell's Mouth, where there is the seasonal Hell's Mouth Cafe. The Path then narrows and turns right at an obvious T-junction. Cross a stile next to a gate and cross the seaward side of a field before continuing easily round Navax and Godrevy Points, the lighthouse becoming a focal point offshore. Keep seaward of the car park and access road and follow the signs along the low cliffs and over the dunes to another car park, at the Godrevy Cafe. Follow the boardwalk from the car park to cross the Red River. Turn left for 30 yards/29m then go right, following the large slate waymarks through the former quarry, now a nature reserve.

Keep ahead through the dunes, following the signposts. Note it is often possible to walk along the beach here but beware the incoming tide which can mean being cut off below the cliffs. If the tide is right, leave the beach at the lifeguard hut near the foot of Black Cliff. If coming through the dunes, keep ahead above the hut. Then, with either option, turn left up some steps just before two chalets. Turn right towards a house, leaving it on the right, and walk along a line of chalets on the left. The Path is slightly overgrown but then opens out at a car park. Follow the access track ahead then bear right onto the raised walkway parallel to the harbour and continue ahead on this level. Descend the steps at the far end and follow the pavement ahead then cross the old swing bridge to the road. Turn right to reach the railway viaduct in the centre of Hayle.

OS Maps: Landranger 203; Explorer 102

	This Walk	Cumulative	This Walk	Cumulative	Grading	Timing
Ascent	617ft	44,055ft	188m	13,428m	Easy	2.5 hours
Distance	6.1mi	232.6mi	9.8km	374.3km		

For detailed directions see our Walking Guide no. 26, Hayle to St Ives.

This Section is never far from roads and houses, so often has a suburban air. However, this is outweighed by the views over the River Hayle estuary and, particularly, by the vistas over the great sweep of St Ives Bay with its vast sandy beaches and dunes, the iconic offshore Godrevy Lighthouse as a focal point and the fabulous sea colours, turquoises, greens and blues, whenever the sun shines on this length.

Directions

A regular bus service links Hayle and St Ives, giving a bus-walk option. In addition, a branch-line railway plies between Lelant and St Ives, and this gives marvellous sea views. This makes for an unusual and especially scenic train-walk option.

Hayle has all facilities, including a railway station on the main line to Penzance. Walk to the viaduct and turn right on the Path immediately before it. Go ahead to Carnsew Road and continue on the pavement, turning right on a narrow Path between housing. Go left at the end then continue to arrive alongside a large lagoon. Keep on to the end then bear left to the road. Continue as the road passes alongside the River Hayle estuary on The Causeway, a birdwatchers' delight. Cross to the far side of the road then back to the riverside again before forking right at the Old Quay House. Under the bridge turn right, signed to St Ives Park and Ride. At the car park attendant's kiosk turn left to a lane, then turn right here. Follow the lane next to the railway and estuary all the way to Lelant Church. Go along the Path next to the church to pass under the railway. Just before the beach turn left along the seaward side of the railway through dunes. (NB. this is also the route of the St Michael's Way, a cross-peninsula path from Lelant to Marazion – a guide leaflet is available at St Ives Tourist Information Centre (TIC)).

Follow the clear Path parallel to the magnificent Porthkidney Beach. Approaching the headland of Carrack Gladden the Path forks – keep right then continue ahead. Descend the road to Carbis Bay, where there are toilets and seasonal refreshments, walking inland of the cafe but seaward of the hotel. Climb over a railway bridge then continue as the Path becomes a minor road. Pass the Path taking St Michael's Way inland then at a little cross-roads go straight ahead, steeply downhill. (Turning right shortly after the St Michael's Way turning down a private, pedestrians only path gives a more scenic alternative to the official route, re-joining at the little cross-roads.) Cross the railway bridge and double back right then left to arrive at Porthminster Beach, just below St Ives railway station.

OS Maps: Landranger 203; Explorer 102

	This Walk	Cumulative	This Walk	Cumulative	Grading	Timing
Ascent	3,428ft	47,483ft	1,045m	14,473m	Severe	7 hours
Distance	13.7mi	246.3mi	22.0km	396.4km		

For detailed directions see our Walking Guide no. 27, St Ives to Zennor and Zennor to Pendeen Watch.

There are no settlements on this Section and the character is lonely and remote. It is also tough going, with rocky scrambles and boggy lengths. But it can only be described as a magnificent length. Stark cliffs, rock pinnacles, tiny scenic coves with translucent water, rugged exposed headlands – all are here. Inland the view is often of empty moorland. This is the Coast Path at its most awe-inspiring. Prepare for its rigours, then enjoy the wonderful experience.

Directions

A regular summer bus service links St Ives and Pendeen village, a little inland of the Coast Path. It also passes through other inland settlements linked by footpath to the Coast Path, principally Zennor, Treen (Gurnard's Head) and Morvah, allowing for various bus-walks options.

A warning: this is a tough and deserted length of the Coast Path. There are no settlements or refreshment facilities, though there are some path links inland to small settlements. The terrain is often rough and rocky and in places can be boggy. But a compensation: this is a length of wonderfully dramatic coastal scenery.

From the path below St Ives railway station keep along as close as possible to the sea and harbour. The official route goes round the green St Ives Head, usually known as The Island. This is reached by following signs to the museum from the far end of the harbour and on through a small car park. From The Island go through the old "Downlong" quarter to Porthmeor Beach and the Tate. There are also short cuts direct to here – follow signs to the Tate.

Go along the rear of Porthmeor Beach then bear off right along the path next to the putting green. The Coast Path now leads out to the rugged Clodgy Point and then on round Hor Point to Pen Enys Point, where it cuts across the neck of the headland. Pass the trig point on Carn Naun, where there are extensive views forward and back, then descend to cross the stream at River Cove. Just beyond the Path passes the offshore Carracks, where seals are regularly seen. Approaching Zennor Head the path forks – keep right to follow the seaward Path round the headland. From Zennor Head the path heads inland – look out for the signed Coast Path descending steeply to the right. If in need of refreshments, or for the bus, continue along the path inland to Zennor, where there is a pub and seasonal cafe.

On the Coast Path, more ups and downs lead to the distinctive headland of Gurnard's Head. The path cuts across its neck, but a diversion onto the headland, an Iron Age fortified site, is worth the effort. There are also diversions inland here to Treen, where refreshments are available at the Gurnard's Head Inn and there is a bus stop.

The Coast Path continues, generally easy to follow if not always an easy walk.
Approaching Bosigran, another Iron Age fortification, head for the high point of the
ridge, following Coast Path signs and keeping on the landward side of a low wall.
At the crest of the ridge head inland and downhill aiming for a stream and building.
Cross the stream on a small bridge near a ruined building then follow the Path uphill,
just seaward of an obvious stone wall. There is a diversion path inland here to a bus stop
at Rosemergy. After heavy rain the Path round here can be boggy.

Further on the Coast Path, look out for a path inland to Morvah for another bus stop if
needed. Otherwise keep on the obvious Coast Path round the back of Portheras Cove
and on to the lighthouse at Pendeen Watch. Pendeen village, with its pubs, cafe, shop,
toilets and bus stop, is about 1 mile/1.5km inland.

Zennor Head

OS Maps: Landranger 203; Explorer 102

	This Walk	Cumulative	This Walk	Cumulative	Grading	Timing
Ascent	1,683ft	49,166ft	513m	14,986m	Moderate	4.25 hours
Distance	9.1mi	255.4mi	14.6km	411.0km		

For detailed directions see our Walking Guide no. 28, Pendeen Watch to Sennen Cove.

This Section offers a wide range of walking experiences. Between Pendeen Watch and Botallack the overriding experience is of Cornwall's coastal mining heritage. This ranges from unattractive early 20th century industrial relics to romantic stone-built cliff-face engine houses, all this next to sheer cliffs and often wild seas. Beyond Botallack is a superb length of scenic exposed cliffs, highlighted by the magnificent headland of Cape Cornwall. This Section has all that is best on the Cornish coast – rugged cliffs, mining relics, translucent water, turquoise coves, purple heather, rocky scrambles, the view of a lighthouse. Then, approaching Sennen Cove, there is a sweep of broad sandy beaches backed by dunes, and the length ends with a scenic harbour and a lifeboat station. A wonderful length.

Directions

A regular summer bus service links Pendeen village, a little inland of the Coast Path, with Sennen Cove. It also serves St Just, inland of Cape Cornwall, which is used as the centre of various Coast Path-based circular walks. Bus-walks are also possible from Geevor and Botallack, reached by footpath from the coast.

From Pendeen Watch the Path goes along the road to the end of the row of cottages, then turns right at a granite marker. (The road continues into Pendeen village, with its range of facilities.) The Coast Path is clear and leads to the old mining area at Geevor. A diversion inland leads to refreshments and toilets at the mining museum, which is itself well worth a visit if possible. Follow the signed track beyond Geevor to the National Trust's Levant Beam Engine House, open for steaming at certain times. From here the official Path follows the clear track parallel to the coast, but a narrower path to seaward with better views leads from the far end of the car park. The two options come together as more mines are passed at Botallack. Look to seaward to see the famous Crowns Mine engine houses perched improbably on the cliff.

Beyond Botallack, as the mines give way, look for the signed Path to the right which leads to the headland at Kenidjack Castle. A lot of the waymarking in this area uses granite stones, perfect for the landscape setting. From the old building on the headland descend left to a track, go left then bear right on a path down to another track. Go left here then turn right to cross the floor of the Kenidjack Valley. Climb to the top and turn right. Ahead now is the distinctive shape of Cape Cornwall, surmounted by its chimney. Turn right immediately before the road and then bear right across a field past the ruins of a chapel to a stone stile. Cross this, turn left and then climb right to reach the top of the headland. Savour the views, then join the Path which descends over the seaward side of the Cape by zigzags and steps to reach the National Coastwatch Institution watchhouse. This recent addition to the Coast Path provides a superb experience. Go to the left of the watchhouse then down the steps and along a path past some stone buildings and through a gate to reach another set of granite steps descending to the right. In the nearby car park are seasonal refreshments and toilets. St Just is about 1 mile/1.5km up the road.

At the bottom of the steps go left then climb right on the track to a road at the top. Bear off right at the sign and follow the clear Path into the Cot Valley. A new route has been established down the valley. For this, turn left at the road and almost immediately right, over a footbridge and past old mine workings, climbing to reach a path which heads to the cove at Porth Nanven. Just before reaching the cove climb left onto the cliffs. There is a good clear cliff-face path to the beach at Gwynver, although with one rocky climb. From Gwynver the Path continues through the dunes behind the sandy beaches, which can be walked at low tide, to the car park at Sennen Cove. This is a popular family and surfing spot with all facilities.

Carn Boel

OS Maps: Landranger 203; Explorer 102

	This Walk	Cumulative	This Walk	Cumulative	Grading	Timing
Ascent	1,542ft	50,708ft	470m	15,456m	Moderate	3.25 hours
Distance	6.3mi	261.7mi	10.1km	421.1km		

For detailed directions see our Walking Guide no. 29, Sennen Cove to Porthcurno.

This is the most westerly length of coast in England. Much of it has the character of moorland meeting the sea, with great granite headlands and massive rock outcrops interspersed with isolated coves with exquisite sea colours. Towards Porthcurno the moorland is replaced by a more pastoral landscape, but the cliffs and coves continue. Much of this Section has a quiet character, interrupted only by the visitor mecca of Land's End.

Directions

Sennen Cove and Porthcurno are linked by a regular bus service, which also goes to Land's End. This allows for a choice of bus-walks and there are also numerous circuits possible based on the Land's End area.

Sennen Cove has all facilities. Leave the village passing the Round House gallery into the car park. Turn left up steps then right, towards the lookout. From here a range of parallel paths all lead to Land's End. Bear right to the First and Last House, at England's most westerly point, then keep seaward of the main complex to the outpost at Greeb Cottage. The complex has toilets and refreshments if needed. The Path goes behind Greeb Cottage; then again a choice of paths all lead towards the beautiful bay of Nanjizal. At the far end of the bay head inland up the track then turn right steeply uphill on a stepped path. After passing through a gate look out for the official, unsigned, Path leaving the main track to go seaward down some rocky steps. The Path descends then climbs to the Coastwatch station on Gwennap Head. The main track also leads here, but less scenically.

The official Path is clear from Gwennap Head down into Porthgwarra. An alternative, in good conditions and for the sure-footed only, is to leave the main Path to the right some 150 yards/140m after the Coastwatch station, then pass the hole of Tol-Pedn-Penwith ("the holed headland of Penwith") before bearing left to re-join the main Path.

Porthgwarra is a charming little hamlet with toilets and seasonal refreshments and unusual passages through the cliffs. Leave along a track next to some cottages, climbing again to the cliffs. The clear Path descends to Porth Chapel, passing St Levan's Holy Well. Continue straight ahead over the bridge, climbing again to arrive at the car park of the unique cliff-face Minack Theatre. Leave by the Path next to the theatre entrance. The Path drops very steeply, with deep steps, to Porthcurno Beach. If in doubt, because of the conditions or possible vertigo, follow the road. At the bottom of the steps keep left above the beach to Porthcurno's facilities.

OS Maps: Landranger 203; Explorer 102

	This Walk	Cumulative	This Walk	Cumulative	Grading	Timing
Ascent	1,381ft	52,089ft	421m	15,877m	Strenuous	3.25 hours
Distance	5.4mi	267.1mi	8.7km	429.9km		

For detailed directions see our Walking Guide no. 30, Porthcurno to Lamorna Cove.

This is a quiet, remote and very scenic Section of cliffs and headlands, punctuated by some picturesque coves and a lighthouse. The larger coves, at each end, Porthcurno and Lamorna, are particularly attractive and are the only access points for cars, so are more popular, Otherwise, the sound of the sea and seabirds are likely to be the only disturbances in this beautiful length.

Directions

A regular bus service goes to Porthcurno and passes about 1 mile/1.5km inland of Lamorna Cove, making a bus-walk feasible. Many undertake one of a variety of circular walks between Porthcurno and Treen using the Coast Path.

Porthcurno has all facilities in summer. The Coast Path leaves at the back of the beach, climbing a steep track to Percella Point before turning to run parallel to the sea. A seaward loop gives a good view of the beautiful Pednvounder Beach, but requires a little scramble to return to the official route. The Path then reaches the neck of Treen Head, or Treryn Dinas, the site of an Iron Age fortification. A cul-de-sac diversion heads for the end and the Logan Rock. Continue on the clear path over the cliff to descend into Penberth Cove, a superb little fishing hamlet with an old capstan. There are toilets but no refreshments.

After climbing away from Penberth the Path continues along the cliff top, with one steep descent and climb at Porthguarnon, then starts to head inland. After passing a seaward house look out for the signed Path to the right which descends into the wooded valley of St Loy and on to the boulder beach. Keep along the top of the beach for 55 yards/50m before leaving up the Path. This climbs to pass above the lighthouse of Tater-du. Approaching Lamorna Point the Path crosses a length of tumbled rocks, making for slow going, until it suddenly descends to the car park at Lamorna Cove. Here are toilets and seasonal refreshments.

Land's End

OS Maps: Landranger 203; Explorer 102

	This Walk	Cumulative	This Walk	Cumulative	Grading	Timing
Ascent	725ft	52,814ft	221m	16,098m	Strenuous then easy	3.5 hours
Distance	9.2mi	276.3mi	14.8km	444.7km		

For detailed directions see our Walking Guide no. 31, Lamorna Cove to Penzance to Marazion.

West of Mousehole this Section is one of lushly vegetated cliffs, but most of it is urban or semi-urban in character as it passes through Newlyn and Penzance. However, it is really defined by its views over the magnificent Mount's Bay, dominated by the iconic sight of St Michael's Mount and its castle, which give this coast a magical character.

Directions

A regular bus service passes about 1 mile/1.5km inland of Lamorna Cove and also serves Newlyn and Penzance, with links possible between Penzance and Marazion, giving a variety of possible bus-walk options.

Lamorna Cove has a seasonal cafe, toilets and, a little way inland, a pub. The Coast Path leaves the cove behind the harbour, bearing right to the cliffs. The well-marked path eventually leads to a road which descends into Mousehole. The road leads to the harbour; however, the official route turns right opposite "Lowena" then continues towards the sea, turning left along a terrace to a car park. It briefly passes along the harbour before turning left then right to reach the main harbour-side road. Mousehole has all facilities and is very picturesque.

At the far end of the harbour go through the car park, on along a concrete walkway then up some steps. Turn right along the road, then along a seaward track to arrive at Newlyn. Follow the road round the harbour and past the fish market, turning right just after the Seamen's Mission to cross a bridge. Bear right past the Tolcarne Inn then follow the promenade to Penzance. Pass the harbour then go right through the large car park to where a walkway leaves from its far right-hand end. Penzance has all facilities, is the end stop of the main-line railway and is the hub of local bus services. The train and bus stations are next to the car park.

The walkway follows the sea wall to the edge of Marazion. At the end of the walkway and cycle route either cross over and follow the road or cross the dunes to a large car park, cross this and continue behind the sea wall into Marazion.

Marazion is the centre for access to St Michael's Mount and is the southern end of the cross-peninsula St Michael's Way from Lelant. The little town of Marazion has all facilities.

OS Maps: Landranger 203; Explorer 103 (Porthleven); Explorer 102 (remainder)

	This Walk	Cumulative	This Walk	Cumulative	Grading	Timing
Ascent	1,916ft	54,730ft	584m	16,682m	Moderate then strenuous	4.75 hours
Distance	10.8mi	287.1mi	17.4km	462.0km		

For detailed directions see our Walking Guide no. 32, Penzance to Marazion to Praa Sands and Praa Sands to Porthleven.

Between Marazion and Cudden Point this Section is dominated by the sweep of Mount's Bay and its iconic focal point of St Michael's Mount. It is a charming length of low cliffs and small fields. East of Cudden Point the Mount is lost but the local landscape is bolder, with craggy headlands, long sandy beaches, inaccessible coves and picturesque cliff-top engine houses.

Directions

There are regular bus services which link Marazion and Porthleven and also serve Perranuthnoe and Praa Sands between the two, making a variety of bus-walks possible, Marazion is a pleasant little town with all facilities and the causeway to St Michael's Mount.

The Coast Path leaves along the main road, following it for some way to the speed restriction sign. Turn right before the cemetery, then bear left on a concrete path down steps and follow the Path to the beach. Cross the top of the beach to some metal steps, climb them and continue ahead. Just after Trenow Cove the Path turns inland. Look out for the signed right turn after 275 yards/250m, which goes back to the low cliffs and on to Perranuthnoe. There are toilets and seasonal refreshments here.

Take the lane on the seaward side of the car park, bearing right and then left into a field. The well-marked path leads to Cudden Point, with magnificent views over Mount's Bay. It descends past Little Cudden to Bessy's Cove, where it joins a track. Go ahead, bearing right at some granite gate posts, then through Prussia Cove on a lane between large stone buildings. Keep ahead on the Path which passes above Kenneggy Sand and then descends to Praa Sands, where there are toilets and seasonal refreshments. Go down the slipway to the beach then along in front of the shop, taking the steps up beside the cafe. Keep along the top of the grassy dunes, turning left when signed at the end then right into a housing estate. At the end bear right and climb to the cliffs. The Path skirts behind Rinsey Head then through a car park and down to a restored engine house. It continues to Trewavas Head, inland of more restored engine houses. Beyond there have been numerous cliff falls – be sure to follow the signed Path. This then enters Porthleven on a lane – fork right entering the town to pass alongside the harbour to its head. Porthleven has all facilities.

OS Maps: Landranger 203; Explorer 103

	This Walk	Cumulative	This Walk	Cumulative	Grading	Timing
Ascent	781ft	55,511ft	238m	16,920m	Moderate	3.25 hours
Distance	5.2mi	292.3mi	8.4km	470.4km		

For detailed directions see our Walking Guide no. 33, Porthleven to Poldhu Cove.

This is a Section mostly of low cliffs with cliff-face paths, long stretches being above extensive beaches. It harbours a couple of unexpected features, firstly in the shape of Loe Bar, a large strip of shingle barring the freshwater Loe Pool from the sea, and secondly in the unusual position of Gunwalloe Church, hidden away in the corner of a sandy cove. Add a cliff-top monument to Marconi, a couple of picturesque coves and the rocky and atmospheric harbour at Mullion Cove and it makes for a fascinating length.

Directions

Porthleven and Mullion village, which is some 0.5 mile/1km from the Coast Path, are both served by regular but separate bus routes, which meet at Helston. The Mullion bus also serves Poldhu Cove, allowing various bus-walks.

Porthleven has all facilities. The Coast Path goes alongside the harbour towards the clock-tower at the end near the pier. Follow the road past this building, going right at the fork and keep on out of the town to a car park. Climb the steps and continue ahead on the track to Loe Bar. Cross the bar to the far side, forking right, downhill, shortly after the memorial. After passing a renovated fishery building the Path arrives at Gunwalloe Fishing Cove. Go ahead onto the National Trust's Baulk Head, then above Halzephron Cove to a road. Bear right to a small car park then go right again, away from the road, on the cliffs down to Gunwalloe Church Cove. There are toilets and seasonal refreshments here. The picturesque church is tucked away at the right-hand end of the cove.

Skirt the beach to a road, then take the signed Path over a footbridge and over the rear of the beach to the Path rising away. Immediately after the car park at the top turn right along the cliff top before returning to the road and dropping into Poldhu Cove, where there is a bus stop, toilets and refreshments. A good path leads inland to Mullion village.

Porthleven Harbour

OS Maps: Landranger 203; Explorer 103

	This Walk	Cumulative	This Walk	Cumulative	Grading	Timing
Ascent	1,631ft	57,142ft	497m	17,417m	Moderate	3.25 hours
Distance	8.2mi	300.5mi	13.2km	483.6km		

For detailed directions see our Walking Guide no. 34, Poldhu Cove To The Lizard.

This is an exposed Section of high, flat-topped cliffs and spectacular coves and bays. The coastal landscape is superb throughout, but punctuated by some real scenic gems, of which Kynance Cove is probably the pick. The combination of steep cliffs, unusual geology and flora, beautiful sea colours and long stretches of easy walking make this a rewarding length. And watch out for choughs, Cornwall's iconic bird now returned to re-colonise this coast.

Directions

A regular bus service links Mullion village with Lizard Town, each settlement about 0.5 mile/1km inland from its respective end, thus giving a possible bus-walk. In addition, there are many easy local circuits based on the Coast Path in the Lizard-Kynance area.

From the road at Poldhu turn right up the driveway signed to the Marconi Centre, leaving this after 110 yards/100m for a path on the right. This passes the Marconi monument on the cliffs then drops down into Polurrian Cove. Climb away past the Polurrian Hotel then right along the Path to the Mullion Cove Hotel. Keep seaward and drop down to the harbour, where there are seasonal refreshments. There are toilets 110 yards/100m up the road.

The Coast Path leaves the cove slightly inland to the right, up the hill just after the cafe. Climb to the cliffs, keeping to the right to hug the coastline. There is an information board on the unique flora and fauna of the area here.

The easy and clear Path rounds Parc Bean Cove and Lower Predannack Cliff. Approaching Vellan Head, be sure to keep close to the coast for the official route – the more obvious track misses the views. After the deep valley at Gew Graze the Path rounds Rill Point and descends to Kynance Cove. The steep descent leads to the beach by the seasonal cafe. There are also toilets here. If the sun is shining the sea is brilliant turquoise.

From the cafe either follow the main track up towards the car park or cross the little beach (at low tide) and climb a partly stepped path to the cliffs, leaving this at a sign pointing right. This passes adjacent to the car park, where the main track arrives, and the Coast Path then continues clearly and easily above Pentreath Beach at Caerthillian and round Old Lizard Head, and on to Lizard Point, England's most southerly point, where there are cafes, gift shops and toilets. The nearby lighthouse is open to visitors at certain times. A path leads inland to Lizard Town, which has all facilities including regular bus services.

OS Maps: Landranger 203 (Lizard); Landranger 204 (remainder); Explorer 103

	This Walk	Cumulative	This Walk	Cumulative	Grading	Timing
Ascent	2,293ft	59,435ft	699m	18,116m	Moderate, strenuous in places	5.75 hours
Distance	10.4mi	310.9mi	16.7km	500.3km		

For detailed directions see our Walking Guide no. 35, The Lizard to Coverack.

This is a Section of cliffs and coves, punctuated by headlands giving excellent views along the coastline. Here and there are areas of sandy beach at the foot of the cliffs, but only at Kennack are they very extensive. This coast is largely sheltered from the worst of the prevailing south-westerly winds, and consequently has a lush, well-vegetated character. This being a relatively unfrequented stretch, substantial lengths are quiet and remote.

Directions

Lizard Town, about 0.5 mile/1km inland of the Coast Path, has a bus service which also passes a little inland of Cadgwith, about half-way along this length, which presents a bus-walk possibility. In addition, there are numerous easy circuits based on The Lizard using the Coast Path which are popular and attractive.

Lizard Point has cafes and toilets, while Lizard Town, inland, has all necessary facilities. Lizard Point has the distinction of being England's most southerly point and is a fine location. The Coast Path leaves the Point alongside the car parking area and on in front of the lighthouse. There is a Heritage Centre at the lighthouse and both lighthouse and Heritage Centre are open to the public at certain times (www.trinityhouse.co.uk). After passing the lighthouse descend to cross a footbridge then climb, passing in front of the Housel Bay Hotel and on past the Lloyds Signal Station, bearing right here. The route passes Bass Point National Coastwatch Institution lookout, the first in the country to be established. At Kilcobben Cove the Path goes behind The Lizard lifeboat station with its boathouse which was completed in 2011. It then arrives at Church Cove. Go left for a short distance then take the Path through the gate on the right. There are some ups and downs to a Path junction just after a stone stile at Polgwidden Cove; keep right here. A little further on the Path skirts the dramatic collapsed cave of the Devil's Frying Pan. Follow the signed Path past the cottages and down into the picturesque little fishing hamlet of Cadgwith.

Cadgwith has a pub, shop, refreshments and toilets. There is a superb little beach here where the fishing boats are hauled up. This is overlooked by a convenient grassy knoll with seats known as The Todn (Cornish for lawn). Walk through Cadgwith and up the hill, turning right on the signed path a little way up. The Path then descends to Poltesco, crossing a footbridge. There is a diversion to the right leading to the attractive and interesting cove, complete with old serpentine works, where the local colourful rock was made into useful items. Climbing out of Poltesco, the Path then joins a road which leads to the beach at Kennack Sands. There are toilets here and seasonal refreshments.

Follow the Path behind the beaches and on to the cliffs to reach the neck of the long promontory of Carrick Lûz, the site of an Iron Age cliff fort. The Path cuts across the neck and then negotiates the steep valley at Downas Cove. Another, shallower valley crossing leads to the end of Black Head and its lookout hut. The Path now descends over the cliffs towards Chynhalls Point going amongst the natural rock outcrops which can be slippery in wet weather. Beyond the Point the Path soon reaches Coverack.

An alternative inland path avoids the slippery Chynhalls Cliff. At the top of the Coast Path descent, the wide alternative path goes through gorse and passes a Sculpture Park, then the edge of a caravan park before arriving at a bungalow on a tarmac road. Turn right towards the hotel and then almost immediately bear left down a narrower path to rejoin the Coast Path at Chynhalls Point.

Reaching the road at Coverack, the Path soon veers off right down some steps to arrive at a car park at the end of the village. Follow the road past the harbour. Coverack, a pretty place, has all facilities, including a regular bus service into Helston.

Red Wall at Bass Point, The Lizard

OS Maps: Landranger 204; Explorer 103

	This Walk	Cumulative	This Walk	Cumulative	Grading	Timing
Ascent	2,192ft	61,627ft	668m	18,784m	Moderate	5.75 hours
Distance	12.9mi	323.8mi	20.8km	521.1km		

For detailed directions see our Walking Guide no. 36, Coverack to Helford.

This is a sheltered Section of the Coast Path. It includes low cliffs facing away from the prevailing winds, but also lengths of pleasant rural field paths, a little inland, necessary to avoid inaccessible coastal working and former quarries. In addition this Section has substantial lengths which fringe a tidal creek and on wooded estuary-side paths passing pretty beaches where the Coast Path reaches the Helford River. While not as dramatic as some Sections, it is an attractive stretch with a quiet charm of its own.

Directions

Separate bus routes from Helston serve Coverack and Helford Passage, across the river via ferry (Good Friday or 1st April to October) from Helford, allowing a bus-walk based on Helston. There is an attractive local circuit using the Coast Path between Helford and Gillan Creek.

There are all necessary facilities at Coverack. The Coast Path follows the road away from the pub and past the harbour, continuing straight ahead on a narrow lane when the road goes left. Look out for the sign pointing right, just before the end of the lane. The Path goes over sometimes boggy ground next to the coast to arrive at Lowland Point. Next, the old workings at Dean Quarry are passed on their seaward side. The well-signed path then arrives at the open area at Godrevy Cove. The next length of coast is inaccessible due to operating quarries, so the Coast Path heads across the open area inland to pick up a signed path going uphill between fields. This leads to the little hamlet of Rosenithon. At the T-junction, turn right on the lane, uphill, turning left into a field just after the right-hand bend. Cross three fields in the same direction, stone stiles between them, to emerge on a lane. Go left then, at a junction, right, which leads to Porthoustock, a coastal hamlet with public toilets.

The route of the next stretch, to another coastal hamlet, Porthallow, is also a rural inland walk. It leaves Porthoustock past the telephone box and up the hill. Where the road bears right go straight ahead on a narrower lane. Go past a row of thatched cottages and over a little grassy bank at the end next to a greenhouse to a kissing-gate. Just past the gate there is a fork in the Path. Bear right and follow the Path climbing to the far top corner of the field to cross a lifting-bar stile and a Cornish stile (a sort of stone cattle grid) into another field. Turn right in this field alongside the hedge, then bear away left at the top to cross another Cornish stile to a road. At the road go left, passing through the tiny hamlet of Trenance. Here the route follows the road round to the right to a T-junction. At the junction go slightly right and immediately left onto an enclosed path which leads to a track between buildings. At the road turn right to arrive at Porthallow.

Porthallow has a pub, toilets and seasonal refreshments. Look out for the marker indicating the half-way point of the Coast Path, equidistant (at 315 miles) from Minehead and Poole. Leave Porthallow along the back of the beach and up the steps.

The Path now follows the coastline, keeping close to the edge round Nare Point and then past a couple of pretty beaches. Moving into the mouth of the Helford River the Path continues alongside its tidal tributary, Gillan Creek. A tidal ferry crosses the creek.

From Easter/1st April to 31st October use the signal board to request the ferry. Telephone 01326 231357 or see page 17 for ferry details.

Otherwise (and for the official Coast Path route), take the lane left from the creekside up the hill to a sharp left-hand bend. Here go straight ahead along the field edge, then bear right over two further fields to a road. Turn right to Carne, at the head of the creek, then right again along the north side of the creek to St Anthony Church. Past the church turn left uphill then shortly right on a farm track which leads into a field. Cross diagonally left to the top of the field to a kissing-gate.

For a short, direct route from here go through the gate and turn left. However, the Coast Path includes an optional extra of a circuit of Dennis Head. For this circuit do not pass through the gate but turn right then almost immediately left over a stile. At the next junction continue straight ahead to reach the end of the headland. The Path circles around the headland, re-joining the outward route to the stile and then the kissing-gate.

Go through the gate and continue along the top of the field. The route now heads up the estuary side of the Helford River through woods and past coves. Towards the end the Path reaches a track – follow to the road and go right here then quickly left. The Path then emerges next to the main car park at Helford. Go down the hill into the village. Helford has a pub and shop and there are toilets at the car park.

Coverack

OS Maps: Landranger 204; Explorer 103

	This Walk	Cumulative	This Walk	Cumulative	Grading	Timing
Ascent	1,397ft	63,024ft	426m	19,210m	Moderate	4.5 hours
Distance	10.3mi	334.1mi	16.6km	537.7km		

For detailed directions see our Walking Guide no. 37, Helford to Falmouth (Ferry).

There are two contrasting parts to this Section. Between Helford and Rosemullion Head it is a sheltered walk alongside the mouth of the beautiful Helford River, with undulating, relatively low cliffs alternating with charming little beaches. Between Rosemullion Head and Falmouth the walk flanks the sweep of Falmouth Bay, with rather larger coves overlooked by the great headland of Pendennis Point at the Falmouth end, crowned by its castle. Over the bay is St Anthony Head lighthouse. None of this is a lonely or remote walk, and the Falmouth end is decidedly urban, but it is never uninteresting and always very scenic.

Directions

Helford Passage and Falmouth are linked by a regular bus service, giving numerous bus-walk options. The short circular walk round Pendennis Head in Falmouth is a great local favourite.

Helford has pub, shop and toilets; Helford Passage, over the river, has a pub and seasonal refreshments. There is a seasonal ferry link. For ferry details see page 17.

Walk around Helford River

If the ferry is not operating, a 13 mile/21km walk around the Helford River is possible. This will add another day to the itinerary. For this route, from Helford take the Path up the hill to arrive at Penarvon Cove. Go round the back of the cove and turn inland up a track to a road. Turn right then left on a track to the permissive path along the atmospheric Frenchman's Creek. At the end take the Path on the right signed to Withan past Frenchman's Pill Cottage, crossing a footbridge. Follow the Path through the woods and aim for the far left corner of the field, taking the stile on the left. Follow the boundary on the left past Withan Farm, then head west over the fields to a lane. Here turn left to a crossroads, turning right here towards Mawgan. The lane joins a larger road; turn right past Gear then down and up into Mawgan-in-Meneage village. Turn right just after the church on the Path towards Gwarth-an-drea then left behind a bungalow to a road. Turn right and at the junction bear right and continue downhill to the bridge at Gweek. There is a shop and pub here. Take the road opposite the Gweek Inn and at Tolvan Cross turn right along a bridleway to a road junction. Go straight ahead, towards Porth Navas. After crossing the stream take the footpath on the left along the field edge to the road.

Follow the road ahead to Nancenoy and Polwheveral. At the crossroads after Polwheveral turn right then after 140 yards/128m take the Path on the left along the field edge then across the field corner to a road junction. Take the Porth Navas road opposite through the village to Trenarth Bridge, then turn right towards Falmouth. At the junction at Trebah turn right, then right again into Bar Road. At the end turn left on a footpath which leads to the Helford River, turning left to the Ferryboat Inn at Helford Passage, the landing place for the ferry from Helford.

Ferry users start from here

Coast Path, Helford Passage - Falmouth

From the Ferryboat Inn, facing the pub, turn right along the river and up to a grassy hill. Keep on to a concrete track and follow this, passing behind Trebah Beach at Polgwidden Cove. Continue on the riverside then through woods to meet a track. Turn right to descend to the little village of Durgan. Go up the road, ignoring one path to the right, until the road turns left and the Path continues straight ahead. Follow this path, arriving at Porth Saxon Beach behind a building and then through a field to Porthallack Beach. The Path then climbs round Toll Point to arrive at a wooded area. At the fork keep right and follow the Path onward to Rosemullion Head, leaving the Helford River behind.

Keep seaward round the headland then descend to go through a small wood and then on, the Path becoming suburban now, to reach Maenporth where there are toilets and refreshments and a bus stop. Turn right behind the cafe and continue to Swanpool, with more toilets and refreshments and another bus stop. Take the Path from the far end of the beach to arrive at Gyllyngvase, then keep along Falmouth's promenade to the far end. The official Path goes around the magnificent Pendennis Point – keep to the seaward road all the way to the end then at the car park descend on the signed Path up the river, parallel to the road above. The Path emerges from woods and passes the Leisure Centre, descending above the docks to a T-junction. Turn right then go ahead under the railway bridge, passing the Maritime Museum and along Falmouth's main shopping street to arrive at the Prince of Wales Pier at the far end. Falmouth, of course, has all facilities, including a rail link to the main line at Truro.

Helford

If you enjoy sleeping, eating or drinking at any business on the Path please sugges[t] they join us as Business Members so that [we] can share their brilliance!

The businesses listed here are all supporters of the
South West Coast Path Association, they have joined as business members
and it would be great if you could show your support for them too. In addition,
businesses are listed with more details on our website: www.southwestcoastpath.org.uk
Find them through our walk finder or our accommodation finder tools.

KEY:

GR Grid Reference
DP Distance from the Path
NT Nearest Town

🐕 Dogs Welcome
🍴 Evening Meal Available
3 Number Of Rooms

🛒 Grocery Shop On Site
📶 Wifi
🚗 Parking

Bed & Breakfasts and Hotels

NAME	OTHER INFO
Smarties Surf Lodge 84 Crantock Street, Newquay, TR7 1JW 📞 07890 125172 ✉ info@smartiessurflodge.co.uk 🌐 www.smartiessurflodge.co.uk	GR: 804 615 — DP: 0.5 miles NT: **NEWQUAY** 🐕 🍴 🛒 Other info:
St George's Country House Hotel St George's Hill, Perranporth, TR6 0ED 📞 01872 572184 ✉ contact@stgeorgescountryhousehotel.com 🌐 www.stgeorgescountryhousehotel.com	GR: SW746533 — DP: 0.25 miles NT: **PERRANPORTH** Offers one night stays 🚗 📶 🍴 Other info:
Kimberley Bed & Breakfast West Polberro, St Agnes, TR5 0SS 📞 01872 552044 ✉ info@kimberleybedandbreakfast.co.uk 🌐 www.kimberleybedandbreakfast.co.uk	GR: 716 511 — DP: 0.25 miles NT: **ST AGNES** 4 🚗 📶 Other info:
Portreath Arms The Square, Portreath, TR16 4LA 📞 01209 842259 ✉ email@theportreatharms.co.uk 🌐 www.theportreatharms.co.uk	GR: 657 453 — DP: 0 miles NT: **PORTREATH** Offers one night stays 7 🚗 📶 🐕 🍴 Other info: Dogs wel[l]come in some rooms by prior arrangemen[t]
Cliff House B&B Cliff Terrace, Portreath, TR16 4LE 📞 01209 843847 ✉ cliffhousebookinginfo@gmail.com 🌐 www.cliffhouseportreath.co.uk	GR: 657 543 — DP: 0 miles NT: **PORTREATH** Offers one night stays 5 🚗 📶 🐕 Other info:
Laity Farm B&B Bridge, Redruth, TR16 4QG 📞 01209 844865 ✉ laityfarm@yahoo.com 🌐 www.laityfarmbandbportreath.wordpress.com	GR: 677 448 — DP: 1 mile NT: **REDRUTH** Offers one night stays 3 🚗 📶 🐕 Other info:
Sandbank House B&B 51 Upton Towans, Hayle, TR27 5BL 📞 01736 752820 ✉ info@sandbank-holidays.co.uk 🌐 www.sandbankhouse.co.uk	GR: 582 400 — DP: 2 miles NT: **HAYLE** 3 🚗 📶 Other info:

NAME	OTHER INFO		
Nanterrow Farm Gwithian, Hayle, TR27 5BP 📞 01209 712282 ✉ nanterrow@hotmail.com 🌐 www.nanterrowfarm.co.uk	GR: 599 412 NT: **HAYLE** Offers one night stays [2] 🚗 📶	DP: 1.25 miles Other info:
Creekside B&B 34 Penpol Terrace, Hayle, TR27 4BQ 📞 01736 753969 ✉ valsherris@hotmail.com 🌐 www.southwestcoastpath.org.uk/creekside-bb-hayle	GR: 558 374 NT: **HAYLE** Offers one night stays [3] 🚗 📶	DP: 0 miles Other info:
The Western Hotel Gabriel Street, St Ives, TR26 2LU 📞 01736 795277 ✉ enquiries@hotelstives.com 🌐 www.hotelstives.com	GR: SW51693 40373 NT: **ST IVES** Offers one night stays [17] 📶 🛒	DP: 0.5 miles Other info: Luggage transfer available - please enquire
Tamarisk Guest House Burthallan Lane, St Ives, TR26 3AA 📞 01736797201/07798 800 930 ✉ tamariskbb@gmail.com 🌐 www.cornwall-online.co.uk/tamariskbandb-stives	GR: 509 405 NT: **ST IVES** Offers one night stays [1] 🚗 📶	DP: 0 miles Other info:
Carlill Guesthouse 9 Porthminster Terrace, St Ives, TR26 2DQ 📞 01736 796738 ✉ carlillguesthouse@hotmail.co.uk 🌐 www.carlillguesthouse.co.uk	GR: 518 403 NT: **ST IVES** Offers one night stays [5] 🚗 📶	DP: 0.25 miles Other info:
Boswednack Manor B&B Zennor, St Ives, TR26 3DD 📞 01736 794183 ✉ boswednack@ravenfield.co.uk 🌐 www.boswednackmanor.co.uk	GR: 443 378 NT: **ZENNOR** Offers one night stays [5] 🚗	DP: 0.5 miles Other info: Evening food at Zennor and Treen pubs
The Gurnard's Head Zennor, St Ives, TR26 3DE 📞 01736 796928 ✉ enquiries@gurnardshead.co.uk 🌐 www.gurnardshead.co.uk	GR: 435 377 NT: **ZENNOR** Offers one night stays 🚗 📶 🐕 🍴	DP: 1 mile Other info: Closed at Christmas
Lamorna House Homestay 8 North Road, Goldsithney, Penzance, TR20 9JY 📞 01736 603532/07834176522 ✉ lamornahouse@gmail.com 🌐 www.lamornahouse.co.uk	GR: NT: **MARAZION** Offers one night stays [2] 📶	DP: 1 mile Other info:
Gypsy Caravan B&B Primrose Cottage, Levant Road, Trewellard, TR19 7SU 📞 01736 787585 ✉ holiday@gypsycaravanbandb.co.uk 🌐 www.gypsycaravanbandb.co.uk	GR: SW3694834116 NT: **TREWELLARD** Offers one night stays [1] 🚗 🐕	DP: 0 miles Other info:
The Old Post House B&B 24 Bosorne Road, St Just, TR19 7LU 📞 07931 139603 ✉ moylefiona@gmail.com 🌐 www.theoldposthousebandb.co.uk	GR: 368 312 NT: **ST JUST** [2] 📶	DP: 0.4 miles Other info: Meditation, yoga and Reiki on offer

NAME	OTHER INFO
Bosavern House St Just, TR19 7RD ☎ 01736 788301 ✉ info@bosavern.com ⊕ www.bosavern.com	GR: 370 304 DP: 0.5 miles NT: **ST JUST** Offers one night stays [10] 🚗 📶 🐕 Other info:
Sunnybank House B&B Seaview Hill, Sennen, TR19 7AR ☎ 01736 871278 ✉ sunnybankhouse@gmail.com ⊕ www.sunnybankhousebandb.com	GR: 366 264 DP: 1 mile NT: **SENNEN** 🍴 Other info:
The Studio 3 Coastguard Cottages, Treen, St Levan, Penzance, TR19 6LQ ☎ 01736 810504 ✉ jeffrey_hardman@sky.com ⊕ www.sennencornwall.com	GR: 351 262 DP: 0.1 miles NT: **TREEN** Offers one night stays [1] 🚗 📶 🐕 Other info:
Treen House B&B Treen, St Leven, Penzance, TR19 6LG ☎ 01736 810379 ✉ hello@treenhousebedandbreakfast.co.uk ⊕ www.treenhousebedandbreakfast.co.uk	GR: 393 230 DP: 0.3 miles NT: **TREEN** Offers one night stays [3] 🚗 📶 Other info:
Bosula House Lamorna, Penzance, TR19 6NZ ☎ 01736 810970 ✉ val@bosula.co.uk ⊕ www.bosulahouse.com	GR: 442 254 DP: 0.75 miles NT: **LAMORNA** Offers one night stays [2] 🚗 📶 Other info: Open Mar-Oct
Mzmia 3 Penlee Close, Praa Sands, Penzance, TR20 9SR ☎ 01736 763856 ✉ marianfoy@hotmail.com ⊕ www.southwestcoastpath.org.uk/mzima-praa-sands	GR: 581 287 DP: 0.5 miles NT: **PENZANCE** Offers one night stays 🐕 🍴 Other info:
Mountview Hotel Longrock, Penzance, TR20 8JJ ☎ 01736 710416 ✉ mountviewhotel@hotmail.co.uk ⊕ www.mountviewhotelcornwall.com	GR: DP: 0 miles NT: **PENZANCE** Offers one night stays [5] 🚗 📶 🐕 🍴 Other info:
St Johns House B&B Boscaswell Downs, Pendeen, Penzance, TR19 7DW ☎ 01736 786605 ✉ moriakeogh@btinternet.com ⊕ www.stjohnshousebedandbreakfast.co.uk	GR: 384 344 DP: 1 mile NT: **PENZANCE** [3] 🚗 📶 Other info:
The Old Chapel B&B Boscaswell Downs, Pendeen, Penzance, TR19 7DR ☎ 01736 786006 / 07789 547806 ✉ geoffgoatherd@aol.com ⊕ www.cornwallfarwest.co.uk/cfwoldchapelbb	GR: 384 344 DP: 1 mile NT: **PENZANCE** Other info:
Sea View House The Valley, Porthcurno, Penzance, TR19 6JX ☎ 01736 810638 ✉ paulinewillows@hotmail.co.uk ⊕ www.seaviewhouseporthcurno.com	GR: 382 228 DP: 0 miles NT: **PENZANCE** [5] 🚗 📶 Other info:

NAME	OTHER INFO	
Sennen Rise	GR: 357 256	DP: 0 miles
Mayon Farm, Sennen, TR19 7AD	NT: **PENZANCE**	
01736 871757		
info@sennenrise.co.uk	[4] [car] [wifi]	Other info:
www.sennenrise.co.uk/our-house		
The North Inn	GR: 382 343	DP: 1 mile
Pendeen, Penzance, TR19 7DN	NT: **PENZANCE**	
01736 788417		
ernestjohncoak@aol.com	[dog] [food]	Other info:
www.thenorthinnpendeen.co.uk		
Number Nine B&B	GR: 473 299	DP: 0.25 miles
9 Regent Square, Penzance, TR18 4BG	NT: **PENZANCE**	
01736 369715	Offers one night stays	
janeclayton27@gmail.com	[2] [wifi]	Other info: Complimentary cream tea on arrival
https://numberninepenzance.jimdo.com		
Cornerways Guest House	GR: 475 307	DP: 0.2 miles
5 Leskinnick Street, Penzance, TR18 2HA	NT: **PENZANCE**	
01736 364645	Offers one night stays	
cornerways.penzance@yahoo.com	[4] [wifi]	Other info:
www.cornerways-penzance.co.uk		
The Tremont Hotel	GR: 466 299	DP: 0.5 miles
Alexandra Road, Penzance, TR18 4LZ	NT: **PENZANCE**	
01736 362614	Offers one night stays	
info@tremonthotel.co.uk	[10] [wifi]	Other info:
www.tremonthotel.co.uk		
Glencree House	GR: 469 297	DP: 0.5 miles
2 Mennaye Road, Penzance, TR18 4NG	NT: **PENZANCE**	
01736 362026		
stay@glencreehouse.co.uk	[wifi]	Other info:
www.glencreehouse.co.uk		
Honeydew Guesthouse	GR: 475 306	DP: 0.2 miles
3 Leskinnick Street, Penzance, TR18 2HA	NT: **PENZANCE**	
01736 364206	Offers one night stays	
info@honeydewguesthouse.co.uk	[4] [wifi] [dog]	Other info: Open all year
www.penzance-bed-breakfast.co.uk		
Wellmore End Cottage	GR:	DP:
Methleigh Bottoms, Porthleven, TR13 9JP	NT: **PORTHLEVEN**	
01326 569310		
wellmoreend-bandb@tiscali.co.uk	[2] [car]	Other info:
www.wellmoreend.com		
The Granary Barn Back Packers & B&B	GR: 637298	DP: 3 miles
Nantrisack Farm, Sithney, Helston, TR13 0AE	NT: **HELSTON**	
07740 514188		
cornwall.backpackers@gmail.com	[car] [wifi]	Other info:
www.cornwall-backpackers.co.uk		
PJ's Bed And Breakfast	GR: 629 262	DP: 0.25 miles
13 The Crescent, Porthleven, Helston, TR13 9LU	NT: **HELSTON**	
01326 722907 / 07745 479151		
info@pjsbedandbreakfast.co.uk	[2] [wifi] [dog]	Other info:
www.pjsbedandbreakfast.co.uk		

NAME	OTHER INFO		
The Top House Inn The Lizard, TR12 7NQ ☏ 01326 290974 ✉ mail@thetophouselizard.co.uk 🌐 www.thetophouselizard.co.uk	GR: 702 125　DP: 0.3 miles NT: **HELSTON** Offers one night stays 8 🛜	Other info: Dogs welcome in pub, not rooms	
Polurrian Bay Hotel - LFH Polurrian Road, Mullion, Helston, TR12 7EN ☏ 01326 240421 ✉ info@polurrianhotel.com 🌐 www.polurrianhotel.com	GR: 67 186　DP: 0.2 miles NT: **MULLION** Offers one night stays 41 🚗 🛜 🐕 🍴	Other info:	
The Old Bakery B&B Main Way, The Lizard, TR12 7NZ ☏ 01326 290755 ✉ robin@lizardforge.co.uk 🌐 ww.southwestcoastpath.org.uk/old-bakery-lizard	GR: 703 128　DP: 0.75 miles NT: **THE LIZARD** 2	Other info:	
Atlantic House B&B Pentreath Lane, The Lizard, TR12 7NY ☏ 01326 290399 ✉ atlantichse@btinternet.com 🌐 www.atlantichouselizard.co.uk	GR: 702 127　DP: 0.25 miles NT: **THE LIZARD** Offers one night stays 3 🛜	Other info:	
Hillside B&B Prazegooth Lane, Cadgwith, TR12 7LA ☏ 01326 290192 ✉ joannaaplin@aol.com 🌐 www.cadgwith-hillside.co.uk	GR: 722 146　DP: 0.1 miles NT: **CADGWITH** 2 🛜 🐕	Other info:	
The Five Pilchards Inn Porthallow, St Keverne, Helston, TR12 6PP ☏ 01326 280256 ✉ fivepilchards@btinternet.com 🌐 www.thefivepilchards.co.uk	GR: 797 231　DP: 0.12 miles NT: **PORTHALLOW** Offers one night stays 4 🚗 🛜 🍴	Other info:	
Penmenner House Bed & Breakfast Penmenner Road, Helston, TR12 7NR ☏ 01326 290315 ✉ contact@penmenner-house.co.uk 🌐 www.penmenner-house.co.uk	GR: SW70121 12069　DP: 0 miles NT: **HELSTON** Offers one night stays 41 🚗 🛜 🐕 🍴	Other info:	
Mullion Cove Hotel Mullion, Helston, TR12 7EP ☏ 01326 240328 ✉ enquiries@mullion-cove.co.uk 🌐 www.mullion-cove.co.uk	GR: 668 180　DP: 0 miles NT: **HELSTON** 4 🚗 🛜	Other info:	
Hellarcher Farm Penmenner Road, The Lizard, Helston, TR12 7NN ☏ 01326 291188 ✉ hellarcher7@btinternet.com 🌐 www.hellarcherfarm.co.uk	GR: 701 123　DP: 0.5 miles NT: **HELSTON** 🐕	Other info:	
Tregonning Lea Laddenvean, St Keverne, Helston, TR12 6QD ☏ 01326 280947 ✉ waltersanger@aol.com 🌐 www.coverack.org.uk/pages/tregonninglea.html	GR: 788 214　DP: 0.75 miles NT: **HELSTON** Offers one night stays 3 🚗 🛜 🐕	Other info:	

NAME	OTHER INFO		
Stormfield B&B The Lizard, Helston, TR12 7NZ 📞 01326 290184 ✉ carol.annetts@hotmail.com 🌐 www.southwestcoastpath.org.uk/stormfield-lizard	GR: 703 126 NT: **HELSTON**	DP: 0.5 miles Other info:	
The Sail Loft B&B Helford, Helston, TR12 6JY 📞 01326 231083 ✉ pamroyall@btinternet.com 🌐 www.southwestcoastpath.org.uk/sail-loft-point-helford	GR: 758 263 NT: **HELSTON** Offers one night stays ⬚1⬚ 🛜	DP: 0 miles Other info:	
Penmarth House Coverack, Helford, TR12 6TQ 📞 01326 280240 ✉ francine@coverack-bandb.co.uk 🌐 www.coverack-bandb.co.uk	GR: SW78062 18559 NT: **HELFORD** Offers one night stays ⬚3⬚ 🚗 🛜	DP: 0.15 miles Other info: Walk-the-Lizard package available	
Trevarn B&B Carninion Road, Mawnan Smith, Falmouth, TR11 5JD 📞 01326 251245 ✉ enquiries@trevarn.co.uk 🌐 www.trevarn.co.uk	GR: 779 284 NT: **FALMOUTH** Offers one night stays ⬚3⬚ 🚗 🛜	DP: 0.75 miles Other info:	
Seaview Inn Wodehouse Terrace, Falmouth, TR11 3EP 📞 01326 311359 ✉ seaviewinn@hotmail.co.uk 🌐 www.seaviewinnfalmouth.co.uk	GR: 808 326 NT: **FALMOUTH** Offers one night stays ⬚3⬚ 🛜 🐾 🍴	DP: 1 mile Other info:	
The Westcott Gyllyngvase Hill, Falmouth, TR11 4DN 📞 01326 311309 ✉ thewestcott@outlook.com 🌐 www.westcottguesthousefalmouth.co.uk	GR: 809 317 NT: **FALMOUTH** ⬚9⬚ 🚗	DP: 0.3 miles Other info:	

Mawnan Smith

Self Catering and hostels

NAME	OTHER INFO	
Sandbanks Holidays 51 Upton Towans, Hayle, TR27 5BL 📞 01736 752 594 ✉ info@sandbank-holidays.co.uk 🌐 www.sandbank-holidays.co.uk	GR: 582 400 DP: 2 miles NT: **HAYLE** 🐕 📶	Other info:
Beachpads Church Lane, Lelant, St Ives, TR26 3DZ 📞 01872 862439 ✉ nicola@beachpads.co.uk 🌐 www.groupaccommodation.com/properties/beach-houses-lelant-st-ives-cornwall	GR: 549 379 DP: 0 miles NT: **ST IVES** 10 🚗 📶 🐕	Other info:
Penhayl Cottage Morreps, Wharf Road, St Ives, TR26 3DU 📞 01736 758227 ✉ penhayl@btinternet.com 🌐 www.penhayl-cottage-cornwall.co.uk	GR: 549 374 DP: 0.1 miles NT: **ST IVES** 2 🚗 📶	Other info: Closed Dec & Jan
Cohort Hostel The Stennack, St Ives, TR26 1FF 📞 01736 791664 ✉ hello@stayatcohort.co.uk 🌐 www.stayatcohort.co.uk	GR: 516 403 DP: 0.5 miles NT: **ST IVES** Offers one night stays 60 📶	Other info:
Lands End Hostel and B&B Mill Barn, Trevescan, Land's End, TR19 7AQ 📞 07585 625774 ✉ lou@landsendholidays.co.uk 🌐 www.landsendholidays.co.uk	GR: SW443378 DP: 0.7 miles NT: **LAND'S END** Offers one night stays 4 🚗 📶	Other info: B&B also available. Open all year
The Lookout Dumbarton Terrace, Mousehole, TR19 6PW 📞 01736 732206 ✉ louisebradley@participate.uk.com 🌐 www.abnb.me/EVmg/OdssCYeI7E	GR: 469 264 DP: 0.1 miles NT: **NEWLYN** Offers one night stays 1 📶	Other info:
Chy Lowena Holiday Cottage 25 Boscaswell Village, Penzance, TR19 7EP 📞 01132 661812 ✉ info@chylowenacornwall.com 🌐 www.chylowenacornwall.com	GR: 378 947 DP: 1 mile NT: **PENZANCE** 3 🚗 📶	Other info:
The Old Vicarage Nansmellyon Road, Mullion, TR12 7DQ 📞 01326 240898 ✉ bandbmullion@hotmail.com 🌐 www.facebook.com/TheOldVicarageHolidayAccomodation	GR: 677 189 DP: 0.5 miles NT: **MULLION**	Other info:
Wireless Cottage Housel Bay, Lizard, Helston, TR12 7AP 📞 0346 800 1895 ✉ enquiries@nationaltrust.org.uk 🌐 www.nationaltrust.org.uk/holidays	GR: 714 119 DP: 0 miles NT: **LIZARD** 1 📶 🐕	Other info: Open all year

NAME	OTHER INFO		
Trenance Farm Cottages Mullion, Helston, TR12 7HB 01326 240639 info@trenancefarmholidays.co.uk www.trenancefarmcottages.co.uk	GR: 672 184 NT: **HELSTON** Other info:	DP: 0.5 miles	
St Anthony Holiday Cottages The Boathouse, St. Anthony, Manaccan, Helston, TR12 6JW 01326 231357 info@stanthony.co.uk www.stanthony.co.uk	GR: 783 256 NT: **HELFORD** Offers one night stays Other info:	DP: 0 miles	
Falmouth Lodge Backpackers 9 Gyllyngvase Terrace, Falmouth, TR11 4DL 01326 319996 : 07525 722 808 judi@falmouthlodge.co.uk www.falmouthbackpackers.co.uk	GR: 810 318 NT: **FALMOUTH** Offers one night stays Other info: 5 mins from the train sation	DP: 0.1 miles	

Campsites and Holiday Parks

NAME	OTHER INFO		
Treago Farm Caravan & Camping Site Treago Farm, Newquay, TR8 5QS 01637 830277 info@treagofarm.co.uk www.treagofarm.co.uk	GR: 781 600 NT: **NEWQUAY** Other info:	DP: 0 miles	
Presingoll Farm Caravan & Camping Site Penwinnick Road, St Agnes, TR5 0PB 01872 552333 pam@presingollfarm.co.uk www.presingollfarm.co.uk	GR: 722 493 NT: **ST AGNES** Other info:	DP: 1.5 miles	
Beacon Cottage Farm Holidays Beacon Drive, St Agnes, TR5 0NU 01872 552347 jane@beaconcottagefarmholidays.co.uk www.beaconcottagefarmholidays.co.uk	GR: 705 502 NT: **ST AGNES** Offers one night stays Other info: Also has 2 Self catering cottages	DP: 0.33 miles	
Ayr Holiday Park Alexandra Road, St Ives, TR26 1EJ 01736 795855 recept@ayrholidaypark.co.uk www.ayrholidaypark.co.uk	GR: 510 405 NT: **ST IVES** Offers one night stays Other info:	DP: 0.5 miles	
Trevalgan Touring Park Trevalgan, St Ives, TR26 3BJ 01736 791892 reception@trevalgantouringpark.co.uk www.trevalgantouringpark.co.uk	GR: 490 401 NT: **ST IVES** Offers one night stays Other info: Open May-Sept	DP: 0.25 miles	
Silversands Holiday Park Gwendreath, Ruan Minor, Helston, TR12 7LZ 01326 290631 info@silversandsholidaypark.co.uk www.silversandsholidaypark.co.uk	GR: SW729169 NT: **MULLION** Other info:	DP: 0.62 miles	

NAME	OTHER INFO	
Teneriffe Farm campsite Predannack, Mullion, Helston, TR12 7EZ ☎ 354 800 1895 ✉ enquiries@nationaltrust.org.uk 🌐 www.nationaltrust.org.uk/holidays	GR: 673 217 DP: 1 mile NT: **MULLION** Offers one night stays 🚗 🐕	Other info: 20 pitches Open Mar-Oct
Little Trevothan Holiday Park Trevothan, Coverack, TR12 6SD ☎ 01326 280260 ✉ holidays@littletrevothan.co.uk 🌐 www.littletrevothan.co.uk	GR: 770 178 DP: 0.5 miles NT: **COVERACK** Offers one night stays 🚗 🐕 🛒	Other info:

Do

NAME	OTHER INFO	
Wild Rambling Zennor, St Ives, TR26 3BY ☎ 07795 654 623 ✉ helen@wildrambling.com 🌐 www.wildrambling.com/explore-cornwall.html	GR: 455 385 DP: NT: **ST IVES** 🐕	Other info:
Jubilee Pool Battery Road, Penzance, TR18 4FF ☎ 07970 565145 ✉ jake@jubileepool.co.uk 🌐 www.jubileepool.co.uk	GR: 476 272 DP: NT: **PENZANCE** 🐕	Other info: Open May-Sept
Meneage Taxis 10 Cunnack Close, Station Road, Helston, TR13 8XQ ☎ 01326 560530 ✉ meneagetaxis@yahoo.com 🌐 www.meneagetaxis.co.uk	GR: DP: NT: **HELSTON**	Other info:
Telstar Taxi & Private Hire Telstar House, Goonhilly Downs, Helston, TR12 6LQ ☎ 01326 221007 ✉ traveltelstar@yahoo.com 🌐 www.telstartravel.co.uk	GR: DP: NT: **HELSTON**	Other info:

Eat and Drink

NAME	OTHER INFO	
Bowgie Inn Ltd West Pentire, Crantock, Newquay, TR8 5SE ☎ 016378 30363 ✉ enquiries@bowgie.com 🌐 www.bowgie.com	GR: 776 606 DP: 0 miles NT: **CRANTOCK** Offers one night stays 🚗 📶 🍽	Other info: Open all year
The Tinner's Arms Zennor, St Ives, TR26 3BY ☎ 01736 796927 ✉ enquiries@tinnersarms.co.uk 🌐 www.tinnersarms.com	GR: 455 385 DP: 0.5 miles NT: **ZENNOR** Offers one night stays 4 🚗 📶 🐕 🍽	Other info: Rooms available

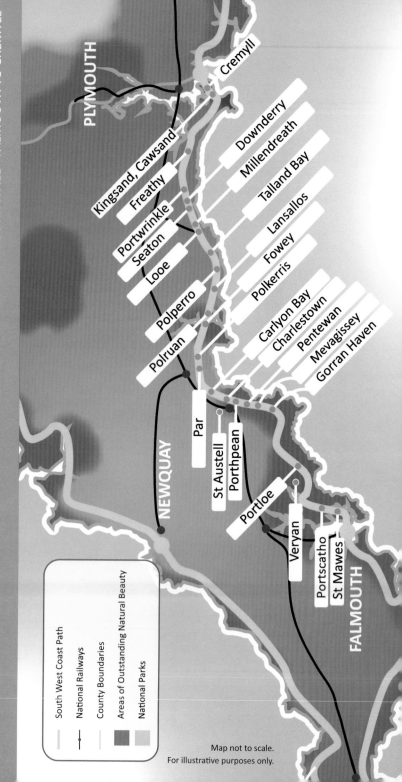

PLYMOUTH

Cremyll

Kingsand, Cawsand

Freathy

Portwrinkle

Seaton

Looe

Polperro

Polruan

Downderry

Millendreath

Talland Bay

Lansallos

Fowey

Polkerris

Carlyon Bay

Charlestown

Pentewan

Mevagissey

Gorran Haven

Par

St Austell

Porthpean

NEWQUAY

Portloe

Veryan

Portscatho

St Mawes

FALMOUTH

South West Coast Path

National Railways

County Boundaries

Areas of Outstanding Natural Beauty

National Parks

Map not to scale.
For illustrative purposes only.

118

South Cornwall
Falmouth to the Tamar

The South Cornwall stretch of coast is relatively sheltered, being either south-east or south-facing and being largely in the lee of the large peninsula of the Lizard. Cliffs of moderate height are found along most of the length, and there are numerous intimate little bays and some quite prominent headlands. In the west the main feature is the superb estuary of the River Fal. Also known as Carrick Roads, this forms one of the largest natural harbours in the world. Walkers will need to take two ferries to cross this superb estuary, which contains the maritime centre of Falmouth. St Austell Bay comprises the central part of this length, the only stretch that lacks the otherwise ubiquitous cliffs. The bay also has the only major length of coastal development on the south coast of Cornwall, based on the town of St Austell. It includes the wonderfully preserved Georgian port of Charlestown, as well as the picturesque traditional fishing town of Mevagissey. To the east, there are attractive estuaries at Fowey and Looe, drowned mouths of river valleys. The great sweep of Whitsand Bay, again backed by cliffs, then leads to the mouth of Plymouth Sound.

River Looe and Looe Beach

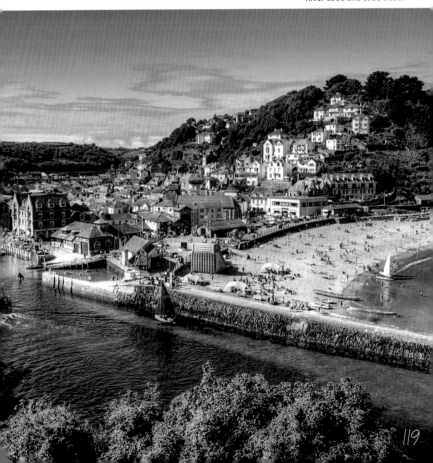

OS Maps: Landranger 204; Explorer 105

	This Walk	Cumulative	This Walk	Cumulative	Grading	Timing
Ascent	974ft	63,998ft	297m	19,507m	Easy	2.75 hours
Distance	6.2mi	340.3mi	10.0km	547.7km		

For detailed directions see our Walking Guide no. 38, St Mawes (Ferry) to Portscatho.

This Section includes a trip on the ferry across the mouth of the River Fal, a treat of scenery and interest in its own right. Beyond, the walk round St Anthony Head is one of superb estuarine and coastal views, followed by an easy but charming path on low cliffs, sheltered from the westerlies, while passing some fine sandy beaches and giving excellent views up the South Cornwall coast.

Directions

A regular bus route serves Portscatho and St Mawes from Truro, which is also linked to Falmouth by bus and train. There is also a very popular circular walk using the Coast Path in the St Anthony Head area and another from Portscatho.

Two ferries are required to cross between Falmouth and the Coast Path at Place, east of the large estuary. The first goes between Falmouth and St Mawes, across the mouth of the main Fal Estuary, sometimes referred to as Carrick Roads. The ferry operates all year from Prince of Wales Pier (year round) and Custom House Quay (summer only). Tel: 01326 741194. For ferry details see page 17.

The second leg of the crossing is the ferry between St Mawes and Place, crossing the mouth of the Fal's tributary, the Percuil River. This ferry operates 1 June – 30 September from 9am – 5pmevery half hour, subject to demand. Tel: 01326 741194. In winter an alternative may be offered by a water taxi service, tel: 07971 846786. For details visit www.stmaweskayaks.co.uk. For ferry details see page 18.

There is also Falmouth Water Taxi service which operates between Falmouth and St Mawes or Place, weather permitting between March and October 9am to 6pm (11.30pm May to September). If needed, it is advisable to telephone 2-3 days in advance in the Summer. Tel: 07522 446659, www.falmouthwatertaxi.co.uk

Information is also available from the Fal River Visitor Information Centre at Prince of Wales Pier, or visit www.falriver.co.uk

If arriving at St Mawes and wishing to proceed to Place when the Place ferry is not operating it is possible to take the regular bus service from St Mawes to Gerrans, walking from here to Place (2.5 miles/4km). For this option, go to Gerrans Church and pick up the walking route described below. Local taxi firms will carry walkers around the peninsula.

Walk between St Mawes and Place

A walking route also exists between St Mawes and Place, via Gerrans. This adds 9 miles/14km to the overall route, effectively an extra day to the itinerary. Leaving the ferry point in St Mawes, turn left along the road. Approaching the castle, take the minor lane left, which leads to a footpath at the end. This becomes a scenic path alongside the Carrick Roads – the Fal Estuary. At the minor road go right then bear left in front of the boatyard and then on a bank above the shore. This leads to the churchyard of St Just in Roseland, a beautiful spot. Pass the church and keep to the Path next to the shore. Follow the Path as it bears right up the hill, signed St Just Lane, to emerge on a road. Turn left, ignoring the first footpath on the right, but take the second a little afterwards. Follow the Path alongside field boundaries, first to the right, then to the left, then to the right again. Go down to the road at the end of the fourth field and turn right to the A3078 at Trethem Mill. Turn left and immediately right after the bridge up some steps and through a small wood. Out of the wood, cross the field diagonally right (bearing 110°) then in the next field bear diagonally right again (bearing 140°), leaving it by a wooded track. Cross the stile at the top and bear diagonally right again (bearing 137°) to meet a hedge, which is followed to a road. Turn right on the road. At the next junction follow the road curving to the right past Polhendra Cottage then turn left through the second gate. Descend towards the bottom of the hedge visible on the opposite side of the valley (bearing 123). Cross the bridge and climb as close as possible with the hedge to the left. Cross the stone steps behind the gorse at the top and bear slightly left across the next two fields (bearing 125) to emerge on a road. Turn right to arrive at Gerrans Church. (Those who have taken the bus from St Mawes will join here – see above.)

At the church fork left into Treloan Lane, keeping ahead past the buildings. Go through the gate at the end of the lane, crossing an open field ahead into another enclosed track, which leads to Porth Farm. At the road turn right then go left at the sign indicating "Footpath to Place by Percuil River". Follow this very scenic path which leads to the ferry landing point then on to Place itself.

Coast Path, Place - Portscatho

At Place, walk up the lane past the gates to the grand house. Turn right into the churchyard of St Anthony Church, passing behind the church and up into a wooded area. Turn right at the track then at the creek look for the sign on the left taking the Path alongside the plantation. The Path now gives superb views over Carrick Roads to Falmouth. Approaching St Anthony Head keep to the Coast Path to the right until passing through the gate towards the lighthouse. Just after the gate climb the steps to the left to the car parking area. There are also toilets here. Leave the car park next to the coast and the superb and easy Path then leads to Portscatho, which has a shop, toilets and pubs, as well as a bus service to St Mawes and Truro.

OS Maps: Landranger 204: Explorer 105

	This Walk	Cumulative	This Walk	Cumulative	Grading	Timing
Ascent	1,674ft	65,672ft	510m	20,017m	Strenuous	3.75 hours
Distance	7.4mi	347.7mi	11.9km	559.6km		

For detailed directions see our Walking Guide no. 39, Portscatho to Portloe.

This is a very quiet Section for the most part. Cliffs are relatively low at first, but increase in height as the great promontory of Nare Head, with its superb views, is approached. The long sandy beaches below the cliffs passed west of Nare Head are replaced by tiny isolated and inaccessible coves east of the headland. This length has a wonderfully remote atmosphere.

Directions

Portscatho and Portloe are both served by regular, but different, bus services, both linking with Truro. There are some local circular walks using the Coast Path around Nare Head, based on the inland village of Veryan.

Portscatho has a shop, pubs, toilets and bus service. The Coast Path leaves past the Harbour Club; keep right just after leaving the village at the footpath junction. The Path goes round the back of Porthcurnick Beach, then up the road on the far side, turning right along the coastal edge. The Path continues to undulate along the coast until it turns inland to reach a road. Turn right, past Pendower Court and down the road to its end at Pendower Beach. Cross the rear of the beach and head for the public toilets, going up the hill and turning right. The Path soon diverts around the rear of the Nare Hotel to a road, descending to Carne Beach. Follow the road round the bend and up the hill for a short way, turning right to return to the cliffs. The Path now heads for Nare Head, via a steep descent and ascent at Tregagle's Hole and past an old fisherman's cottage. A short diversion at the top of Nare Head reveals some stunning coastal views.

The Path now goes round the seaward edge of Rosen Cliff and over the valley behind Kiberick Cove to Blouth Point. At the point enter a field and keep left for a short way before bearing right, downhill, towards some trees. The Path zigzags upward to pass Broom Parc and then goes through a field to round Manare Point. After this it is downhill going over a short uneven section before joining a tarmac path which descends into Portloe. The village is very picturesque and has pubs and toilets as well as a bus service.

Portloe

OS Maps: Landranger 204; Explorer 105

	This Walk	Cumulative	This Walk	Cumulative	Grading	Timing
Ascent	2,841ft	68,513ft	866m	20,883m	Strenuous then easy	5.75 hours
Distance	12.2mi	359.9mi	19.6km	579.2km		

For detailed directions see our Walking Guide no. 40, Portloe to Mevagissey.

This is a quiet Section of mostly high cliffs, often covered in lush vegetation. Towards Gorran Haven these cliffs reduce in height. The section includes the great headland of Dodman Point, from where there are views to the Lizard in one direction and Devon in the other on a clear day. Below the cliffs are some sandy beaches, often all but inaccessible. This is a coastline for those preferring remoteness.

Directions

There are some excellent circular walks using the Coast Path at Dodman Point and linking to Gorran Haven, giving a variety of options here.

The scenic little harbour village of Portloe has toilets, pubs and a bus service. The Coast Path leaves behind the Lugger Hotel, leaving the road to reach a prominent converted chapel. Pass this then climb steeply to the cliffs. After a quite strenuous length the Path arrives at West Portholland. Follow the road above the shore to a junction, then turn right to East Portholland. There are toilets here and a seasonal cafe and shop. Pass the cottages at the far end and climb behind them on a clear path to a field, turning right down the field edge. The Path leads to a road which descends to Porthluney Cove. Here are toilets and seasonal refreshments and the picturesque setting is enhanced by the presence of Caerhayes Castle just inland. Walk behind the beach and turn right into parkland. Climb behind the field-edge trees then go to the right and follow the field edge to the woods. After crossing the rocky ridge at Greeb Point the Path descends to a road behind Hemmick Beach. Cross the bridge and go right, climbing to the headland of Dodman Point ("The Dodman"), with its memorial cross and superb views. The Path stays clear above the lovely sands of Bow or Vault Beach, then rounds the headland of Pen-a-maen to enter Gorran Haven. This little harbour village has a shop, pub and toilets. There is a Gorran community bus which runs 4 days a week www.gorranbus.org which walkers have recommended to us and can be hailed anywhere along its route.

Leave Gorran Haven up Church Street, turning right into Cliff Road. At the top of the hill, follow to the end of the road and a small wooden bridge will lead to a stile into the field, which leads to the cliffs. The clear Path leads to Chapel Point, where it crosses the tarmac access road to follow the Path along the coast into Portmellon. Follow the road uphill and go down through the park on the right on entering Mevagissey. Steps descend to the harbour. Mevagissey is the archetypal Cornish fishing village and has all facilities.

OS Maps: Landranger 204; Explorer 105 (western half); Explorer 107 (eastern half)

	This Walk	Cumulative	This Walk	Cumulative	Grading	Timing
Ascent	2,434ft	70,947ft	742m	21,625m	Strenuous then easy	5 hours
Distance	10.7mi	370.6mi	17.2km	596.4km		

For detailed directions see our Walking Guide no. 41, Mevagissey to Charlestown.

The western half of this Section has a relatively remote feel, enhanced by some quite strenuous climbs and some attractive cliffs and headlands. To the east the coastline is more urbanised but with beaches and the lovely Georgian docks of Charlestown found among the houses, golf courses and clay industry. The cliff-top path between Porthpean and Charlestown was reinstated in late 2011, avoiding two miles of road diversion.

Directions

There are bus routes from St Austell to Charlestown and Par, one of these routes also serving Mevagissey, so that a range of bus-walks is possible.

The attractive fishing village of Mevagissey has all facilities. The Coast Path goes along the back of the harbour and then turns right along its eastern side before forking left steeply uphill. After crossing some playing fields, pass seaward of the houses then continue along the undulating cliffs to descend behind the ruined fish cellars at Portgiskey Cove. Continue uphill along the seaward and far field boundaries to a fenced path at the top. Turn right here, parallel to the road. At the entrance to Pentewan Sands Holiday Park follow the B3273 road pavement and turn first right before the petrol station, signposted to Pentewan. There are a few shops, toilets, pub and café in the village. The official route then follows the road through Pentewan and up the hill for about 100 yards/90m, taking the first turn sharp right along The Terrace and along a narrow path at the end to arrive at the cliffs. A more interesting alternative turns right, away from the road into the harbour area just after the public toilets then, immediately after the last cottage, goes left steeply uphill, through gardens, to arrive at the official route on the cliffs.

After some 1.25 miles/2km the Path descends through a wood and reaches a track. Turn right here to arrive at another track just behind the remote Hallane Mill Beach. Turn left here then quickly right, climbing back up the cliffs to arrive at Black Head. A diversion from the memorial stone goes to the tip of this atmospheric location. Continuing from Black Head the Path enters Ropehaven Woods with some confusing paths – it is important to follow the waymarking. Entering the wood turn right down a rocky and sometimes slippery path, then left. Go left again onto a walled path, ignoring descending paths on the right, to arrive beside a cottage and emerge onto a track. Go right here then leave the road to the right just after a parking area and follow the cliff-top path down, up and down again to Porthpean. Walk along the promenade to the far end and climb the steps to rejoin the newly reinstated cliff-top path all the way to Charlestown.

Charlestown has a fascinating Georgian harbour, the home of a group of tall ships, and has refreshments, toilets, pubs and buses. Note that the official Coast Path does not cross the dock gate at the mouth of the harbour, though many people use that route.

On the east side climb the Path and on to reach a suburban road for a short way, soon forking off right over a long grassy area. Arriving at a large car park above Carlyon Bay Beach keep seaward then cross the beach access road where a new resort is being developed and continue ahead on the low cliffs. Keep seaward of the golf course to approach the old china clay works at Par Docks. At the little beach at Spit Point turn inland and follow the narrow path past the works and then turn right alongside a railway line to emerge on a road. Turn right along the pavement past the docks entrance and under a railway bridge. Turn right at the junction, signposted to Fowey, over a level crossing and then under another railway bridge before forking right on the road, Par Green. If closed, turn left alongside the harbour, right at the end and right again to return to the coast.

To continue beyond Par on the Coast Path, walk along Par Green, looking for house no.52 and follow the Path signed on the right. Par has all facilities, including a mainline railway station; for the station turn left at the far end of Par Green along Eastcliffe Road.

Mevagissey Spring

OS Maps: Landranger 200 or 204; Explorer 107

	This Walk	Cumulative	This Walk	Cumulative	Grading	Timing
Ascent	1,132ft	72,079ft	345m	21,970m	Moderate	3 hours
Distance	6.8mi	377.4mi	10.9km	607.4km		

For detailed directions see our Walking Guide no. 42, Charlestown to Fowey.

This Section goes out to the prominent Gribbin Head. The west side of the headland is relatively exposed, mostly on high cliffs, with views west over St Austell Bay. The east side is more indented and sheltered, the cliffs lower, and the Path passes numerous scenic little sandy coves. At its eastern end the Path enters the lovely part-wooded estuary of the River Fowey, culminating in the atmospheric little town of Fowey.

Directions

Par and Fowey are linked by two bus routes giving a half-hourly service, making this a bus-walk option. In addition, a popular local circular walk from Fowey takes in Gribbin Head, using the waymarked Saints' Way path with the Coast Path.

Par has all facilities, including a mainline railway station. For the Coast Path walk along the road called Par Green and follow the Path which leaves the road next to no.52. After crossing the private clay haul road, fork right along a grassy path immediately before the chalet park. Follow this path before turning left then quickly right along the road to a small car park at the western end of the sands of Par Beach. Walk along the back of the beach to another car park at the far, eastern end. This is Polmear; a pub and buses are to be found on the road outside the car park.

The Coast Path crosses the car park to a footbridge and then up the cliffs and continues on to the little harbour village of Polkerris. Here are a pub, toilets and restaurant. The Path continues from the back of the beach, up a ramp to join a zigzag path through woods to the top. The Path now continues to the Daymark on Gribbin Head (or "The Gribbin"). The tower is open to visitors on some summer Sundays. From the Daymark follow the Path downhill to the scenic cove at Polridmouth ("Pridmouth"), said to have inspired the setting for Daphne du Maurier's "Rebecca". Cross behind the beach on the stepping stones and turn right into the woods, then on over cliff-top fields and past a couple of small coves to arrive at another woodland. Look out for the Path on the right, which goes past St Catherine's Castle and gives superb views upriver to Fowey. Now follow the Path down the woodland track and behind Readymoney Cove before following the road into Fowey.

Note that it is possible to walk Coast to Coast across Cornwall between Fowey and Padstow on the north coast using the Saints' Way. A guidebook is available from Fowey Tourist Information Centre (TIC).

OS Maps: Landranger 200 or 204 (Fowey); Landranger 201 (remainder); Explorer 107

	This Walk	Cumulative	This Walk	Cumulative	Grading	Timing
Ascent	1,939ft	74,018ft	591m	22,561m	Strenuous	3.5 hours
Distance	7.1mi	384.5mi	11.4km	618.8km		

For detailed directions see our Walking Guide no. 43, Fowey to Polperro.

This is a connoisseur's Section – it is quiet and remote; it is scenic, with beautiful large sandy bays and smaller coves plus impressive headlands; it is started and finished at superbly picturesque locations, the Fowey estuary at one end and Polperro at the other; and it is quite hard work, emphasising that nothing this good should come too easily.

Directions

Polruan and Polperro are linked by a bus service, giving a bus-walk option, though unfortunately it does not operate at weekends. There is a popular scenic circular walk (the Hall Walk) taking in Fowey and Polruan and using two ferries, an estuary tributary valley and the Coast Path.

Fowey is a charming little town, well worth exploring, with all facilities. The crossing of the river to Polruan on the opposite bank is by foot ferry. In summer it usually operates from Whitehouse Quay, below the Esplanade opposite Fowey Hotel, while in winter and in summer early mornings and evenings it operates from Town Quay (centre of Fowey). The ferry operates all year except Christmas Day at 5-10 minute intervals, telephone 01726 870232. For ferry details see page 18.

At Polruan, a picturesque little place, go up the steps next to The Lugger. Turn right at the top in West Street then turn left up Battery Lane. At the grassy area keep left by the wall then through the car park parallel to the coast to a signed path on the right. After around 2 miles/3km the Path passes above and behind the impressive Lantic Bay, climbing steeply at the far end. There is a higher path here, going to the top of the hill and turning right, or a lower one, turning off right 30 yards/28m before the top, dropping then climbing again to meet the higher path (ignore beach turnings to the right). The Path goes out around Pencarrow Head then behind an old watch house to descend and pass behind two charming and remote coves at Lansallos West and East Coombes. After climbing past a marker warning shipping of an offshore rock more ups and downs follow until the Path approaches the almost hidden inlet of Polperro. Follow the waymarked path to arrive at a rocky outlook point – go left here then fork right to descend to the harbour. Polperro, an impossibly picturesque harbour village, which figures justifiably in most picture books and calendars of Cornwall. It has all facilities.

OS Maps: Landranger 201; Explorer 107

	This Walk	Cumulative	This Walk	Cumulative	Grading	Timing
Ascent	774ft	74,792ft	236m	22,797m	Moderate	2.25 hours
Distance	5.0mi	389.5mi	8.0km	626.8km		

For detailed directions see our Walking Guide no. 44, Polperro to Looe.

The cliffs on this Section, never really lofty, tend to decrease in height towards the east. This is a relatively sheltered length passing around lush bays, while offshore, Looe Island is a seaward focal point from the eastern end. Here, also, extensive rocky platforms are exposed at low tide. These factors, and the popularity of Polperro and Looe, have made this a justifiably popular length of coast.

Directions

There is a bus route between Polperro and Looe, making a bus-walk a popular option here.

Polperro is a popular visitors' destination with all facilities. The Coast Path crosses the stone bridge behind the harbour then turns right along The Warren. Climb out of the village upwards along the main path to the top and turn left where way head is fenced off, onto the narrow path to the second stile. Go over the stile and turn left on to the track on the field edge to highway. Turn right, walk down road, which becomes a path, to the beach at Talland Bay. There are toilets and seasonal refreshments here. Pass behind the beach, going left then right by the public toilets and behind a second beach to a small car parking area. The Path climbs back to the cliffs from here – keep well back from the crumbling edge. It then continues very clearly (ignore all turnings towards the beach) eventually arriving at the end of a suburban road at Hannafore, the western end of Looe. Continue along the road, or the lower promenade; there are toilets and seasonal refreshments along here. At the end a short stretch of road with no pavement turns alongside the mouth of the Looe River. Take steps down on the right to the riverside of West Looe. There is a seasonal and tidal ferry from here to East Looe, the main part of the town, as an option. Otherwise continue along the West Looe riverside and over the bridge, turning right into East Looe's main street. Looe has buses to Plymouth and a branch to the mainline railway at Liskeard - for the station turn left after the bridge. Between them, East and West Looe have all necessary facilities.

The old fishermans net loft of Polperro

OS Maps: Landranger 201; Explorer 107 (western half); Explorer 108 (eastern half)

	This Walk	Cumulative	This Walk	Cumulative	Grading	Timing
Ascent	1,965ft	76,757ft	599m	23,396m	Strenuous, moderate in places	4.5 hours
Distance	7.7mi	397.2mi	12.4km	639.2km		

For detailed directions see our Walking Guide no. 45, Looe to Portwrinkle.

Quiet and relatively remote cliff lengths in the western and eastern parts of this Section are separated by a low-level, suburban length, or by an optional route via sea wall and beach between Seaton and Downderry. The western cliffs are covered in lush vegetation, scrub and woodland, and there are stretches where the sea is only glimpsed through the trees. The eastern cliffs are more open and give some superb views along the coast in both directions, with the distinctive Rame Head a focal point.

Directions

A bus service connects Seaton, Downderry and Portwrinkle, making a bus-walk option possible over the eastern end of this section. Further bus-walk options may be possible with a change of bus from Looe at Hessenford (inland from Looe).

From East Looe's town centre, turn up Castle Street (Ship Inn on the corner) and keep climbing until it becomes a footpath above the sea. Continue, then at a road turn right, passing Plaidy Beach, and continue until just after the road veers left inland. Here go right, up a steep tarmac path then ahead at the top until the road turns left. The Coast Path descends steps between houses to Millendreath Beach. There are refreshment facilities here. On the far side go up the cul-de-sac road and climb the sunken lane to reach another road. After 50 yards (45m) turn right and take the signed route left through twin gates across a drive. Follow the Path ahead through woods to rejoin the road. Turn right on the road and keep ahead past the Monkey Sanctuary onto a narrow lane. At the crest of this lane turn right and cross the field, going left on the far side to follow the Path until it arrives at the lane again. Turn right to descend to Seaton beach. Turn right and along the road behind the beach, where there are toilets and seasonal refreshments.

Although the official path follows the narrow and busy road up the hill to Downderry, if the tide is not high it is preferable to walk along the top of the sea wall from Seaton and then the beach, taking one of the choice of footpath links into Downderry, where there are pubs, shops, toilets and seasonal refreshments. Note that the most easterly link path shown on the OS map is currently closed. Follow the road to the eastern end of Downderry, where it turns inland, and take the signed path right, which zigzags steeply upward. A superbly scenic cliff-top path, with several ups and downs, continues until it arrives at a road just above Portwrinkle. Turn right to descend to the village and the quiet sea-front road. The Jolly Roger Cafe and Bistro is open all year in Portwrinkle or other facilities are at Crafthole, a 10 minute walk uphill inland.

OS Maps: Landranger 201; Explorer 108

	This Walk	Cumulative	This Walk	Cumulative	Grading	Timing
Ascent	2,169ft	78,926ft	661m	24,057m	Moderate	5.75 hours
Distance	13.2mi	410.4mi	21.2km	660.5km		

For detailed directions see our Walking Guide no. 46, Portwrinkle to Cawsand and Cawsand to Cremyll (Plymouth Ferry).

This is a Section of great interest rather than spectacular drama. There is a golf course, a gunnery range, a cliff face of wooden chalets and an historic Country Park. It also includes the magnificent and atmospheric Rame Head, which is a significant landmark for many miles along the coast in both directions, the charming twin villages of Cawsand and Kingsand and some superb views, including Plymouth Sound and, indeed, the city itself.

Directions

A bus route links Cawsand to Cremyll, part-way along the section, and also runs along the coast road adjacent to the Coast Path between Tregantle and Rame Head, giving various bus-walk options. There are a number of popular circular walks using the Coast Path based on Mount Edgcumbe Country Park, next to Cremyll, and also around Rame Head.

From Portwrinkle walk up the road, past the first footpath, which leads to the beach, then turn right on the signed path opposite the golf club. After climbing, the Path goes along the seaward side of the golf course. After leaving the golf course the Path begins to rise towards the Tregantle Firing Ranges. When firing is not taking place it is possible to walk an excellent, well-signed permissive path through the ranges. At the time of going to print non-firing weekends (Friday to Sunday inclusive) for 2018 had not been confirmed, but will normally alternate throughout the year. But please note that live firing may still take place on these weekends if operational requirements demand. In addition there is no live firing on Bank Holiday weekends nor on any day in August. Other non-firing days are known up to two weeks in advance - telephone The Ranges on 01752 822516 during office hours to check. If live firing is in progress red flags will be raised and the access gates locked - do not proceed into the range. If open, keep closely to the marked path and, at the far end of the range path, emerge through another security gate onto the National Trust's cliff-top path.

If the range path is closed, continue on the official Coast Path through a field to a road, where the Path initially continues inside the hedge before joining the road further along. The road is usually quite busy so take care. There is the compensation of a magnificent view up the Tamar to Plymouth from the car parking area here, where there is often a refreshment van. Follow the road (past Tregantle Fort entrance) then turn right at the first road junction and continue along the road to the cliffs (passing where the range path emerges).

The Coast Path is then off-road, along National Trust land, before it rejoins the road for about 1.25 miles/2km. The signed path then leaves the road again to descend onto the sloping cliff face, although this cliff length had to be closed in 2013 because of subsidence, the Coast Path continuing on the road. There is a cafe just off the Path down the cliff at this point. If open, the Path undulates quite steeply and meanders unexpectedly among chalets and gardens – keep alert for the waymarking – climbing back to the road. The route then descends gently across the cliff slope to Polhawn Cove at the base of Rame Head. After crossing a private access road for Polhawn Fort the Path climbs to reach the headland. The official Coast Path route omits the very end, with its medieval chapel, but the easy climb is worthwhile for the views and the atmosphere.

A good cliff path then goes to Penlee Point, where there are the first views of Plymouth Sound. Bear left to reach a road then fork off to the right on the signed Path through woods to descend to the charming little village of Cawsand, with pubs, toilets, shops and refreshments. Go through the village square to Garrett Street and continue, turning right in front of the Post Office having, imperceptibly, crossed into Kingsand. At The Cleave turn left then first right up Heavitree Road, which leads to a gate on the right into Mount Edgcumbe Country Park. Continue through the park to a road, turning right then almost immediately left, forking uphill through woods. After a woodland drive there is a waymarked diversion to avoid a cliff fall, the route climbing left to a higher level path before continuing parallel to the coast. Once around the fallen cliff the Path descends to the foreshore of Plymouth Sound. Keep on the signed Path up and through a deer gate then back down towards the shore to follow into an Italianate garden, past the Orangery of Mount Edgcumbe House (refreshments), and out through the park gates to the ferry point. Cremyll has a pub and toilets, but most will use it as the staging point for the ferry across the Tamar to Plymouth, an interesting excursion in its own right.

Portholland

If you enjoy sleeping, eating or drinking at any business on the Path please sugge[st] they join us as Business Members so tha[t] can share their brilliance!

The businesses listed here are all supporters of the South West Coast Path Association, they have joined as business members and it would be great if you could show your support for them too. In addition, businesses are listed with more details on our website: www.southwestcoastpath.org.uk Find them through our walk finder or our accommodation finder tools.

KEY:

GR Grid Reference
DP Distance from the Path
NT Nearest Town

🐕 Dogs Welcome
🍴 Evening Meal Available
3 Number Of Rooms

🛒 Grocery Shop On Site
📶 Wifi
🚗 Parking

Bed & Breakfasts and Hotels

NAME	OTHER INFO	
Ship & Castle Hotel The Waterfront, St Mawes, TR2 5DG 📞 01326 270401 ✉ 🌐 www.shearings.com	GR: 847 330 DP: 0.2 miles NT: **ST MAWES** 54 📶 🍴	Other info:
Braganza B&B Grove Hill, St Mawes, TR2 5BJ 📞 01326 270281 ✉ enquiries@braganza-stmawes.co.uk 🌐 www.braganza-stmawes.co.uk	GR: 846 331 DP: 0.25 miles NT: **ST MAWES** Offers one night stays 5 🚗 📶 🐕	Other info:
Corfingle B&B Portloe, Truro, TR2 5QU 📞 01872 501388 ✉ carol_sherwood@hotmail.co.uk 🌐 www.southwestcoastpath.org.uk/corfingle-bb-portloe	GR: 937 393 DP: 0 miles NT: **PORTLOE** Offers one night stays 2 📶	Other info:
Treverbyn House B&B Pendower Road, Veryan, TR2 5QI 📞 07826 826959 / 01872 501201 ✉ info@treverbyn.co.uk 🌐 www.treverbyn.co.uk	GR: 914 393 DP: 1 mile NT: **VERYAN** Offers one night stays 5 🚗	Other info: Open fro[m] March
Trenona Farm Holidays Ruan High Lanes, Truro, TR2 5JS 📞 01872 501339 ✉ pam@trenonafarmholidays.co.uk 🌐 www.trenonafarmholidays.co.uk	GR: SW915411 DP: 1 mile NT: **VERYAN** Offers one night stays 4 🚗 📶 🐕	Other info: Self-cater[ing] available
The Rosevine Portscatho, Truro, TR2 5EW 📞 01872 580206 ✉ nicola@providencehospitality.co.uk 🌐 www.rosevine.co.uk	GR: 879 362 DP: 0.2 miles NT: **TRURO** Offers one night stays 15 🚗 📶 🐕 🍴	Other info: Op[en] all year
Broom Parc B&B Veryan, Truro, TR2 5PJ 📞 01872 501803 ✉ lindsay@broomparc.co.uk 🌐 www.broomparc.co.uk	GR: 930 389 DP: 0 miles NT: **TRURO** Offers one night stays 🚗 📶 🐕	Other info:

NAME	OTHER INFO	
Lower Penvose B&B Porthholland,Tregony, Truro, TR2 5SS ☎ 01872 501789 ✉ penvose@mail.com ⊕ www.penvose.co.uk	GR: 949 415 DP: 0.5 miles NT: **PORTHHOLLAND** Offers one night stays [3] 🚗 📶 🍴	Other info:
Treveor B&B 10 Perhaver Park, Gorran Haven, PL26 6NZ ☎ 01726 843777 ✉ wabennett2901@gmail.com ⊕ www.southwestcoastpath.org.uk/treveor-gorran-haven	GR: 011 418 DP: 0 miles NT: **GORRAN HAVEN** Offers one night stays [2] 🚗 📶 🐕	Other info:
Mevagissey Bay Hotel Polkirt Hill, Mevagissey, PL26 6UX ☎ 01726 843453 ✉ info@mevagisseybayhotel.co.uk ⊕ www.mevagisseybayhotel.co.uk	GR: SX0163544402 DP: 0 miles NT: **MEVAGISSEY** Offers one night stays [11] 🚗 📶	Other info:
The Tremarne Hotel The Tremarne Hotel, Polkirt Hill, Mevagissey, PL26 6UY ☎ 01726 842213 ✉ info@tremarne-hotel.co.uk ⊕ www.tremarne-hotel.co.uk	GR: 015 443 DP: 0.3 miles NT: **MEVAGISSEY** 🍴	Other info:
Tregorran Guest House Cliff Street, Mevagissey, PL26 6QW ☎ 01726 842319 ✉ info@tregorran.co.uk ⊕ www.tregorran.co.uk	GR: 015 451 DP: 0.2 miles NT: **MEVAGISSEY** Offers one night stays [6] 🚗 📶	Other info:
Honeycombe House 51 Polkirt Hill, Mevagissey, PL26 6UR ☎ 01726 843750 ✉ enquiries@honeycombehouse.co.uk ⊕ www.honeycombehouse.com	GR: SX 016 445 DP: 0 miles NT: **ST AUSTELL** Offers one night stays [5] 🚗 📶	Other info:
The Cornwall Hotel Spa & Estate Pentewan Rd, Tregorrick, St Austell, PL26 7AB ☎ 01726 874 051 ✉ enquiries@thecornwall.com ⊕ www.thecornwall.com	GR: DP: 2 miles NT: **ST AUSTELL** 🚗 📶 🍴	Other info:
Fowey Hall Hotel - LFH Hanson Drive, Fowey, PL23 1ET ☎ 01726 833866 ✉ diane.viljoen@luxuryfamilyholidays.com ⊕ www.foweyhallhotel.co.uk	GR: 120 514 DP: 0.5 miles NT: **FOWEY** Offers one night stays [36] 🚗 📶 🐕 🍴	Other info:
Hormond House B&B 55 Fore Street, Polruan, PL23 1PH ☎ 01726 870853 ✉ bellacornwall@outlook.com ⊕ www.hormondhouse.com	GR: 126 508 DP: 0.5 miles NT: **FOWEY** Offers one night stays 📶 🐕	Other info:
Meadow View B&B 6 Long Meadow Views, Fowey, PL23 1ES ☎ 07736 066319 ✉ info@foweybedandbreakfast.co.uk ⊕ www.foweybedandbreakfast.co.uk	GR: 119 521 DP: 0.75 miles NT: **FOWEY** Offers one night stays 🚗 📶	Other info: Vegetarian, vegan, gluten/ dairy free and other diets catered for
The Strand 61 Tehidy Road, Tywardreath, PL24 2QD ☎ 07792062471 ✉ j.askew439@btinternet.com ⊕ www.thestrandbnb.com	GR: 083 542 DP: 2 miles NT: **FOWEY** 🚗 📶 🐕	Other info: Cooked breakfast included, washing service, packed lunches

NAME	OTHER INFO	
Wellingtons Guest House 59 Tavern Barn, Fowey, PL23 1EG ☎ 01726 833232 / 07764465992 ✉ contact@wellingtons-fowey.co.uk 🌐 www.wellingtons-fowey.co.uk	GR: 120 521 DP: 0.5 miles NT: **FOWEY** Offers one night stays [4] [🚗] [📶] [🐕]	Other info: Contact direc[t] for reduction info
The House On The Props B&B Talland Street, Polperro, PL13 2RE ☎ 01503 272310 ✉ houseonprops@btinternet.com 🌐 www.houseontheprops.co.uk	GR: 208 509 DP: 0.1 miles NT: **POLPERRO** [3] [📶] [🐕] [🍴]	Other info: Dogs by prior arrangement
Hannafore Point Hotel Marine Drive, Looe, PL13 2DG ☎ 01503 263273 ✉ stay@hannaforepointhotel.com 🌐 www.hannaforepointhotel.com	GR: 256 528 DP: 1 mile NT: **LOOE** Offers one night stays [37] [🚗] [📶] [🐕] [🍴]	Other info:
Hendersick Farm House Portlooe, Looe ☎ 01503 263207 ✉ hendersick@gmail.com 🌐 www.hendersickfarmhouse.com	GR: 239 523 DP: 0.3 miles NT: **LOOE** Offers one night stays [3] [🚗] [📶]	Other info:
Woodlands B&B St Martins Road, Looe, PL13 1LP ☎ 01503 264405 ✉ lundyfishlock@googlemail.com 🌐 www.looedirectory.co.uk/woodlands.htm	GR: 254 542 DP: 1 mile NT: **LOOE**	Other info:
The Bungalow B&B Cliff Road, Portwrinkle, PL11 3BY ☎ 01503 230334 ✉ fiona.harvey334@btinternet.com 🌐	GR: SX3550054180 DP: 0 miles NT: **PORTWRINKLE** Offers one night stays [2] [🚗] [📶]	Other info:
Coombe House B&B Coombe Farm, Fourlanesend, Cawsand, Torpoint, PL10 1LR ☎ 01752 823925 ✉ info@coombehouse-cawsand.co.uk 🌐 www.coombehouse-cawsand.co.uk	GR: 429 512 DP: 0.5 miles NT: **CAWSAND** Offers one night stays [5] [🚗] [📶] [🍴]	Other info:
Edgecombe Arms Cremyll, Torpoint, PL10 1HX ☎ 01752 822294 ✉ jacqui.southw@btconnect.com 🌐 www.edgcumbearms.co.uk	GR: 453 534 DP: 0 miles NT: **TORPOINT** [4] [🚗] [📶] [🍴]	Other info:
Treliddon Farm Downderry, Torpoint, PL11 3DP ☎ 01503 250288 ✉ 🌐 www.treliddon-farm.co.uk	GR: 320 550 DP: 1 mile NT: **TORPOINT** [🐕]	Other info:

Campsites and Holiday Parks

NAME	OTHER INFO	
Highertown Farm Campsite Lansallos, Looe, PL13 2PX ☎ 0355 800 1895 ✉ enquiries@nationaltrust.org.uk 🌐 www.nationaltrust.org.uk/holidays	GR: 174517 — DP: 1 mile NT: **LANSALLOS** Offers one night stays	🚗 🐕 — Other info: 30 pitches. Open Mar-Oct
Camping Caradon Touring Park Trelawne, Looe, PL13 2NA ☎ 01503 272388 ✉ enquiries@campingcaradon.co.uk 🌐 www.campingcaradon.co.uk	GR: SX2177754106 — DP: 2 miles NT: **LOOE** Offers one night stays	🚗 📶 🐕 🍴 🛒 — Other info:
Great Kellow Farm Caravan & Campsite Lansallos, Polperro, PL13 2QL ☎ 01503 272387 ✉ enquiries@greatkellowfarm.co.uk 🌐 www.greatkellowfarm.co.uk	GR: 203 520 — DP: 1 mile NT: **LOOE** Offers one night stays	🐕 — Other info:

Do

NAME	OTHER INFO	
Walk Kernow Nordic Walking Three Milestone, Truro, TR3 6SR ☎ 07540 478919 ✉ walkkernow@gmail.com 🌐 www.walkkernow.co.uk	GR: — DP: miles NT: **FALMOUTH**	🐕 — Other info:

Eat and Drink

NAME	OTHER INFO	
Coast Path Cafe Coast Path, Gorran Haven, St Austell, PL26 6JN ☎ 07512 543735 ✉ geoff.cooke@icloud.com 🌐 www.facebook.com/Coast-Path-Cafe-287587094719036	GR: 014 416 — DP: miles NT: **GORRAN HAVEN**	🚗 📶 — Other info:
The Par Inn The Par Inn, 2 Harbour Road, Par, PL24 2BD ☎ 01726 815695 ✉ mattybailey1@hotmail.co.uk 🌐 www.parinn.co.uk	GR: 074 535 — DP: 0.1 miles NT: **PAR**	1 🍴 — Other info:

Self Catering and hostels

NAME	OTHER INFO		
Towan Cottage St Anthony, Porthscatho, Truro, TR2 5EX ☎ 0344 800 1895 ✉ enquiries@nationaltrust.org.uk 🌐 www.nationaltrust.org.uk/holidays	GR: 868 329 DP: 1 miles NT: **ST MAWES** 5 📶 🐕 Other info: Open All year		
Porthscatho Holidays Ltd 4 The Quay, Truro, TR2 5DG ☎ 01326 270900 ✉ info@portscathoholidays.co.uk 🌐 www.portscathoholidays.co.uk	GR: DP: NT: **TRURO** Other info:		
SeaSpray Cottage & Cabin East Portholland, St Austell, PL26 6NA ☎ 01872 501187 ✉ seaspraycornwall@gmail.com 🌐 www.seaspraycornwall.co.uk	GR: DP: 0 miles NT: **ST AUSTELL** Offers one night stays 1 🚗 📶 🍴 Other info:		
Eden's Yard Backpackers 17 Tregrehan Mills, St Austell, PL25 3TL ☎ 01726 814907 ✉ info@edensyard.uk 🌐 www.edensyard.uk	GR: 043 544 DP: 2 miles NT: **ST AUSTELL** Offers one night stays 14 🚗 📶 🍴 Other info:		
Treargel Retreats The Barn, Hendersick Farm, Portlooe, PL13 2HZ ☎ 01503 598932 ✉ info@treargel.com 🌐 www.treargel.com	GR: SX236520 DP: 0.6 miles NT: **PORTLOOE** 3 Other info:		
The Old Coach House Windsworth, St Martin, Looe, PL13 1NZ ☎ 01503 262671 ✉ stay@windsworth.org.uk 🌐 www.windsworth.org.uk	GR: 228 208 DP: 0 miles NT: **LOOE** 3 🚗 🐕 Other info: Woodburner and solar-powered		
1 Fisherman's Cottage Higher Row, Kingsand, Torpoint, PL10 1NL ☎ 01752 823110 ✉ enquiries@southwestshortstays.co.uk 🌐 www.southwestshortstays.co.uk	GR: 434 506 DP: 0 miles NT: **KINGSAND** Offers one night stays 2 📶 Other info: B&B also available		

Millendreath Beach

Near Fowey

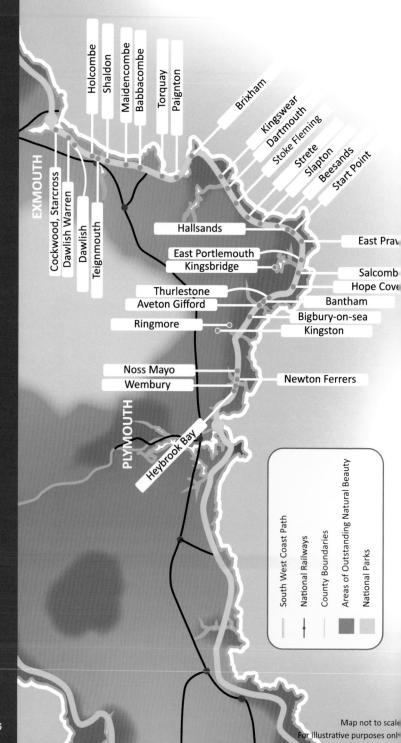

Holcombe
Shaldon
Maidencombe
Babbacombe
Torquay
Paignton

Brixham

Kingswear
Dartmouth
Stoke Fleming
Strete
Slapton
Beesands
Start Point

EXMOUTH

Cockwood, Starcross
Dawlish Warren
Dawlish
Teignmouth

Hallsands

East Portlemouth
Kingsbridge

East Prav

Salcomb
Hope Cove

Thurlestone
Aveton Gifford

Bantham

Ringmore

Bigbury-on-sea
Kingston

Noss Mayo
Wembury

Newton Ferrers

PLYMOUTH

Heybrook Bay

South West Coast Path

National Railways

County Boundaries

Areas of Outstanding Natural Beauty

National Parks

Map not to scale
For illustrative purposes onl

138

South Devon
Plymouth to the Exe

(Sections 47-57)

In the west of this length is the estuary of the River Tamar with the major naval port of Plymouth, the biggest urban area on the South West Coast Path but full of historic interest. East of Plymouth the coast is largely characterised by cliff scenery cut by some attractive estuaries, the drowned mouths of wooded river valleys – the Yealm, Erme, Avon, Kingsbridge and Dart estuaries. As well as the ups and downs of the cliffs these estuaries present the walker with a number of ferry crossings and one ford. This southernmost part of Devon forms the area known as the South Hams. East of the Dart and the attractive and historic town of Dartmouth the coast becomes an area of low, mostly red sandstone cliffs. This length, the "Riviera", is largely occupied by towns based on tourism such as Paignton, Torquay, Teignmouth and Dawlish, and being east-facing is mostly sheltered. Much of this length presents an almost continuously developed coastline. The major estuary of the River Exe forms the eastern boundary of this length.

Brixham Harbour

OS Maps: Landranger 201; Explorer 108

	This Walk	Cumulative	This Walk	Cumulative	Grading	Timing
Ascent	463ft	79,389ft	141m	24,198m	Easy	3.5 hours
Distance	7.5mi	417.9mi	12.1km	672.5km		

For detailed directions see our Walking Guide no. 47, Admiral's Hard (Plymouth) to The Barbican and The Barbican to Mount Batten.

This is an urban walk along the waterfront of one of the country's prime historical maritime cities. It is therefore quite different to the vast majority of the Coast Path, but is nevertheless well worth doing. The view over Plymouth Sound, flanked on both sides by cliffs, is inspiring, and often referred to as the finest urban vista in the country. Elsewhere are lengths of waterside industry, historic quays and modern marinas, making this a fascinating excursion.

Directions

A range of urban bus services runs throughout Plymouth, including to and from Admiral's Hard, the ferry point for Cremyll, and Mount Batten. Though not on the same route, they link in the city centre. There is also a ferry link across the mouth of the River Plym between the historic Sutton Harbour and Mount Batten. These links make a range of public transport-walks possible.

The Coast Path from Cremyll uses the ferry across the Tamar. The ferry operates all year, weather, tide and other circumstances permitting, generally at 30 minute intervals. Telephone 01752 822105. For ferry details see page 18.

Plymouth's Waterfront Walk is enhanced by a variety of information plaques and pieces of artwork relating to the city's history. A companion guidebook "Plymouth's Waterfront Walkway" is available free of charge from us, you will just pay postage.

Most of the route is waymarked by white bands on lamp-posts, red metal marker signs and pavement signs.

From the ferry walk up the road and turn right, going round the car park into Cremyll Street and on to the gates of the Royal William Yard. Enter the Yard via the walkway to the right of the main entrance and go through the Yard following the sea wall. (There is a ferry from the Royal William Yard to the Barbican that will also stop at Mount Batten on request for those who want a short cut). At the far corner of the Yard's sea wall climb the Eric Wallis Memorial Steps to Devil's Point Park. Follow the Path around the Park, overlooking Drake's Island and Plymouth Sound to reach the Artillery Tower, now a restaurant. At this point bear inland into Durnford Street and continue past the Royal Marines Barracks, turning right immediately after them. Continue along Millbay Road then, after the entrance to Millbay Docks, turn right into West Hoe Road. Fork right off here into Great Western Road, then bear off right down a narrow path along the shoreline. The Path returns to the road; here turn right to walk along the Hoe promenade all the way to The Barbican and Sutton Harbour, Plymouth's original harbour. Above on the left, away from the Coast Path but worth a visit, are the lighthouse of Smeaton's Tower, Drake's statue and other points of interest.

At The Barbican on the right are the Mayflower Steps, the site of the Pilgrim Fathers' embarkation. The large pontoon on nearby Commercial Wharf is the ferry point for Mount Batten, an unofficial short cut direct to the end of the Section.

The ferry operates all year, telephone 07930 838614. For ferry details see page 18.

Continuing on the Coast Path Waterfront Walk, walk across the lock gates at the entrance to Sutton Harbour, past the Marine Aquarium and then along Teat's Hill Road past the entrance to Queen Anne's Battery. At Breakwater Road, just after the entrance to Victoria Wharves, turn right up a narrow hill and footpath and down to the industrial Cattedown Wharf area. Continue past warehouses, then left along Shapters Way, right into Maxwell Road and along Finnigan Road to Laira Bridge. Turn right to cross the River Plym then, at the first roundabout, turn right (at the rhinoceros!) Go right, into Breakwater Road, and continue for about 500 yards/450m then turn left, still in Breakwater Road, to the entrance to Yacht Haven Quay Boatyard. To the left of a mesh fence is a path, signed as the Coast Path, which is followed to Oreston Quay. At the quay walk past the grassy area into Marine Road then left into Park Lane. Turn left at the top of the hill, and this path descends to Radford Lake. From here a Coast-to-Coast walk goes to Lynmouth on the north coast, following the Erme-Plym Trail and the Two Moors Way. Guidebooks are available at Ivybridge Tourist Information Centre (TIC).

Go across the causeway with its old mini castle folly and turn right. Follow the Path along then left and at a junction turn right down Hexton Hill Road to Hooe Lake. Skirt the lake, going along Barton Road and then turn left on a path to Turnchapel. Go through the village, bearing left at the Clovelly Bay Inn, up the hill then turn right down steps to the marina and over the slipway and along the shoreline to Mount Batten and the Sutton Harbour ferry. There are toilets, refreshments and a pub here. The short walk along the breakwater is very popular, although not part of the Coast Path.

Plymouth Hoe

OS Maps: Landranger 201; Explorer OL20

	This Walk	Cumulative	This Walk	Cumulative	Grading	Timing
Ascent	1,260ft	80,649ft	384m	24,582m	Easy	3 hours
Distance	7.5mi	425.4mi	12.1km	684.6km		

For detailed directions see our Walking Guide no. 48, Mount Batten to Warren Point (Yealm Ferry).

This is a Section of low cliffs, much of it overlooking Plymouth Sound. Below the cliffs are extensive areas of rock platform and offshore the Great Mew Stone becomes a focal point. Caravan and chalet sites and suburban villages are never far away and this is never a lonely Section. Towards its eastern end, as the cliffs rise somewhat, is the picturesque mouth of the River Yealm, forming a dramatic wooded gap in the cliffs.

Directions

Separate bus routes serve Mount Batten and Wembury village, and also Heybrook Bay, midway along this section, all from Plymouth city centre, allowing bus-walk options. There is a popular circular walk using the Coast Path between Wembury and Warren Point and a longer, full-day circular using the Erme-Plym Trail between Wembury and Mount Batten plus the Coast Path.

Mount Batten has toilets and refreshments, as well as a direct ferry link to and from Plymouth's Sutton Harbour. From Mount Batten the Coast Path heads over the little hill and past the old fort tower to the grassy area at Jennycliff, where there are more toilets and refreshments. Stay to the lower side of the field and at the end of the grass, from the stone "doormat" to Plymouth use the renovated steps down and stairs up again to access woodland. The Path then undulates and emerges above Fort Bovisand. Descend steeply to a road and turn left; there are seasonal refreshments here. Follow round to the right and up to pass seaward of the chalets, past a cafe and toilets and on round the point and so to Heybrook Bay. There is a pub a little way up the road here, as well as a bus stop. Keep right and follow the Path above the shore around Wembury Point and on to Wembury Beach. Yet more toilets and refreshments await here and the bus stop, together with pub and shop, are in the village a little way inland.

From Wembury Beach a Coast-to-Coast walk goes to Lynmouth on the north coast, following the Erme-Plym Trail and the Two Moors Way. Guidebooks are available from Ivybridge Tourist Information Centre (TIC).

Continuing on the Coast Path, climb seaward of the church and along the now higher cliffs to a junction of paths at the Rocket House. The Path going inland from here leads to Wembury village and its facilities. For the Coast Path, bear right, downhill, to reach the ferry point. Note that operating times on this ferry can be limited – see page 18 and Walk 49.

OS Maps: Landranger 201 (western end); Landranger 202 (remainder); Explorer OL20

	This Walk	Cumulative	This Walk	Cumulative	Grading	Timing
Ascent	1,466ft	82,115ft	447m	25,029m	Easy then strenuous	5.75 hours
Distance	10.3mi	435.7mi	16.6km	701.2km		

For detailed directions see our Walking Guide no. 49, Noss Mayo (Yealm Ferry) to Mothecombe.

This is a fine Section of high-level coastal cliffs, cut mid-way by the substantial and extremely picturesque estuary of the River Erme. The western end is a particularly good length, since the superb cliff coastline is easily accessed by a scenic former carriage route. Beyond that a series of descents and ascents, some quite steep, accentuate the dramatic landscape of the coastline. At the eastern extremity is the tidally insular Burgh Island, a focal point on this part of the coast. Because of its remoteness and strenuous nature, much of this section has a quiet character which will specially appeal to those in search of a lonely coastline.

Directions

A bus route links Noss Mayo, near the western end of this length, with Battisborough cross, a little way inland from the eastern end, making a bus-walk feasible. There is a very popular local walk using the Coast Path on the carriage drive from Noss Mayo.

The ferry at Wembury's Warren Point operates three ways over the River Yealm and its tributary Newton Creek. Warren Point is thus linked with both Newton Ferrers and Noss Mayo, and these two points with each other. For the Coast Path the link between Warren Point and Noss Mayo is needed. The ferry operates seasonally and at limited times – telephone 01752 880079. For ferry details see page 18.

There is a signal board to summon the ferryman by the steps at Warren Point or the slipway at Noss Mayo. Alternatively, telephone beforehand.

Because of the somewhat limited nature of the ferry it may be necessary to make alternative arrangements to reach Noss Mayo. Both Wembury and Noss Mayo have a regular bus service to and from Plymouth, so it is possible to use these services as a link, perhaps combining with an overnight stop in Plymouth. Alternatively, local taxi companies are available.

It is also possible to walk round the Yealm Estuary from ferry point to ferry point. This is a distance of some 9 miles/14.5km, effectively adding an extra day or half day to the itinerary.

Walk around the Yealm Estuary

Walk uphill inland from the ferry steps to the house at the top, the Rocket House. Continue inland along the track, which in turn becomes a road. Where the road bears sharp right go ahead along a public footpath into a field, then keep ahead alongside a high wall. At the end of the wall, after two gates, bear left (bearing 330) across fields, then go down a few steps. The now enclosed path goes left then right to arrive at a road. This is Knighton, on the outskirts of Wembury. The bus stop for Plymouth is a little way to the left, just before the pub.

To continue the walking route around the estuary cross the road at Knighton to a minor lane, following it left to another junction. Turn right here and continue until the road meets another, more major, road. Cross this road, going ahead and left for a short way then turn right on a signed footpath. This is part of a waymarked route, the Erme-Plym Trail, and is shown on the OS Explorer OL20 map. Follow the waymarked route across fields, over Cofflete Creek, next to a lane and on to the village of Brixton. Turn right and follow the road through the village to Brixton Church then back on the Erme-Plym Trail up Old Road, along a suburban road, over fields, along a minor lane then over more fields to arrive at another village, Yealmpton. On reaching the A379 road at Yealmpton the Erme-Plym Trail is now abandoned. Here, turn right along the A379 then quickly left, into Stray Park. At the bottom bear right along a tarmac path then, when it arrives at a road, turn left along a stony track. At the footpath sign continue ahead, eventually emerging at a road by a car park. Turn left along the road to cross Puslinch Bridge then follow the road up the hill. Take the footpath on the right near the top of the hill, crossing a couple of fields to a road. Turn right and continue to meet a more major road, which is followed ahead to Newton Ferrers. At the edge of the village turn left down the road signed to Bridgend and Noss Mayo, and at the junction at the head of the creek keep to the right. Follow the riverside road, forking right into Noss Mayo. Keep on the road round Noss Creek and continue on the creekside road out of the village until this becomes a track. A signed path on the right leaves the track for the ferry point.

Coast Path, Noss Mayo-River Erme

From the ferry point, follow the Path westward through the woods as it climbs to meet a track, an old carriage drive. (NB if refreshments are needed here, turn left and continue for about a mile to Noss Mayo village, where there are two pubs and seasonal toilets). The drive continues through woods, past a row of former coastguard cottages, into more woods, then on a superb cliff-face shelf round Mouthstone Point. Further on keep right where the more obvious path bears left inland to a car park, the drive continuing round Stoke Point and on to Beacon Hill. A series of ups and downs now ensues as the Path approaches the estuary of the River Erme, which has been fairly described as England's most unspoiled river estuary, and is possibly the most attractive. The Path crosses the top of a small beach then passes through a short woodland stretch to arrive at Mothecombe slipway on the Erme. There are seasonal refreshments a little way inland.

There is no ferry at the River Erme. It is usually possible to wade the river 1 hour either side of low water along the old ford and, under normal conditions, at low tide the water is about knee deep and the river bed is of sand with pebbles. The crossing is between grid references 614 476 and 620 478, ie the road by the row of coastguard cottages at Mothecombe and the end of the inland road to Wonwell Beach. However, great care should be taken as heavy rains or high seas can make conditions dangerous. Low water is approximately at the same time as at Devonport; see tide tables on pages 20-26.

Alternatively, it is possible to walk round the estuary. There are no riverside rights of way and for the most part minor roads must be used. The distance is approximately 8 miles/13km, adding an extra half day to the itinerary.

Walk round the Erme Estuary

From the slipway follow the road inland, following signs to Holbeton. Go through the village and leave on the minor lane to Ford and then Hole Farm. At the sharp bend after this farm follow the waymarked Erme-Plym Trail to the A379 and across the River Erme at Sequer's Bridge. Then leave the waymarked trail, continuing very carefully along the A379 for a couple of hundred yards/metres, before turning right on the lane signed to Orcheton. Follow this for about 2 miles/3km then turn right, following signs for Wonwell Beach. Follow the lane downhill to arrive at the estuary.

OS Maps: Landranger 202; Explorer OL20

	This Walk	Cumulative	This Walk	Cumulative	Grading	Timing
Ascent	1,860ft	83,975ft	567m	25,596m	Moderate	2.75 hours
Distance	9.3mi	445.0mi	15.0km	716.2km		

For detailed directions see our Walking Guide no. 50, Mothecombe to Thurlestone.

While the western end of this Section is relatively remote, in the east it is a well-used and popular Section, never far from residential and holiday accommodation. It is a length of low cliffs and sandy beaches, the coastline providing some interesting seascapes. These include views of the tidal Burgh Island, the estuary of the River Avon, the distinctive holed Thurlestone Rock and the headland of Bolt Tail. At the end of the Section, Hope Cove is a charming little settlement with a picturesque harbour and an old centre of historic cottages.

Directions

A regular, if infrequent, bus service links Thurlestone and Hope Cove, making a bus-walk option possible on the eastern part of this Section. There are popular short circular walks using the Coast Path between Bantham and Thurlestone.

For details of crossing the River Erme, see Section 49. On the eastern side, just inland of Wonwell slipway a path leaves the lane into the woods then continues above the shore, emerging on cliffs which rollercoaster up and down to the holiday park at Challaborough and then Bigbury-on-Sea. There are toilets here and also the year-round Café. On Burgh Island offshore, reached by walking across the sands or by unusual sea tractor, is a pub.

From the main facilities at Bigbury-on-Sea the Coast Path goes along the road, turning right immediately after the car park entrance to follow a short cliff-top length which re-joins the road further up. Cross the road and follow the path along the field edge next to the road. Leave the field where signed and cross the road, passing through Folly Farm and down the cliffs to the flat open area of Cockleridge Ham. At the edge is the ferry point for the crossing of the mouth of the River Avon.

The ferry is seasonal and operates at limited times and not at all on Sundays – telephone 01548 561196. For ferry details see page 18. The ferryman is alerted by waving. It must be noted that if the ferry is not operating on arrival the river should NOT be forded, despite its sometimes benign appearance.

Alternatively, there is a waymarked walk round the estuary between Bigbury-on-Sea and Bantham. This route, the Avon Estuary Walk, is signed with blue waymarks and adds about 8 miles/13km to the route, or another half day to the itinerary. The route is shown on OS Explorer map OL20.

Avon Estuary Walk

Continue up the road, without turning into Folly Farm, for a further 60 yards/55m and then turn right. The Path reaches the golf course, turning left on a track then off this to the right, down another track past Hexdown Farm. Follow this track to the bottom then go left along a drive which eventually arrives at a road. There is a permissive path alongside the road and at the end of this a path goes right over a field, through the top of a wood then downhill over another field to a road alongside the estuary. This tidal road is then followed to Aveton Gifford on the A379.

At high tide there is a waymarked diversion which crosses the tidal road on arriving at it and re-joins it next to the village. From Aveton Gifford cross the Avon on the A379 then take the first lane on the right, which becomes a track and continues to Stadbury Farm. Bear left approaching the farm onto a footpath, following field edges towards the valley bottom to cross Stiddicombe Creek. Enter the wood on the right and climb to leave at the far top corner. Follow the top edge of fields then cross a farm track and a stream to a junction of paths. Turn right and continue to Bantham village, where there is a pub, shop, toilets and seasonal refreshments.

Coast Path, Bantham-Hope Cove

From the ferry point go through the car park and round the edge of the dunes of Bantham Ham. Follow the shore, leaving the dunes and climbing past the edge of Thurlestone Golf Club to descend to Thurlestone Sands. Cross a long footbridge at an inland lagoon (South Milton Ley), pass public toilets and seasonal refreshments then join a road for a short stretch before turning back to the shoreline and over low cliffs to Outer Hope, where there are all facilities in season. Follow the Path behind the little harbour and down to the old lifeboat station at Inner Hope, where the bus stop is situated. Buses to Kingsbridge leave from here. A little inland is the old village centre of Inner Hope, at The Square, a picture-postcard location worth seeing before leaving.

Hope Cove

OS Maps: Landranger 202; Explorer OL20

	This Walk	Cumulative	This Walk	Cumulative	Grading	Timing
Ascent	1,506ft	85,481ft	459m	26,055m	Strenuous	4 hours
Distance	8.1mi	453.1mi	13.0km	729.2km		

For detailed directions see our Walking Guide no. 51, Thurlestone to Salcombe.

This is a very scenic Section of the coast, largely comprising quite spectacular high cliffs soaring above tiny, mostly inaccessible coves. Near both ends are dramatic headlands, Bolt Tail in the west and Bolt Head in the east, offering superb coastal views in their respective directions. At the eastern end this Section turns into the mouth of the estuary of Salcombe Harbour, and there is the contrast of softer, sandy bays. This is a length which is never really remote, but never really busy.

Directions

Separate bus routes serve Hope Cove and Salcombe from Kingsbridge and Malborough, a few miles inland, making a bus-walk feasible from there. There are numerous local circuits using the Coast Path based on Hope Cove and Salcombe, as well as Bolberry and Soar.

Leave Hope Cove from the old lifeboat station at Inner Hope up the signed Coast Path and out to the magnificent viewpoint of Bolt Tail, where the ramparts of an Iron Age cliff fort are crossed to reach the end. The Path doubles back along the cliff top over Bolberry Down and then down to the splendid Soar Mill Cove (there are seasonal refreshments inland from here). Climbing from the cove a long level stretch of easy walking follows. Keep along the cliff top and as the Path approaches Bolt Head pass through a couple of gates, staying on the closest path to the cliff top as possible. A steep descent will then lead to the headland, where a sharp turn leads to the cliff-face path round Starehole Bay and then on to the Courtenay Walk below rocky pinnacles. Passing into woodland at the National Trust's Overbecks property the Path joins a road which is followed past South Sands and North Sands – toilets and seasonal refreshments at both – and then on into Salcombe town centre. For a variation, there is a summer ferry service between South Sands and Salcombe. The town is a renowned yachting centre and has all facilities.

Lookout over Starehole Bay

southwestcoastpath.org.uk

OS Maps: Landranger 202; Explorer OL20

	This Walk	Cumulative	This Walk	Cumulative	Grading	Timing
Ascent	2,251ft	87,732ft	686m	26,741m	Strenuous	6.75 hours
Distance	12.6mi	465.7mi	20.3km	749.5km		

For detailed directions see our Walking Guide no. 52, Salcombe to Torcross.

This is a superb section of walking. Part of it is on exposed cliff faces, the sometimes stark cliffs contrasting with numerous tiny sandy coves below. A significant length in the middle is on an old "raised beach", a low shelf a little above the sea giving an easy passage here. In the east the Path crosses the rocky spine of Start Point, behind its lighthouse, a dramatic stretch, before following a lush, sheltered length into Torcross.

Directions

Salcombe and Torcross are both on regular bus routes to and from Kingsbridge, a little inland, making a bus-walk possible from that town. There is also a popular local circuit using the Coast Path from the Salcombe Ferry.

Salcombe has all necessary facilities. The ferry across the estuary leaves from steps next to the Ferry Hotel, a little way downstream from the town centre. The ferry operates all year; tel: 01548 842061 or 01548 560558. For ferry details see page 18.

From the ferry point on the eastern side, where there are toilets and refreshments, the Coast Path follows the road down the estuary side then, after crossing the rear of the beach at Mill Bay (toilets), passes the refreshment facilities at Gara Rock (call 01548 844810 for details), then follows a clear cliff Path to Prawle Point. The Path goes to the Coastwatch lookout at the very end, then descends to follow the "raised beach" shelf just above the waves before a short inland length to avoid a cliff fall leads to Lannacombe Beach. Beyond here a dramatic length goes along and up to the rocky ridge leading to Start Point, the Path dropping to the lighthouse access road. From the car park at the top the Path bears off right down the cliff face to Hallsands, passing above the old ruined village. A short diversion to the viewpoint is both instructive and interesting. The Path continues over low cliffs to Beesands, where there is a pub, toilets and seasonal refreshments. Continue along the shingle ridge then behind an old quarry to descend into Torcross, with a panoramic view of Slapton Ley ahead on the descent. Torcross has all facilities, and buses to Plymouth, Kingsbridge and Dartmouth.

Start Point

OS Maps: Landranger 202; Explorer OL20

	This Walk	Cumulative	This Walk	Cumulative	Grading	Timing
Ascent	1,493ft	89,225ft	455m	27,196m	Easy then strenuous	4.75 hours
Distance	10.3mi	476.0mi	16.6km	766.0km		

For detailed directions see our Walking Guide no. 53, Torcross to Dartmouth.

Something like a quarter of this Section consists of the low shingle ridge known locally as the Slapton Line, cutting off the freshwater lake of Slapton Ley from the sea. Most of the remainder of the Section is cliffs and coves, partly looking to the sea and partly to the outer reaches of the picturesque wooded Dart Estuary.

Directions

A regular bus service runs along the coast road which is, for much of the Section, adjacent to the Coast Path. With stops at most obvious locations this gives numerous bus-walk options. There is also a very popular and scenic circular walk using the Coast Path between Dartmouth and the mouth of the Dart Estuary.

From Torcross, with all facilities, the Coast Path runs along the shingle ridge. The official route is on the landward side but it is possible, if more tiring, to walk along the seaward side. After the Strete Gate car park, look out for the fingerpost signing the new section of Coast Path, opened in summer 2015. Follow the path along the cliff top and through the woods to the A379. It is now necessary to walk along this and for the next 400 yards/365m.

Follow the main road through Strete village (pub – closed at time of writing – and shop) then, just after the village end, take the path to the right which passes over fields and a footbridge to reach a high point above the sea. Continuing parallel to the coast for a while it then heads inland over a deep valley, crossing the main road and over more fields to a lane. Descend the lane then leave it across more fields until, after crossing the main road again, the picturesque cove of Blackpool Sands is reached. There are toilets and seasonal refreshments. Follow the path uphill through the woods then the route enters and meanders along various paths in the village of Stoke Fleming (pub, shop and toilets), arriving at the village hall. Cross the main road again and follow a lane to a National Trust car park. From here a scenic cliff path proceeds, latterly through woods, to reach the Dart Estuary and arrive at Dartmouth Castle. An estuary-side path passes the adjacent church and joins the road which is followed into the town. Look out for some steps on the right just after the public toilets before reaching the centre; the steps lead down to Bayards Cove through its little castle and on to the Embankment at the town centre. Dartmouth, of course, has all facilities.

OS Maps: Landranger 202; Explorer OL20

	This Walk	Cumulative	This Walk	Cumulative	Grading	Timing
Ascent	2,992ft	92,217ft	912m	28,108m	Strenuous	5.75 hours
Distance	10.9mi	486.9mi	17.5km	783.6km		

For detailed directions see our Walking Guide no. 54, Dartmouth (Kingswear) to Brixham.

This is a Section of superb cliff scenery, tough going in places and often quite lonely. In the west, near the mouth of the Dart, are substantial wooded areas but further along the cliffs become higher and more open. This makes for a dramatic, steeply undulating landscape ending at the sea in steep cliff faces.

Directions

A regular bus service links Brixham and Kingswear, on the east side of the Dartmouth Ferry, making a bus-walk possible. There is also a popular circuit using the Coast Path based on Kingswear.

Walkers have two ferry options from Dartmouth town centre to cross the river, the Lower Car Ferry, which also carries foot passengers, and the Dartmouth Passenger Ferry. The Lower Car Ferry operates all year on a continuous service telephone 01803 752342. The Dartmouth Passenger Ferry also operates all year on a continuous service telephone 01803 555872. For ferry details see page 19.

From either ferry landing point in Kingswear, follow the Coast Path signposts, turning left along Beacon Road then right up Church Hill and down Beacon Lane. Continue out of the village. After some 1.25 miles/2km turn right down steps and undulate sometimes steeply into and through woodland to the old Battery buildings at Froward Point. Here the Path descends steeply to the right from the corner of an old lookout building, passing World War II searchlight and gun positions before continuing along the cliffs. Pass Pudcombe Cove, by the National Trust Coleton Fishacre Gardens, and then on over Scabbacombe Head and past Scabbacombe Sands and Man Sands and over Southdown Cliff to Sharkham Point – this is a particularly strenuous length. Passing holiday accommodation the Path arrives at Berry Head, a Napoleonic fortified area. Divert to the end of the headland to see the unusually squat lighthouse. Berry Head has toilets and year round refreshments available at the Guardhouse Café. From here descend past an old quarry to a road, where there are further refreshment facilities. Turn right then go right again through the Shoalstone Car Park and along above the shoreline, returning to the road before descending steps to Brixham Breakwater. Follow the promenade to the harbour. Brixham has all facilities.

OS Maps: Landranger 202: Explorer OL20 (western half); Explorer 110 (eastern half)

	This Walk	Cumulative	This Walk	Cumulative	Grading	Timing
Ascent	1,972ft	94,189ft	601m	28,709m	Moderate	6 hours
Distance	13.2mi	500.1mi	21.2km	804.8km		

For detailed directions see our Walking Guide no. 55, Brixham to Paignton and Paignton to Babbacombe.

This is mostly an urban Section, passing along the shoreline of the "English Riviera", or Tor Bay. There is a mixture of grand terraces, open green parkland, amusement parks and the elegant white buildings overlooking the sea at Torquay. At the western end there is also the old fishing town of Brixham and at the other end the almost rural wooded cliffs around Babbacombe. All in all, this is a surprisingly diverse Section.

Directions

A range of bus routes runs throughout the Torbay area, including one which follows the coast road between Brixham and Torquay, and another linking Torquay to Babbacombe. As a result, a wide variety of bus-walks is possible. A pleasant alternative is the Torquay to Brixham ferry which runs regularly.

Leaving Brixham by the fish market, the Coast Path initially passes a car park and gardens before passing two small coves and climbing into woodland which takes the path to Elberry Cove. From here it passes behind the sweep of Broadsands, climbing by the railway viaduct at the far end to proceed alongside the steam railway line to the promenade at Goodrington. At the far end climb through ornamental gardens and go down a road to Paignton Harbour and so along the promenade. Paignton's railway station is inland of the pier. Turn inland at Hollicombe, at the far end of Preston Sands, going through a park to the main sea-front road which is followed to Torquay Harbour. Torquay Station is inland a little before the harbour.

Cross the pedestrian bridge across the harbour and climb the hill, turning right at the Hotel on the signed path which leads to the open area at Daddyhole Plain. Descend to the sea-front road at Meadfoot Beach, climbing again at Ilsham Marine Drive. Take the cliff path round Thatcher Point to Hope's Nose. A cul-de-sac path goes to the end of this low headland.

From Hope's Nose follow the path inland of the road, crossing the road to the Bishop's Walk, which in turn arrives at a car park above Anstey's Cove. The path now goes round the edge of the grassy downs on Walls Hill, bearing off right to descend to Babbacombe Beach. Cross a wooden footbridge to Oddicombe Beach then climb by the cliff railway to reach Babbacombe's facilities at the top.

OS Maps: Landranger 202; Explorer 110

	This Walk	Cumulative	This Walk	Cumulative	Grading	Timing
Ascent	2,090ft	96,279ft	637m	29,346m	Strenuous	3.75 hours
Distance	6.4mi	506.5mi	10.3km	815.1km		

For detailed directions see our Walking Guide no. 56, Babbacombe to Teignmouth.

This is a tough Section of almost constant ups and downs. The characteristic red cliffs of this part of Devon are often quite high and quite sheer, though unfortunately the terrain is such that sea and cliff views are perhaps less frequent than would be wished. Its strenuous nature makes it a relatively quiet Section, except for the two ends, although it is never far from roads or housing.

Directions

A regular bus service links Babbacombe and Teignmouth, making a bus-walk an option.

From Babbacombe, a pleasant suburb of Torquay with all facilities, the Coast Path descends next to the cliff railway and then soon climbs again to avoid a cliff fall. This diversion takes the path up a grassy area to a main road where it turns right, then right again into Petitor Road. At the bottom turn left on the Coast Path again, which soon descends onto a cliff face before reaching the wooded valley at Watcombe. Cross the track running down the valley and on through a wooded length to a short rocky stretch, turning right at a junction before reaching the car park at Maidencombe. There is a pub and toilets here. Turn right after the car park and keep on the rollercoaster path which eventually climbs to go alongside the coast road, then quickly leaves it to pass alongside fields to a track. Turn right and go round the wooded Ness headland, with super views ahead, descending to the promenade at Shaldon, on the estuary of the River Teign.

The ferry service across the River Teign operates throughout the year, weather permitting. For ferry details see page 19.

Walk, Shaldon-Teignmouth

If the ferry is not operating, continue inland along the riverside roads to Shaldon Bridge and cross the Teign. On the Teignmouth side turn right into Milford Park, through Bitton Sports Ground into Park Hill, cross into Bitton Avenue then into Clay Lane and right into Willow Street. At the end bear left then right into Quay Road, then right to go along the Strand and right to the Harbour Beach and the ferry point. Teignmouth has all facilities, including a mainline rail station and buses to Exeter.

OS Maps: Landranger 192; Explorer 110

	This Walk	Cumulative	This Walk	Cumulative	Grading	Timing
Ascent	488ft	96,767ft	149m	29,495m	Easy	3 hours
Distance	8.0mi	514.5mi	12.9km	828.0km		

For detailed directions see our Walking Guide no. 57, Teignmouth to Exmouth.

This Section primarily comprises two fairly large seaside towns, flanked by a coastline of high red cliffs at one end and marshes and a sand bar at the other. Running through it, often next to the Coast Path, is possibly the most scenic part of Brunel's GWR railway line, the embankment of which forms the sea wall for much of this length. This is a busy, largely urban and much used Section with an historic importance to the tourist trade.

Directions

A regular bus service links Teignmouth and Starcross, the ferry point for Exmouth, and also passes through Dawlish and Dawlish Warren. As there are also stations on the railway line at these places, bus or train-walks are options here.

From the ferry point at Teignmouth, or from the town centre, go to the car park at The Point, jutting out into the Teign Estuary, and begin by walking along the promenade. Leaving the town the Coast Path continues between railway and sea below the red cliffs to the end, where it descends steps to pass under the railway and then up Smugglers Lane to the A379 road at the top.

High water route, Teignmouth-Smugglers Lane

With a high sea and an onshore wind the far end of the promenade can become very wet, and at exceptionally high tides the steps at Smugglers Lane may become impassable. In these cases, immediately after leaving the town fork left and cross the railway on a footbridge on Eastcliff Walk, and this path eventually reaches the A379 which is then followed ahead to meet the official path at the top of Smugglers Lane.

Coast Path, Smugglers Lane-Dawlish Warren

Use the footway on the inland side of the A379 and walk for about 150 yards/135m before turning right into Windward Lane, going immediately left on a path which skirts fields before returning to the A379. Bear right into Old Teignmouth Road, which in turn returns to the A379 then, very soon, turn right into a park through some railings and follow the Path around its edge which then zigzags down to the shoreline. Follow the sea wall through Dawlish, past the station – all facilities are found beyond the railway here. The Coast Path then continues on the sea wall between railway and sea, again below the red cliffs, to Dawlish Warren. Just before the amusement area at Dawlish Warren, cross the obvious railway footbridge to a car park, turn right and follow to the main road.

High water route, Dawlish-Dawlish Warren

Occasionally, at the highest tides, it becomes impossible to proceed along the sea wall for a short stretch just beyond the station. In this case, from the sea wall, cross the footbridge immediately after the end of station platform and follow the path up to the A379. Turn right and continue alongside the road until the Path passing a line of shops to reach Warren Road. Turn right here crossing over Pinewood Close to reach a path going through a small wood. Follow this path, locally known as Lady's Mile, as it follows the line of coast above the sea wall. Continue to follow this path until you reach the main road in Dawlish Warren to pick up the Coast Path here.

Coast Path, Dawlish Warren-Starcross

The Coast Path does not go around the large sand spit at Dawlish Warren itself, jutting out into the mouth of the River Exe, or the marshes behind it, but if there is time this can be an exhilarating experience. Otherwise continue along Warren Road on the pavement, then opposite the entrance to Dawlish Warren Sandy Park join the cycleway and footpath to Cockwood Harbour. After following the road around the harbour join the A379. Cross the road and follow the footpath and cycleway to Starcross, and the ferry point to Exmouth. Starcross has all facilities.

The ferry operates mid-April – end October, telephone 01626 862452 or 07974 022536. For ferry details see page 19. If there is no ferry operating on arrival at Starcross, there are several options to reach Exmouth.

Option 1: Explorer Water Taxi – this runs daily 1st April until 31st October. Check their web site before travelling as times vary: www.exeplorerwatertaxis.co.uk

Option 2: Bus or train from Starcross to Exeter, bus or train from Exeter to Exmouth.

Option 3: Walk from Starcross to Turf Lock following the waymarked Exe Estuary Trail on the riverside road and footpath (3 miles/5km), then ferry Turf Lock-Topsham and bus or train from Topsham to Exmouth.

Ferry operates seasonally – telephone 07778 370582. For ferry details see page 19.

Option 4: Walk from Starcross to Topsham Lock following the waymarked Exe Estuary Trail on the riverside road and footpath and Exeter Canal towpath (4.5 miles/7km), then ferry Topsham Lock-Topsham and bus or train from Topsham to Exmouth.

Ferry operates seasonally – telephone 01392 274306 (office) or 07801 203338 (ferryman). For ferry details see page 19.

Teignmouth

If you enjoy sleeping, eating or drinking at any business on the Path please suggest they join us as Business Members so that we can share their brilliance!

The businesses listed here are all supporters of the South West Coast Path Association, they have joined as business members and it would be great if you could show your support for them too. In addition, businesses are listed with more details on our website: www.southwestcoastpath.org.uk Find them through our walk finder or our accommodation finder tools.

KEY:

GR Grid Reference
DP Distance from the Path
NT Nearest Town

Dogs Welcome
Evening Meal Available
3 Number Of Rooms

Grocery Shop On Site
Wifi
Parking

ed & Breakfasts and Hotels

NAME	OTHER INFO	
.dgecombe Guesthouse 0 Pier Street, West Hoe, Plymouth, PL1 3BT 01752 660675 enquiries@edgcumbeguesthouse.co.uk www.edgcumbeguesthouse.co.uk	GR: 473 537	DP: 0.1 miles
	NT: **PLYMOUTH**	
	🛜	Other info:
The Mariners Guest House 11 Pier Street, West Hoe, Plymouth, PL1 3BS 01752 261778 enquiries@marineguesthouse.co.uk www.marinersguesthouse.co.uk	GR:	DP: 0 miles
	NT: **PLYMOUTH**	
	Offers one night stays	
	8 🛜	Other info: Sauna available
Sea Breezes Guest House 28 Grand Parade, Plymouth, PL1 3DJ 01752 667205 stay@plymouth-bedandbreakfast.co.uk www.plymouth-bedandbreakfast.co.uk	GR: 472 536	DP: 0 miles
	NT: **PLYMOUTH**	
	Offers one night stays	
	🛜	Other info:
The Rusty Anchor Guest House 30 Grand Parade, Plymouth, PL1 3DJ 01752 663924 enquiries@therustyanchor-plymouth.co.uk www.therustyanchor-plymouth.co.uk	GR: 472 536	DP: 0 miles
	NT: **PLYMOUTH**	
	🐕	Other info:
Raleigh Stile B&B Hexton Hill Road, Hooe, Plymouth, PL9 9WA 01752 492232 enquiries@stormplymouth.co.uk www.raleighstyle.co.uk	GR: 499 526	DP: 0 miles
	NT: **PLYMOUTH**	
		Other info:
Wembury Bay B&B 2 Warren Close, Wembury, PL9 0AF 01752 863392 pwgreenwood59@gmail.com wemburybaybedandbreakfast.yolasite.com	GR: 523 488	DP: 0.1 miles
	NT: **PLYMOUTH**	
	Offers one night stays	
	3 🚗 🛜	Other info: Pub and shop 10 mins walk
Ferry Stop Bed & Breakfast 1 Barton Close, Wembury, PL9 0LF 01752 863710 lorraine.pitcher123@btinternet.com www.southwestcoastpath.org.uk/ferrystop-bb-wembury	GR: 527 494	DP: 0.75 miles
	NT: **WEMBURY**	
	Offers one night stays	
	1 🚗 🛜 🐕	Other info:

NAME	OTHER INFO	
37 Kingfisher Way 37 Kingfisher Way, Oreston, Plymouth, PL9 7RU ☎ 07769 652720 ✉ nickatkins7@hotmail.com ⊕ www.southwestcoastpath.org.uk/37-kingfisher-way-oreston-plymouth	GR: 503 531 ┊ DP: 0 miles NT: **WEMBURY**	Other info: 2 🚗 📶
Thorn House B&B Thorn, Wembury, Plymouth, PL9 0EQ ☎ 01752 862494 ✉ thornhouseuk@gmail.com ⊕ www.airbnb.co.uk/rooms/4592914?guests=1&adults=1&children=0&infants=0&s=NGG3eqlM	GR: 541 490 ┊ DP: 1 mile NT: **WEMBURY** Offers one night stays	Other info: 3 🚗 📶 🍴
Cellars B&B Cellars, Passage Wood Road, Noss Mayo, PL8 1EU ☎ 01752 872771 ✉ suespoonerrogers@btinternet.com ⊕ www.southwestcoastpath.org.uk/cellars-noss-mayo	GR: 534 475 ┊ DP: 0 miles NT: **NOSS MAYO** Offers one night stays	Other info: 🚗 📶 🐕
Worswell Barton Farmhouse B&B Noss Mayo, Plymouth, PL8 1HB ☎ 01752 872977 ✉ info@worswellbarton.co.uk ⊕ www.worswellbarton.co.uk	GR: 536 471 ┊ DP: 1 mile NT: **NOSS MAYO** Offers one night stays	Other info: 5 🚗 📶
The Ivy Barn B&B Fore Street, Holbeton, PL8 1NA ☎ 01752 830484 ✉ theivybarn@gmail.com ⊕ www.theivybarnbnb.co.uk	GR: 613 501 ┊ DP: 2 miles NT: **HOLBETON** Offers one night stays	Other info: 6 🚗 📶 🐕
Kimberley B&B Ringmore, Kingsbridge, TQ7 4HJ ☎ 01548 811115 ✉ info@kimberley-annex.co.uk ⊕ www.kimberley-annex.co.uk	GR: 652 461 ┊ DP: 1 mile NT: **BIGBURY-ON-SEA** Offers one night stays	Other info: Cooked breakfast 2 🚗 📶 🐕
Tanfield B&B Grand View Road, Hope Cove, TQ7 3HF ☎ 01548 561555 ✉ info@hopecove.com ⊕ www.hopecove.com	GR: 678 402 ┊ DP: 0.3 miles NT: **HOPE COVE**	Other info: 🐕
Rocarno B&B Grenville Road, Salcombe, TQ8 8BJ ☎ 01548 842732 ✉ rocarno@aol.com ⊕ www.rocarno.co.uk/homepage.php	GR: 736 388 ┊ DP: 0 miles NT: **SALCOMBE**	Other info:
Shute Farm South Milton, Kingsbridge, TQ7 3JL ☎ 01548 560680 ✉ shutefarmdevon@gmail.com ⊕ www.shutefarm.co.uk	GR: 699 432 ┊ DP: 1.5 miles NT: **SALCOMBE** Offers one night stays	Other info: Will pick up & drop off walkers between Salcombe and Bantham 3 🚗 📶
Waverly B&B Devon Road, Salcombe, TQ8 8HL ☎ 01548 842633 ✉ pauline@waverleybandb.co.uk ⊕ www.waverleybandb.co.uk	GR: 738 388 ┊ DP: 0.1 miles NT: **SALCOMBE** Offers one night stays	Other info: 5 🚗 📶 🐕

NAME	OTHER INFO	
Ashleigh House Ashleigh Road, Kingsbridge, TQ7 1HB 01548 852893 reception@ashleigh-house.co.uk www.ashleigh-house.co.uk	GR: 730 438 / DP: 3 miles NT: **KINGSBRIDGE** 🐕	Other info:
Down Farm Chivelstone, Kingsbridge, TQ7 2NQ 01548 511234 downfarm@btinternet.com www.downfarm.co.uk	GR: 806 377 / DP: 0.25 miles NT: **KINGSBRIDGE** Offers one night stays ③ 🚗 🛜 🐕 🍴	Other info: Evening meals by prior arrangement. Conditions for dogs.
Holywell B&B St Ann's Chapel, Bigbury, TQ7 4HQ 01548 810308 holywellstores@msn.com www.holywell-bigburybedandbreakfast.co.uk	GR: 663 472 / DP: 2.5 miles NT: **KINGSBRIDGE** Offers one night stays ③ 🚗 🛜 🐕 🛒	Other info: Pub across the road. Pick up from the coast path available
Summerwinds B&B Marine Drive, Bigbury on Sea, Kingsbridge, TQ7 4AS 01548 810669 pritchard212@btinternet.com www.southwestcoastpath.org.uk/summerwinds-bigbury	GR: 651 442 / DP: 0 miles NT: **KINGSBRIDGE**	Other info:
The Cricket Inn Beesands, Kingsbridge, TQ7 2EN 01548 580215 enquiries@thecricketinn.com www.thecricketinn.com	GR: 819 403 / DP: 0 miles NT: **KINGSBRIDGE** Offers one night stays ⑦ 🚗 🛜 🍴	Other info:
The Old Post Office South Milton, Kingsbridge, TQ7 3JQ 07760 225717 toposouthmilton@hotmail.co.uk x www.theoldpostofficesouthmilton.co.uk	GR: 700 426 / DP: 1.25 miles NT: **KINGSBRIDGE** Offers one night stays ④ 🛜	Other info:
Valseph Beesands, Kingsbridge, TQ7 2EJ 01548 580650 / 07890 197673 valseph@btinternet.com www.beesandsbandb.co.uk	GR: 819 406 / DP: 0 miles NT: **KINGSBRIDGE** Offers one night stays ① 🚗 🛜	Other info:
Welle House B&B East Prawle, Kingsbridge, TQ7 2BU 01548 511151 enquiries@wellehouse.co.uk www.wellehouse.co.uk	GR: 778 364 / DP: 0.5 miles NT: **KINGSBRIDGE** 🐕	Other info:
Camelot B&B 61 Victoria Road, Dartmouth, TQ6 9RX 01803 833805 jjwright@talktalk.net www.southwestcoastpath.org.uk/camelot-bb-dartmouth	GR: 874 512 / DP: 0.5 miles NT: **DARTMOUTH** Offers one night stays ③ 🛜	Other info:
Cladda House B&B and Self-catering Apartments Dartmouth, TQ6 9EF 01803 835957 / 07967 060003 bandb@cladda-dartmouth.co.uk www.cladda-dartmouth.co.uk	GR: 871 511 / DP: 0.5 miles NT: **DARTMOUTH** ⑥ 🚗 🛜 🐕	Other info: See website for self-catering contact details
Eight Bells B&B South Embankment, Dartmouth, TQ6 9BB 01803 839506 lizhelyer20@gmail.com dartmouthbandb@gmail.com	GR: 878 511 / DP: 0.15 miles NT: **DARTMOUTH** Offers one night stays ② 🛜	Other info:

NAME	OTHER INFO		
Fairholme B&B Bay View Estate, Stoke Fleming, TQ6 0QX ☏ 01803 770356 ✉ stay@fairholmedartmouth.co.uk 🌐 www.fairholmedartmouth.co.uk	GR:	DP: 0.1 miles	
	NT: **DARTMOUTH**		
	Offers one night stays		
	3 🚗 📶		Other info:
Roxburgh House B&B Dartmouth Road, Strete, Dartmouth, TQ6 0RW ☏ 01803 770870 ✉ ingrid@roxburghhouse.co.uk 🌐 www.roxburghhouse.co.uk	GR: 840 468	DP: 0 miles	
	NT: **DARTMOUTH**		
	Offers one night stays		
	3 📶 🐕		Other info: If the local pub not open, will drive walkers to a nearby pub!
Beacon House B&B Prospect Steps, South Furzeham Road, Brixham, TQ5 8JB ☏ 01803 428720 ✉ enquiries@beaconbrixham.co.uk 🌐 www.beaconbrixham.co.uk	GR: 924 563	DP: 0 miles	
	NT: **BRIXHAM**		
	Offers one night stays		
	4 🚗 📶		Other info: Sea views from all bedrooms
Brixham House 130 New Road, Brixham, TQ5 8DA ☏ 01803 853954 ✉ stay@brixhamhouse.co.uk 🌐 www.brixhamhouse.co.uk	GR: 916 555	DP: 0.5 miles	
	NT: **BRIXHAM**		
	Offers one night stays		
	6 🚗 📶 🐕		Other info:
Driftwood B&B 11 Prospect Road, Brixham, TQ5 8HS ☏ 01803 858 915 / 07711 771462 ✉ stay@driftwoodbandb.co.uk 🌐 www.driftwoodbandb.co.uk	GR: 924 562	DP: 0.15 miles	
	NT: **BRIXHAM**		
	4 🚗 📶		Other info:
The Smugglers Haunt Hotel Church Hill East, Brixham, TQ5 8HH ☏ 01803 853050 ✉ info@smugglershauntdevon.co.uk 🌐 www.smugglershauntdevon.co.uk	GR: 923561	DP: 1 mile	
	NT: **BRIXHAM**		
	Offers one night stays		
	14 📶		Other info:
Westbury Guest House 51 New Road, Brixham, TQ5 8NL ☏ 01803 851684 ✉ westburyguesthouse@gmail.com 🌐 westburyguesthouse.com	GR: 920 559	DP: 0.2 miles	
	NT: **BRIXHAM**		
	Offers one night stays		
	6 🚗 📶		Other info:
Higher Gitcombe Boutique B&B Cornworthy, Totnes, TQ9 7HH ☏ 01803 712990 ✉ info@highergitcombe.co.uk 🌐 www.highergitcombe.co.uk	GR: 821 542	DP: 6 miles	
	NT: **TOTNES**		
	Offers one night stays		
	🚗 📶 🍴		Other info:
Bay Esplanade Hotel The Esplanade, Sands Road, Paignton, TQ4 6EG ☏ 01803 556333 ✉ 🌐 www.shearings.com	GR: 890 603	DP: 0 miles	
	NT: **PAIGNTON**		
	83 🚗 📶 🍴		Other info: Open all year
Elberry Farm Broadsands, Paignton, TQ4 6HJ ☏ 01803 842939 ✉ enquiries@elberryfarm.co.uk 🌐 www.elberryfarm.co.uk	GR: 899 570	DP: 0.25 miles	
	NT: **PAIGNTON**		
	Offers one night stays		
	4 🚗 📶 🐕 🍴		Other info:
The Clifton at Paignton 9-10 Kernou Road, Paignton, TQ4 6BA ☏ 01803 556545 ✉ enquiries@cliftonhotelpaignton.co.uk 🌐 www.cliftonhotelpaignton.co.uk	GR:	DP: 0.01 miles	
	NT: **PAIGNTON**		
	Offers one night stays		
	12 🚗 📶 🍴		Other info:

NAME	OTHER INFO	
Coastguard Cottage 84 Babbacombe Downs, Babbacombe, TQ1 3LU ☎ 01803 311634 ✉ sheila.besidethesea@googlemail.com 🌐 www.babbacombebandb.co.uk	GR: 927 653	DP: 0.3 miles
	NT: **TORQUAY**	
	Offers one night stays	
	[3]	Other info:
Bay Torbay Hotel Torbay Road, Torquay, TQ2 5EY ☎ 01803 295218 ✉ 🌐 www.shearings.com	GR: 916 635	DP: 0.2 miles
	NT: **TORQUAY**	
	[111] [📶] [🍽]	Other info: Open all year
The Millbrook Guest House 1 Old Mill Road, Torquay, TQ2 6AP ☎ 01803 297394 ✉ info@themillbrook.co.uk 🌐 www.themillbrook.co.uk	GR: 904 642	DP: 0.5 miles
	NT: **TORQUAY**	
		Other info:
Garway Lodge Guest House 79 Avenue Road, Torquay, TQ2 5LL ☎ 01803 293126 ✉ info@garwaylodge.co.uk 🌐 www.garwaylodge.co.uk	GR: 904 645	DP: 1.5 miles
	NT: **TORQUAY**	
	Offers one night stays	
	[6] [🚗] [📶] [🐕]	Other info: Early breakfast on request
The Haldon Guest House 6 Beach Road, TQ4 6AY ☎ 01803 551120 ✉ stay@haldonguesthouse.co.uk 🌐 www.haldonguesthouse.co.uk	GR: 891 608	DP: 0.3 miles
	NT: **TORQUAY**	
	Offers one night stays	
	[7] [📶] [🍽]	Other info:
Aveland House Aveland Road, Babbacombe, TQ1 3PT ☎ 01803 326622 ✉ enquiry@avelandhouse.co.uk 🌐 www.avelandhouse.co.uk	GR: 921 652	DP: 0.5 miles
	NT: **BABBACOMBE**	
	Offers one night stays	
	[🚐] [📶] [🍽]	Other info:
Lynton House 7 Powderham Terrace, Teignmouth, TQ14 8BL ☎ 01626 774349 ✉ stay@lyntonhouseteignmouth.com 🌐 www.lyntonhouseteignmouth.com	GR: 939 725	DP: 1 mile
	NT: **TEIGNMOUTH**	
	Offers one night stays	
	[12] [📶] [🐕]	Other info:
The Thornhill Mere Lane, Seafront, Teignmouth, TQ14 8TA ☎ 01626 773460 ✉ stay@thethornhill.co.uk 🌐 www.thethornhill.co.uk	GR: 944 730	DP: 0 miles
	NT: **TEIGNMOUTH**	
	[10] [📶] [🐕]	Other info:
The Blenheim 1 Marine Parade, Dawlish, EX7 9DJ ☎ 01626 862372 ✉ blenheimholidays@btconnect.com 🌐 www.theblenheim.uk.net	GR:	DP: 0 miles
	NT: **DAWLISH**	
	Offers one night stays	
	[11] [🚗] [📶] [🐕]	Other info: Limited parking, free carpark nearby
The Croft Guest House Cockwood Harbour, Starcross, Exeter, EX6 8QY ☎ 01626 890282 ✉ croftcockwood@aol.com 🌐 www.thecroftcockwood.com	GR: SX9754880855	DP: 0 miles
	NT: **DAWLISH**	
	Offers one night stays	
	[8] [🚗] [📶] [🐕]	Other info: 10% Discount on Food at The Anchor Inn & The Ship Cockwood

Self Catering and hostels

NAME	OTHER INFO	
The Mill Cottage Wembury, Plymouth, PL9 0HP ☎ 0348 800 1895 ✉ enquiries@nationaltrust.org.uk 🌐 www.nationaltrust.org.uk/holidays	GR: NT: **WEMBURY** ③	DP: 0 miles **Other info:** Parking nearby. Open all year
Carswell Cottages Carswell Farm, Holberton, PL8 1HH ☎ 01752 830020 ✉ enquiries@carswellcottages.com 🌐 www.carswellcottages.com	GR: 589 477 NT: **NOSS MAYO** ⑤ 🚗 📶 🐕	DP: 0.3 miles Other info:
Mount Folly Farm Mount Folly Farm, Bigbury on Sea, TQ7 4AR ☎ 01548 810267 ✉ info@bigburyholidays.co.uk 🌐 www.bigburyholidays.co.uk	GR: 660 446 NT: **BIGBURY-ON-SEA** Offers one night stays 🚗 🐕	DP: 0.1 miles Other info:
Ocean Reach Bolberry Down, Salcombe, TQ7 3DY ☎ 07718 187469 ✉ oceanreach@outlook.com 🌐 www.oceanreach.eu	GR: NT: **HOPE COVE** ⑦ 🚗 📶 🐕	DP: 0 miles Other info:
Bolberry Farm Cottages Marlborough, Salcombe, TQ7 3DZ ☎ 07718 187469 ✉ info@bolberryfarmcottages.co.uk 🌐 www.bolberryfarmcottages.co.uk	GR: 690 392 NT: **HOPE COVE** ⑦ 🚗 📶 🐕	DP: 1 mile Other info:
Toad Hall Cottages Abbots Quay, Prince of Wales Rd, Kingsbridge, TQ7 1DY ☎ 01548 202020 ✉ property@toadhallcottages.co.uk 🌐 www.toadhallcottages.co.uk	GR: NT: **KINGSBRIDGE**	DP: Other info:
Blackadon Barn Holiday Cottages Bittaford, Ivybridge, PL21 0HB ☎ 01752 897034 ✉ info@blackadonbarns.co.uk 🌐 www.blackadonbarns.co.uk	GR: 665 577 NT: **IVYBRIDGE** 🚗 📶 🐕	DP: 6 miles Other info:
Kittiwake Cottage East Prawle, Kingsbridge, TQ7 2BY ☎ 07980310696 ✉ kittiwakecottage@btinternet.com 🌐 www.kittiwakecottage.com	GR: 781 364 NT: **EAST PRAWLE** ②	DP: 0.5 miles Other info:
Kiln Nook Kiln House, Kiln Lane, Stokenham, Kingsbridge, TQ7 2SQ ☎ 07756 177466 ✉ kilnnookbookings@gmail.com 🌐 www.kilnnook.co.uk	GR: 805 430 NT: **TORCROSS** ① 🚗 📶	DP: 1 mile Other info:
Cofton Holidays Starcross, Dawlish, EX6 8RP ☎ 01626 890111 ✉ mellony@coftonholidays.co.uk 🌐 www.coftonholidays.co.uk	GR: 967 802 NT: **DAWLISH** Offers one night stays 🚗 📶 🐕 🛒	DP: 0.7 miles Other info:

Eat and Drink

NAME	OTHER INFO	
The Old Mill Café Church Road, Wembury, Plymouth, PL9 0HP ☏ 01752 863280 ✉ m1llcafe@btconnect.com ⊕ www.oldmillwembury.co.uk	GR: 520 487	DP: 0 miles
	NT: **PLYMOUTH**	
	🐕	Other info:
The Odd Wheel Knighton Road, Wembury, PL9 0JD ☏ 01752 863052 ✉ theoddwheel@btconnect.com ⊕ www.theoddwheel.co.uk	GR: 527 496	DP: 1 mile
	NT: **WEMBURY**	
	🚗 📶	Other info:
The Cove Café Bar Harbour Lights, Hope Cove, TQ7 3HQ ☏ 01548 561376 ✉ hello@thecovedevon.co.uk ⊕ www.thecovedevon.co.uk	GR: 675 400	DP: 0.1 miles
	NT: **HOPE COVE**	
	🚗 📶 🐕 🍴	Other info:
Queens Arms Slapton Slapton, Kingsbridge, TQ7 2PN ☏ 01548 580800 ✉ queensarms@slapton.org ⊕ www.queensarmsslapton.co.uk/#about	GR: 821 449	DP: 0.5 miles
	NT: **KINGSBRIDGE**	
	🐕 🍴	Other info:
Coast @ Gara Rock East Portlemouth, Salcombe, TQ8 8FA ☏ 01548 845945 ✉ concierge@gararock.com ⊕ www.gararock.com	GR: 752 371	DP: 0.3 miles
	NT: **EAST PORTLEMOUTH**	
	🚗 📶 🐕 🍴	Other info:
The Guardhouse Cafe Berry Head Nature Reserve, Brixham, TQ5 9AW ☏ 01803 855778 ✉ info@guardhousecafe.com ⊕ www.guardhousecafe.com	GR: 943 564	DP: 0 miles
	NT: **BRIXHAM**	
	🚗 📶 🐕	Other info:
Terrace Cafe Bar at Living Coasts Torquay Harbourside, Beacon Quay, Torquay, TQ1 2BG ☏ 01803 202470 ✉ ⊕ www.livingcoasts.org.uk	GR: 918 631	DP: miles
	NT: **TORQUAY**	
	🚗 📶	Other info:
Salty Dog Kiosk Smugglers Lane, Holcombe, EX7 0JL ☏ 07707 923 757 ✉ tq14@icloud.com ⊕ saltydogkiosks.business.site	GR: 957 747	DP: 0 miles
	NT: **TEIGNMOUTH**	
	🚗 📶 🐕	Other info: Special treats menu for doggies
The Strand Cafe 1 Strand, Shaldon, TQ14 0DL ☏ 01626 872624 ✉ info@thestrandcafebistro.co.uk ⊕ www.thestrandcafebistro.co.uk	GR:	DP: 0 miles
	NT: **SHALDON**	
	🐕	Other info:

Campsites and Holiday Parks

NAME	OTHER INFO		
Bolberry House Farm Caravan & Camping Park Bolberry, Marlborough, Kingsbridge, TQ7 3DY 📞 01548 561251 ✉ enquiries@bolberryparks.co.uk 🌐 www.bolberryparks.co.uk	GR: 695 391	DP: 0.25 miles	
	NT: **KINGSBRIDGE**		
			Other info:
Caravan at South Bay Holiday Park St Mary's Rd, Brixham, TQ5 9QW 📞 01626 821221 ✉ hsbarrow@uwclub.net 🌐	GR: 926 548	DP: 0.25 miles	
	NT: **BRIXHAM**		
	Offers one night stays		
			Other info: Prepaid breakfast choice available
Longmeadow Farm Coombe Road, Ringmore, Shaldon, TQ14 0EX 📞 01626 872732 ✉ anne@longmeadowfarm.co.uk 🌐 www.longmeadowfarm.co.uk	GR: 922 721	DP: 0.75 miles	
	NT: **SHALDON**		
	Offers one night stays		
			Other info:

Do

NAME	OTHER INFO		
Wembury Cars 1 Barton Close, Wembury, Plymouth, PL9 0LF 📞 01752 863710 ✉ lorraine.pitcher123@btinternet.com 🌐	GR: 527 494	DP: 1 mile	
	NT: **WEMBURY**		
	Offers one night stays		
			Other info: Local pub & shop nearby
Heart And Sole Wellbeing 3 Beachdown, Challaborough, Bigbury, TQ7 4JB 📞 07876 774397 ✉ sandra@heartandsolewellbeing.co.uk 🌐 www.heartandsolewellbeing.co.uk	GR: 649 449	DP: 0.1 miles	
	NT: **BIGBURY-ON-SEA**		
			Other info:
Paignton Zoo Totnes Road, Paignton, TQ4 7EU 📞 01803 697500 ✉ 🌐 www.paigntonzoo.org.uk	GR: 875 599	DP: 1.5 miles	
	NT: **PAIGNTON**		
			Other info:
Living Coasts Torquay Harbourside, Beacon Quay, Torquay, TQ1 2BG 📞 01803 697500 ✉ marketing.manager@paigntonzoo.org.uk 🌐 www.livingcoasts.org.uk	GR: 918 631	DP: 0 miles	
	NT: **TORQUAY**		
			Other info: Cafe on site

Brownstone Daymark, Orionid Meteor Shower

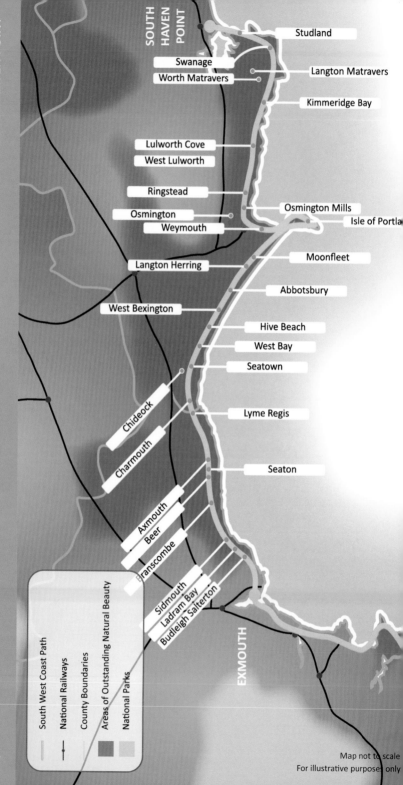

SOUTH HAVEN POINT

Studland

Swanage

Worth Matravers

Langton Matravers

Kimmeridge Bay

Lulworth Cove

West Lulworth

Ringstead

Osmington

Osmington Mills

Weymouth

Isle of Portla

Langton Herring

Moonfleet

Abbotsbury

West Bexington

Hive Beach

West Bay

Seatown

Chideock

Lyme Regis

Charmouth

Seaton

Axmouth

Beer

Branscombe

Sidmouth

Ladram Bay

Budleigh Salterton

EXMOUTH

South West Coast Path

National Railways

County Boundaries

Areas of Outstanding Natural Beauty

National Parks

Map not to scale
For illustrative purposes only

The Jurassic Coast
Exmouth to South Haven Point (Poole Harbour) (Sections 58-70)

Geology is both the curse and the boon of this part of the South West Coast Path. As a curse, the geology means the cliffs are vulnerable to slippage, especially in the Sidmouth area, in the Undercliffs and in West Dorset. This has meant that several diversions, necessary but hardly ideal, have had to be put in place for the Coast Path. However, as a boon, the Jurassic Coast's exposed and accessible layers of geological history have made it a textbook example for a wide range of coastal features. These features are also landscape highlights – the classic red cliffs of East Devon; the undisturbed nature reserve of the Seaton-Lyme Regis Undercliffs; the great shingle bar of Chesil Beach backed by the semi-freshwater lagoon of the Fleet; the fortress-like monolith of the Isle of Portland, jutting into the English Channel; the textbook arch of Durdle Door; the erosion of soft rock once the harder limestone has been broken through forming hollowed-out bays, as at Lulworth Cove; the offshore Purbeck stone stacks at Handfast Point. In addition, the Jurassic Coast contains a number of classic holiday towns; Exmouth, Sidmouth, Lyme Regis, Weymouth and Swanage. This length also contains some taxing gradients for walkers including the climb to the highest point on the south coast of England, Golden Cap, as well as the challenge of the military firing ranges east of Lulworth Cove with its frequent closures.

OS Maps: Landranger 192; Explorer 115

	This Walk	Cumulative	This Walk	Cumulative	Grading	Timing
Ascent	722ft	97,489ft	220m	29,715m	Moderate	3 hours
Distance	5.4mi	519.9mi	8.7km	836.7km		

For detailed directions see our Walking Guide no. 58, Exmouth to Budleigh Salterton.

This is a well-used and popular Section, never far from houses and passing a large caravan site and a golf course on the way. Most of this length is on relatively low cliffs and in the west these give excellent views over the mouth of the Exe and the great sandy bar of Dawlish Warren. Further east, the high point of West Down Beacon gives exceptionally fine panoramic views, while beyond the Beacon the Path becomes more enclosed. It is an easy-going Section of some variety, ideal for those not wishing to explore remote or strenuous lengths.

Directions

A regular bus service links Exmouth and Budleigh Salterton, making this a good bus-walk option. In addition, a summer service links Exmouth with Sandy Bay, approximately mid-way along the section, giving another, shorter bus-walk.

Exmouth has all facilities, including a railway station connecting to Exeter. The Coast Path follows the promenade from the redeveloped docks area at the mouth of the Exe, which is also the ferry landing point. Continue to the cliffs at Orcombe Point then climb the steps and continue on the cliff top, passing the Jurassic Coast marker and on to the Caravan Site at Sandy Bay. Follow the fence line inland of the Straight Point rifle range then climb to the high point at West Down Beacon. The Path then descends, seaward of the golf course though offering relatively few sea views on this stretch. Approaching Budleigh Salterton, a charming and traditional small town, the Path turns inland then almost immediately, at a junction, goes right to descend to the end of the promenade. The shops, pubs and other facilities are immediately inland of the Path, which continues towards the distinctive line of pine trees to the east of the town.

Budleigh Salterton

OS Maps: Landranger 192; Explorer 115

	This Walk	Cumulative	This Walk	Cumulative	Grading	Timing
Ascent	1,037ft	98,526ft	316m	30,031m	Moderate then strenuous	3.5 hours
Distance	7.1mi	527.0mi	11.4km	848.1km		

For detailed directions see our Walking Guide no. 59, Budleigh Salterton to Sidmouth.

Most of this pleasant Section is on relatively low red cliffs with attractive views inland over an undulating pastoral countryside as well as seaward. However, there are contrasts at both ends. The western end skirts the narrow, marsh-fringed estuary of the River Otter while the eastern end includes a wooded cliff top and high cliffs on the appropriately named High Peak and Peak Hill. This is a pleasant and quietly popular Section.

Directions

A regular bus service links Budleigh Salterton and Sidmouth, making a bus-walk a possible.

Budleigh Salterton, a town with something of an olde-world air, has all facilities. The Coast Path goes along the promenade to the car park at the eastern end. Progress east seems tantalisingly close, but the River Otter, with no bridge at its mouth, bars the way. The Path passes through a gate at the rear riverside corner of the car park and follows the riverside path until it meets a road. Turn right and cross the River Otter on the road bridge, then bear right to follow the Path back downriver to the sea.

The Path is clear to the caravan site at Ladram Bay, where there are toilets and seasonal refreshments. Here, descend across a field to the beach access track, going left then immediately right, past a pub and on to climb into woodland at High Peak. Here, the Path goes behind the very top, emerging on a track. Turn right and climb again to the open land at Peak Hill. Follow the Path down the cliff through woodland to a road, turn right then keep right along an old road then onto a large grassy area down to a zigzag Path next to the white Jacob's Ladder. At the bottom follow the seafront path to reach the main esplanade. Sidmouth is an elegant Regency town and has all facilities.

Above Sidmouth

southwestcoastpath.org.uk

OS Maps: Landranger 192; Explorer 115 (most); Explorer 116 (eastern end)

	This Walk	Cumulative	This Walk	Cumulative	Grading	Timing
Ascent	2,408ft	100,934ft	734m	30,765m	Severe then strenuous	5.5 hours
Distance	10.3mi	537.3mi	16.6km	864.7km		

For detailed directions see our Walking Guide no. 60, Sidmouth to Branscombe and Branscombe to Seaton.

This is a Section of lofty cliffs cut by deep and narrow valleys, making for a magnificent coastal landscape but a testing one to walk. In the west the cliffs are characteristically red, but this changes quite abruptly along the length as the Section reaches the most westerly chalk cliffs in England, appropriately bright white. Add an elegant Regency town, a charming picture-postcard village and a quaint fishing town and the result is a length of great attraction.

Directions

A regular bus service links Sidmouth with Seaton, making a bus-walk possible. There are also regular, if less frequent, bus links to Branscombe and Beer along the length giving further options.

The Coast Path passes along the elegant esplanade at Sidmouth to the footbridge over the mouth of the River Sid at the eastern end. Some dramatic cliff falls have occurred just east of Sidmouth and a well-signed diversion is necessary past housing until, at the top of Laskeys Lane, it turns back to the cliff top. A steep climb up Salcombe Hill is soon followed by an equally steep descent and climb through the Salcombe Regis valley. The Path skirts behind the hollow of Lincombe then descends to the beach at Weston Mouth. A short way along the beach the Path leaves to climb steeply back to the cliffs and a good level stretch, which eventually turns inland to meet a track. This descends to Branscombe Mouth, where there are refreshments and toilets. Beyond Branscombe the official Path passes among some holiday chalets then along an undercliff path, with imposing cliffs rearing above, before climbing to the cliff top at Beer Head. These are the most westerly chalk cliffs in England. An alternative route from Branscombe Mouth climbs up the valley side and proceeds directly along the cliff top to Beer Head.

Follow the signed Path from Beer Head, past a caravan site and into the village behind the beach. Beer, an attractive fishing village, has all facilities. Climb the Path on the east side of the beach to the cliff top, descending to a road and down to Seaton Hole. If the tide is low, walk along the beach to the end of the promenade at Seaton. If not, an inland diversion must now be taken. A cliff fall caused by the extreme wet weather in 2012 necessitated permanent closure of the previous Coast Path route. At Seaton Hole turn left on to Old Beer Road and walk approximately 220 yards/200m inland towards Beer. Turn right on a path through woodland to arrive at the B3172 Beer Road and turn right here. After approximately 875 yards/800m, leave Beer Road and take the Path on the right through the Chine and on to the promenade and into Seaton, which has all facilities, including bus services to Exeter and Lyme Regis.

OS Maps: Landranger 193; Explorer 116

	This Walk	Cumulative	This Walk	Cumulative	Grading	Timing
Ascent	1,401ft	102,335ft	427m	31,192m	Moderate	3.5 hours
Distance	7.1mi	544.4mi	11.4km	876.1km		

For detailed directions see our Walking Guide no. 61, Seaton to Lyme Regis.

Some changes have occurred to part of this length following the storms of winter 2013-14. After crossing a golf course then cliff land the route now climbs to a superb viewpoint known as Goat Island, part of the old cliff top which was subject to a massive cliff fall in 1839. From here the path descends into the Axmouth-Lyme Regis Undercliff. This length, a National Nature Reserve, has been undisturbed since that cliff fall and is effectively a wilderness area of virtually virgin woodland and dense scrub, often with an almost eerie character. For most of this part the sea will not be visible. It is an odd and impressive experience, delighting some, but frustrating others.

Directions

Leave Seaton at the east end, using the old concrete bridge to cross the River Axe. Turn inland along the road then turn right up the golf course access road, past the club house then across the fairway to the end of a lane. Turn right off the lane to reach the cliffs, and the Path then rises to the vantage point of Goat Island, with its magnificent views. Continue across the grassy area then follow the Path as it descends through woodland to enter the strange world of the Undercliff.

This old landslip is a National Nature Reserve, being an area of virtual wildlife wilderness. The Path through the Undercliff rarely offers sea views and can feel almost claustrophobic in places. There are no escape routes inland nor safe paths to the sea shore. However, the route is well waymarked and the maps on the Natural England display boards show walkers their exact location; no one should ever feel lost and many find it an exhilarating experience.

Eventually the Path emerges on cliffs and is then waymarked down through woods to arrive adjacent to Lyme Regis's scenic harbour, the Cobb. Lyme Regis is a charming and attractive town and has all facilities.

The Cobb, Lyme Regis

OS Maps: Landranger 193; Explorer 116

	This Walk	Cumulative	This Walk	Cumulative	Grading	Timing
Ascent	3,097ft	105,432ft	944m	32,136m	Moderate then strenuous	3 hours
Distance	10.0mi	554.4mi	16.1km	892.2km		

For detailed directions see our Walking Guide no. 62, Lyme Regis to West Bay.

A major feature of this Section is the large number of cliff slippages caused by a combination of wet weather and geology. This means that the route between Lyme Regis and Charmouth (approximately 3 miles/4.5km) relies on a footpath diversion. However, the remainder of this Section is a superb coastal experience, climbing as it does over the top of Golden Cap, the highest point on the entire south coast of England, with views to match as well as a challenging steep climb!

Directions

A regular bus service between Lyme Regis, Charmouth, Chideock (which is about 0.75 mile/1.25km inland of Seatown) and West Bay makes a variety of bus walks possible.

Lyme Regis to Charmouth

Major diversions have had to be put in place in this Section, especially between Lyme Regis and Charmouth to avoid the cliff falls that have occurred. It looks likely that these diversions will remain in place for 2018. However, for up-to-date details check the Association's website (www.southwestcoastpath.org.uk).

Lyme Regis is a charming and attractive town with all facilities. From the Cobb harbour proceed along the esplanade to the small car park at Cobb Gate and the Millennium Clock Tower: the town centre is on your left. Continue along the new sea wall, passing seaward of the Millennium Theatre for approximately 550 yards/500m, turn up the large flight of steps on the left that lead to Charmouth Road car park. Cross the car park to the main road (A3052), then turn right uphill past the Football Club beyond, which, opposite the cemetery, go through a pedestrian gate to follow the footpath across fields to a lane. Turn left and after 100 yards/90m turn right at a sign through woods to emerge on a road near Timber Hill.

Preferred Diversion, Lyme Regis-Charmouth

Several public footpaths are shown on the Ordnance Survey map seaward of the current Coast Path. These cross The Spittles, Black Ven and the edge of the golf course but are all impassable and closed due to active landslips, which make this a hazardous area. Since the major cliff falls of 2001, this part of the walk has been shown as a 'diversion' in the expectation that the Path could be reinstated along the cliff top. However, the ongoing instability of the cliffs has meant that this has not been possible, and so the Path will continue to be routed inland and across the golf course.

So, once you've re-joined the road, turn right and follow the road uphill for 600 yards/ 550m past the entrance to the Golf Club until you reach a fingerpost pointing the route across the golf course. Follow the Path across the golf course to the woods on the far side. From here there are proposals to change the route on to Charmouth that it is hoped will be implemented in 2018, so check with southwestcoastpath.org.uk/routechanges for latest information and look out for new signage.

The proposed new route will turn right and run along the edge of the golf course before descending into Charmouth. Until this is implemented the Coast Path turns left at this point to run north-east through the woods to re-join the A3052. Turn right to the roundabout then take the road signposted to Charmouth and shortly after the junction take steps on the right to a stile and public footpath. Follow the waymarked direction up the field to the former Lily Farm, now holiday accommodation. Cross a stile, hidden to the right of the farm gate and pass between the buildings and the Dutch barn on the left. After the buildings cross a field to arrive after 25 yards/23m at a tarmac lane (Old Lyme Hill). Turn right and after 90 yards/80m turn left to arrive at Old Lyme Road.

Go left along Old Lyme Road and after 80 yards/70m turn right into Westcliffe Road, which is a public right of way for pedestrians. Descend steeply for 330 yards/300m to a junction with Five Acres. Bear right here and at the end of the cul-de-sac take a footpath going forward into a narrow lane. Shortly it reaches a wider road (Higher Sea Lane). Turn right and continue ahead, ignoring various signs pointing off the lane, continuing round the bend to the west in the lane that rises for some 130 yards/120m to an oak signpost on the left. Here leave the lane through a metal gate to re-join the Coast Path, descending over grassy slopes to Charmouth Beach, with its toilets and refreshments.

Beach route, Lyme Regis to Charmouth

It is possible to walk along the beach between Lyme Regis and Charmouth, but this is not recommended. Mudslides midway along mean that the route is very narrow and only passable at low tide. As such IT SHOULD ONLY BE ATTEMPTED AFTER CHECKING TIDE TABLES AND ON A FALLING TIDE. Many people are cut off or get stuck trying to cross one of the innocuous looking mud flows and have to be rescued.

Coast Path, Charmouth East to Seatown (Chideock)

From the Jurassic Coast Heritage Centre on the seafront at Charmouth (well worth a visit) the route crosses a footbridge and climbs the obvious green path up to Stonebarrow. After a couple of moderate hills, the route starts the long, steep climb to Golden Cap, the highest point on England's south coast, but the climb is rewarding as the views from the top are spectacular. At the top go slightly left to the trig point which then leads to the long and steep descent. Approaching Seatown, the Coast Path detours slightly inland before it emerges at Seatown, which has toilets and a pub. A shop and other facilities are at Chideock, 0.75 mile/1.25km inland.

From Seatown the Coast Path climbs the cliff slope on its way to the high point of Thorncombe Beacon. There is a descent to the little beach at Eype then a further climb and descent to the harbour at West Bay, which has most facilities.

OS Maps: Landranger 193 (western half); Explorer 116 (western half)
Landranger 194 (eastern half); Explorer OL15 (eastern half)

	This Walk	Cumulative	This Walk	Cumulative	Grading	Timing
Ascent	275ft	105,707ft	84m	32,220m	Strenuous then moderate	6.25 hours
Distance	9.3mi	563.7mi	15.0km	907.2km		

For detailed directions see our Walking Guide no. 63, West Bay to Abbotsbury.

From West Bay a sheer red sandstone cliff rises from the sea, looking almost artificial in its straight lines. Then the coastline subsides to a low level and the Coast Path loses its ups and downs. It can still be hard work here though, as the shingle of what is the far western end of Chesil Beach tests the legs.

Directions

A regular bus service links West Bay with Abbotsbury, and also calls at Burton Bradstock along the length of this Section, giving various bus-walk options. A popular circular walk based on Abbotsbury uses the Coast Path as well as the South Dorset Ridgeway.

At West Bay go round the back of the harbour, pass to the right of the church and ahead to the West Bay public house, opposite which is the Coast Path sign pointing to the surprisingly steep cliff. Arriving at Burton Freshwater the Path runs between the caravan park and the beach and is well signed. Following major cliff falls in the summer of 2012 the Coast Path has been reopened along Burton Cliff, although a short inland diversion is necessary around the hotel leading to Burton Beach where there are refreshments and toilets. Further on, the Path passes inland of Burton Mere before coming to West Bexington, where there are toilets and seasonal refreshments.

See Section 71 for details of the alternative Inland Coast Path (South Dorset Ridgeway) between West Bexington and Osmington Mills.

The Coast Path continues along the back of the beach, later passing another car park with toilets and seasonal refreshments and some 200 yards/185m beyond this it turns inland to Abbotsbury. There are alternative routes either going into the village or going south and east of Chapel Hill and missing the village. A permissive Path alternative leaves the Coast Path and leads direct to the famous Swannery. Abbotsbury is a beautiful stone-built village with much of historic interest and most facilities.

Burton Bradstock

OS Maps: Landranger 194; Explorer OL15

	This Walk	Cumulative	This Walk	Cumulative	Grading	Timing
Ascent	955ft	106,662ft	291m	32,511m	Easy. Chesil Beach route strenuous	4 hours official route
Distance	10.9mi	574.6mi	17.5km	924.7km		

For detailed directions see our Walking Guide no. 64, Abbotsbury to Weymouth.

This is an untypical Section of the Coast Path. In the west, there is an inland rural high-level field route, giving views over the unusual feature of Chesil Beach and the landlocked Fleet behind. To the east, the Path runs along the banks of the Fleet, with pleasant views over this attractive feature, but with views of the sea largely cut off by the shingle bank of Chesil Beach. Although never far from houses or roads, this is often a very quiet Section.

Directions

Buses to and from Abbotsbury and Ferry Bridge link at Weymouth for a potential bus-walk.

It is possible to walk direct from the beach near Abbotsbury to Ferry Bridge at Wyke Regis along the length of Chesil Beach. If this is intended, start at the beach at the inland turn (Walk 63) to Abbotsbury, continuing along the beach. However, note that:

1. It is not possible to get off the beach before Ferry Bridge

2. It is extremely hard and slow walking

3. It is necessary to check that firing is not scheduled at the nearby Chickerell Rifle Range; check the web page which is updated monthly – www.gov.uk/government/publications/chickerell-firing-times. Alternatively telephone the Commandant on 01305 831930

4. The beach is closed to visitors from 1st May to 31st August for the bird nesting season

Although the Coast Path does not pass through Abbotsbury most walkers will visit the attractive village and its facilities. From the village leave West Street on the Path going south adjacent to Chapel Lane Stores. Continue on to Nunnery Grove to the signed Coast Path, which now goes inland but is well signed and enjoyable with some excellent views. After Horsepool Farm on the edge of Abbotsbury the Path climbs onto the ridge. After about a mile/1.5km, turn right off the ridge then left after Hodder's Coppice. Cross a minor road then follow the field headland east then south to the north-east corner of Wyke Wood. The Path then heads for the edge of the Fleet – be aware approaching Rodden Hive that the Path suddenly goes through a hedge on the left. From here the Path follows the edge of the Fleet. At Tidmoor Point follow the red and white posts, unless it is necessary to divert inland because of firing. The diversion is well marked. Approaching Wyke Regis there is a minor deviation behind an MOD Bridging Hard, then the Path arrives at the A354 road adjacent to Ferry Bridge, the access for the Isle of Portland at Wyke Regis, a suburb of Weymouth.

OS Maps: Landranger 194; Explorer OL15

	This Walk	Cumulative	This Walk	Cumulative	Grading	Timing
Ascent	1,112ft	107,774ft	339m	32,850m	Moderate	6 hours
Distance	13.0mi	587.6mi	20.9km	945.6km		

For detailed directions see our Walking Guide no. 65, The Isle of Portland.

Portland is different. Different from the rest of Dorset and from the rest of the Coast Path. An almost-island jutting out into the English Channel, joined to the mainland only by the end of Chesil Beach, it has an isolated air. Formed of limestone, it has been extensively quarried and these workings, some still operational, characterise much of the landscape. Elsewhere, former military buildings and those of Verne Prison and the Young Offenders' Institution are prominent. Portland has a rugged beauty and is well worth exploring with superb views and a rich natural and historic heritage.

Directions

Bus routes run the length of Portland in the summer season (June-September) making a variety of bus-walks possible. There is also a regular bus from Weymouth to Portland throughout the year. This Section is, in any event, a circular walk. Check on local bus information.

From Ferry Bridge cross the causeway onto Portland; this is done by simply following the shared footway/cycleway alongside the A354 road or alternatively by crossing the bridge on the A354 to beyond the boatyard. Then walking along the raised bed of the old railway on the eastern bank to near the end of the causeway at the roundabout for the access road to Osprey Quay and here returning to the footway/cycleway. At the southern of the two roundabouts at Victoria Square take the main road south and shortly turn right into Pebble Lane then left just before the public toilets. Continue and bear right up onto the promenade. About half way along, at the floodgates, cut back sharp left then right, following Coast Path signs up a steep tarmac path, past the school and up the steep path in the grass incline to the steps to the terraced path that was once the old road. Bear off right onto the signed Path running between quarry banks and the cliff face, leading to 3 miles/5km of airy cliff-top walking to Portland Bill. Two short lengths of the Coast Path above West Wears have remained closed since January 2013 following movement in the cliffs. Follow the signed diversions as you proceed along the old quarrymen's tramway. At Portland Bill, as well as the lighthouse, are refreshments, toilets and buses.

Continue around the end of the low headland then start northwards, seaward of the wooden chalets, to follow a winding path along the top of low cliffs to join a road above Freshwater Bay after about 1.5 miles/2.5km. Turn right on the road (use the footway on the west side of the road) for 600 yards/550m, past Cheyne Weares car park to a signpost on the right. Follow the zigzag path into the undercliff area and follow the waymarking through disused quarry workings to Church Ope Cove.

Ascend the stepped and signed Path up to Rufus Castle. Here the South West Coast Path also becomes the England Coast Path, the first section of which, from here to Lulworth Cove, was formally opened on 30th June 2012. The signposting now usually indicates simply "Coast Path". Some, but not all, of the improvements to the route that the Association sought on Portland can now be walked and the new route is described below. Unfortunately the major alignment around the north-east corner of Portland was not resolved because of legal complications with Portland Ports plc and security issues.

After Rufus Castle the Coast Path soon joins the track bed of the former Weymouth to Easton railway line. This is then followed northwards for some 1,585 yards/1,450m to a pair of signposts. Here, turn left to follow a rocky path that climbs up the cliffs to what appears to be an isolated chimney seen on the skyline above. At the top turn sharp right along the prison road northwards and through a gap in a high wall. On the right is the Old Engine Shed, soon to be converted into a visitor centre. On reaching a narrow road the official route is signed across the road and takes a route across open ground passing disused quarries to reach the perimeter fence of the Verne prison. However, the Association's preferred route here, which is all on public rights of way, can be followed thus:

At the road turn right and just over the brow of a hill turn left on an access track to compounds. Continue ahead on a grassy path towards a large pinnacle of rock (Nichodemus Knob) after which, at the "rock falls" sign, bear left steeply up onto the higher escarpment, heading for a large communications mast. At the high wire perimeter fence turn left and follow it along then round to the right, to reach the south entrance to Verne Prison. Here rejoin the route of the England Coast Path.

Take a path through a little gap to the left of the entrance, passing beside railings and down steep steps. Bear right along a path that traverses under the grassy banks.

The Path drops downhill towards houses to a waymark post. Ignore the left fork and continue on the level on a grass path which then passes through an underpass below a road. Descend steeply towards Castletown down the Merchant's Incline (a former quarry tramway), crossing two footpaths and a road. Pass under a footbridge and through another underpass to reach an access road and turn left to a roundabout.

Continue ahead for some 30 yards/27m and then cross to turn right down Liberty Road, signposted to Portland Castle. Go past the castle entrance to the car park and turn right towards the harbour, heading for five black posts. Here join the footway/cycleway to follow the harbour-side to the Sailing Academy, the venue of the sailing events at the 2012 Olympics. Continue on the footway/cycleway to reach the roundabout on the A354 road. From here follow the former railway trackbed to the boatyard before the bridge over the mouth of the Fleet and follow the footway alongside the road to Ferry Bridge.

View to Portland

southwestcoastpath.org.uk

OS Maps: Landranger 194; Explorer OL15

	This Walk	Cumulative	This Walk	Cumulative	Grading	Timing
Ascent	2,385ft	110,159ft	727m	33,577m	Easy to moderate to strenuous	6.25 hours
Distance	14.4mi	602.0mi	23.2km	968.8km		

For detailed directions see our Walking Guide no. 66, Weymouth to Lulworth Cove.

This section is part of the first section of the England Coast Path. The signposting generally only refers to "Coast Path".

The western part of this Section is a well-trodden walk through the seaside town of Weymouth with its working harbour, sandy beach and attractive Georgian sea front. East of the town is a length of relatively low cliffs but then at White Nothe, two thirds of the way along the section, the coastal geology changes. East of here is a rollercoaster of often sheer white cliffs, the length punctuated by the iconic landmarks of Durdle Door and Lulworth Cove. Both ends of this Section are busy, but in the centre is an often quiet and remote length.

Directions

A bus service from Weymouth to Osmington (and on to Wool) enables access to the Coast Path mid-way along the Section, allowing some bus-walk options.

From Ferry Bridge the coast path follows the foot/cycle path on the route of the old Weymouth to Portland railway (the Rodwell Trail) and passes inland of the sailing centre. Shortly afterwards follow the Coast Path signs and bear off right and then left to walk up the road (old castle road), passing Sandsfoot Gardens and café on your right. Turn right into Belle Vue Road. At the end of Belle Vue Road turn right into Redcliff View then turn left onto the signed path across a grassed area, passing to the left of the Portland Stone monument erected in memory of Thomas Fowell Buxton (1786-1845), Abolitionist & Social Reformer. Follow the Path to the right of the housing estate, cross the pedestrian bridge over Newtons Road at Newtons Cove and follow the Path to and through Nothe Gardens towards Nothe Fort. (Alternatively, for a route closer to the sea turn right down the steps just beyond the seasonal ice cream kiosk and follow the lower path, Jubilee Walk.)

Before reaching the fort take the signed path left past the public conveniences. Cross the fort access road to the foot path and follow the signed path left until you reach steps on your right heading down to Weymouth harbourside. Turn left at the foot of the steps. There is a seasonal ferry (rowing boat) which crosses the harbour by Weymouth Sailing Club. If you don't take the ferry, walk along the harbour and cross the Town Bridge (a lifting bridge which opens at set times of the day to give access to Weymouth Marina). Take the steps at the end of the bridge down to the other side of the harbour to walk towards the Pavilion Theatre. Before reaching the Pavilion turn off left to follow the Esplanade along Weymouth's sea front to reach Overcombe. Here you leave the beach behind. Walk up the minor road towards Bowleaze Cove. After passing the Spyglass Inn the route bears right to cross the crest of the grassed public open space to reach the Beachside Centre at Bowleaze Cove. Follow the signed path through the Beachside Leisure Centre. The Path passes to the right of the Riviera Hotel and then on to Redcliff Point. The Path skirts around an education and adventure centre at Osmington and then goes on to Osmington Mills

See Section 71 for details of the alternative Inland Coast Path (South Dorset Ridgeway) between West Bexington and Osmington Mills.

At Osmington Mills turn right and walk down the road to the Smugglers Inn. The Path goes through the pub garden, across a bridge in front of the pub and then round to the back of the pub where the Path crosses a field and passes through an area of scrub and then along the cliffs towards Ringstead. After walking through a wooded area, you reach Ringstead.

At Ringstead follow the graveled track in front of some houses, then bear left on the tarmac road. Turn right just before the car park and café and toilets (both seasonal). Follow the Path towards White Nothe. Shortly after the church (St Catherine's By the Sea) at Holworth the official path goes straight on, forming two sides of a triangle. (The former path bears off to the right and is still useable, but it can become muddy in wet weather.) At the top of a short incline turn right to continue to follow the Coast Path, signed White Nothe.

Turn left through a kissing gate into a field. Follow the Path and bear right through scrub and up a series of steps. Continue on to White Nothe where you pass in front of the former coastguard cottages. From here follow the Path along the cliffs towards Durdle Door. The route is straightforward to follow but does involve some particularly severe gradients.

Just below the car park and caravan park at Durdle Door turn right at the bridle gate and follow the Path to Lulworth Cove, descending a stone pitched path into the car park. Lulworth Cove has toilets and refreshments and most facilities are found here or at West Lulworth, a little way inland.

Walk to the left of the Visitor Centre and then right to walk round the back of the Visitor Centre. At a junction of roads take the Path leading to Stair Hole, with its spectacular upturned rock formations, and then on to the Commemorative Stone marking the inauguration of the Jurassic Coast as a World Heritage Site. Walk down a series of steps, turning left at the Boat Shed Café, to the shore of the Cove itself.

Lulworth Bay

OS Maps: Landranger 194 (most); Landranger 195 (eastern end); Explorer OL15

	This Walk	Cumulative	This Walk	Cumulative	Grading	Timing
Ascent	2,002ft	112,161ft	610m	34,187m	Severe	4 hours
Distance	7.1mi	609.1mi	11.4km	980.2km		

For detailed directions see our Walking Guide no. 67, Lulworth to Kimmeridge.

The coast of this Section is of geological interest and importance, largely formed by lines of relatively hard limestone having been breached at intervals to form coves and bays as the sea erodes the softer rocks behind. The result is a dramatic coastline of white cliffs and darker coloured coves, some prominent headlands and a succession of extremely steep slopes. Inland, the landscape of the military ranges has been unchanged by farming for some seventy years, though it is perhaps a little too obviously military in a few places.

Directions

Lulworth Cove and Kimmeridge village (inland from Kimmeridge Bay) have extremely limited bus services to Wareham, Corfe Castle and Swanage, which could provide a bus-walk option.

IMPORTANT: Note that this Section passes through the Lulworth Army Firing Ranges. Before deciding to walk this Section, check that the Ranges are open. PLEASE BE AWARE THE OFFICIAL COAST PATH FOR THIS SECTION MAY BE CLOSED TO WALKERS DURING THE WEEK. However most weekends and during school holidays it is normally open, but please read the section below to check the dates when walkers are allowed access along the official Coast Path.

The Lulworth Range walks, including the Coast Path between Lulworth Cove and Kimmeridge Bay, plus access to Tyneham village, are open to the public every weekend.

LULWORTH RANGE WALKS AND TYNEHAM VILLAGE OPENING TIMES 2018

The Lulworth Range walks and Tyneham Village are open to the public every weekend, except for the following: • 13 and 14 January 2018 • 24 and 25 February 2018 • 17 and 18 March 2018 • 13 and 14 October 2018 • 10 and 11 November 2018 • 8 and 9 December 2018

In addition to the weekends, they are open every day during the following periods; all dates are inclusive:

- Easter 2018 - 30 March 2018 to 15 April 2018
- Spring Break 2018 - 26 May 2018 to 3 June 2018
- Summer 2018 - 27 July to 2 September 2018
- Christmas 2018 - 22 December 2018 to 7 January 2019

The exhibitions in Tyneham school and Tyneham church are open from 10am until 4pm.

When no firing is taking place, the gates to the Range Walks are opened as near to 9am on the Saturday morning as possible and remain open until 8am on the Monday morning.

The Elmes Grove gate that allows vehicle access to Tyneham is opened at 9am daily when no firing is taking place and is closed at dusk each evening.

For further information on Lulworth ranges firing times, phone 01929 404816

The abandoned village and its historical exhibition are 0.5 mile/800m inland of the Coast Path, and worth the diversion. The gates to the walks are opened as near to 9am on the Saturday morning as possible and remain open until 08.00 on the Monday morning when open only at weekends. The gate to Tyneham is locked each night at dusk. For any further information telephone 01929 404819 or 01929 404712, 8am-5pm, Monday to Friday.

If the Ranges are closed, it is recommended that schedules are re-arranged so that the Coast Path is walked when open. If, however, this is not possible, two alternative inland diversions are shown below. If using these routes you are strongly advised to carry OS 1:25,000 Explorer Map OL15 (Purbeck and South Dorset).

Coast Path – Lulworth Cove – Kimmeridge Bay

The eastbound Coast Path from Lulworth Cove no longer leaves from behind the café adjacent to the beach – both the café and the adjacent cliffs were destroyed in the storms of the winter of 2013-14. This resulted in closure of the original path. Take the road inland up through the village and after passing the entrance to the main car park and café, take the narrow higher road northward past the properties on the east side of the road. After the last house take a signed footpath eastwards steeply uphill to join a path southwards that contours around the hill to re-join the old Coast Path route as it climbs around the cliff edge at the top of the cove. The Coast Path then turns south-eastwards and descends to the east side of the cove. As an alternative, tide permitting, walking the beach avoids considerable ascent and descent. At most states of the tide this is possible. Then take the Path going up from the far side of the cove beach to re-join the Coast Path which rises steeply on the eastward cliff edge to the beginning of the Army Ranges. The route onward is straightforward – just follow the yellow topped posts through the ranges to arrive at Kimmeridge Bay. Here are toilets and seasonal refreshments (or all year refreshments in the village 0.6 mile/1km to the north). There is a new museum in Kimmeridge which is worth visiting – https://jurassiccoast.org/ discovering/the-etches-collection. Note that currently there is no access to the 'Fossil Forest' (near Lulworth Cove) due to a small cliff collapse. The MOD are expected to repair this early in 2018.

If Ranges Closed – Alternative Option 1 (13.5 miles/22.0km)

This route is safer and quieter but more strenuous than Option 2; it uses mainly rights of way plus some permissive paths. It should be noted that this route is not specifically signed or waymarked as an official alternative to the Coast Path.

Leave Lulworth Cove as described above for the Coast Path and where the revised route of the Coast Path leaves to the east continue ahead on a footpath parallel to the B3070 road. At the end of the footpath return to the road and follow it inland, forking right, before taking the next road on the left just after a bus shelter (GR 825 807). In 100 yards/90m turn right on to a footpath that heads uphill for 0.75 mile/1.2km. At the second junction of paths turn right (east) and after 100 yards/90m turn left (north) to pass Belhuish Coppice and Belhuish Farm. On reaching the B3071 road at GR835 832 cross the road and take the track opposite. Ignore the first path junction to the north-east and continue downhill to the eastern boundary of Burngate Wood (GR 845 828).

Turn north-east on a permissive path (blue) past Park Lodge and go across the road at GR 855 832 onto a bridleway. Continue along the bridleway for just over 2 miles/3.4km to GR 866 856 to join a minor road from Highwood veering north and later north-east to meet an east-west road at GR 871 861. Walk east along the road then fork right (signposted Stoborough) at GR 883 856. Go over the crossroads (seat) with the B3070 road at GR 886 855 (*Route Option 2 joins this route at this location) and walk east for a further 1.5 miles/2.5km along Holme Lane to GR 909 854 (about 330 yards/300m before railway underbridge) and turn southwards onto diverted Doreys Farm bridleway (see Option 1A below), which is followed for 1.25 miles/2.1km before turning right onto Creech Road.

Turn right and in 0.9 miles/1.5km after Creech Grange the road climbs steeply for 0.6 miles/1.0km to the Steeple Viewpoint car park. Just before the car park turn left at GR 905 817 on a bridleway that falls steeply southwards to re-join the same road. As the road levels out, at a left hand bend at GR 907 812, take the bridleway/access road ahead that leads south through Steeple Leaze Farm. About 200 yards/185m south of the farm take the narrow footpath that heads up steeply south through woods to a bridleway on the ridge. Turn left through a gate and look for a narrow path on the right raking steeply downhill and then across three fields towards the coast ahead and Kimmeridge Bay, where the Coast Path is joined at a T-junction.

Option 1A (This avoids 0.6 miles/1.0km of road walking.)

On Doreys Farm bridleway (see above), after emerging from Bridewell Plantation (GR 914 839), (where a fine house comes into view through trees on the left), go through the first field gate on the right onto the east side of Grange Heath. Initially the route is indistinct and the ground can be wet in and after inclement weather. However, head south-west across the heath and in some 160 yards/146m a good gravel path will be found that winds its way across Grange Heath. Although this is described as a permissive path on some maps legal access is as shown, as this area is designated as Access Land. Follow the path south-west across the heath to join a bridleway that runs south-east passing a farm to join Creech Road by a telephone box. Turn right on the road and in 0.3 miles/0.5km pass Creech Grange and then follow the details set out in the final paragraph of Option 1 above.

If Ranges Closed – Alternative Option 2 (12 miles/19km)

This option is mainly road walking, and care is needed on narrow bends. Leave the Cove to West Lulworth on the B3070, then turn right to East Lulworth and beyond, keeping to the B3070 for some 3 miles/5km to GR 886 855. Here turn right along Holme Lane to GR 911 854. From here, follow the route described from (*) in Option 1 above.

OS Maps: Landranger 195; Explorer OL15

	This Walk	Cumulative	This Walk	Cumulative	Grading	Timing
Ascent	1,597ft	113,758ft	487m	34,674m	Strenuous	3.25 hours
Distance	7.1mi	616.2mi	11.4km	991.7km		

For detailed directions see our Walking Guide no. 68, Kimmeridge to Worth Matravers.

This section mostly hugs the coast running along high cliff tops. Because of the Kimmeridge Clays that are a feature of this section of the coast, in places the Path can be claggy and slippery after wet weather. There is a particularly steep cliff at Houns-Tout. Towards the eastern end, this length is dominated by St Aldhelm's Head, a flat-topped headland surmounted by an old chapel, which gives extensive views. This is a tough Section with a remote character.

Directions

Bus-walks are not easily undertaken on this Section. Circular walks using the Coast Path, based on inland villages such as Kimmeridge or Kingston, are possible.

The Coast Path from Kimmeridge Bay eastwards is straightforward, although care may be needed where small lengths have slipped, cracked or may be close to the cliff top. Just beyond Kimmeridge the Clavell Tower has been relocated 27 yards/25m inland and an improved Coast Path installed. There is a very steep climb to Houns-Tout and the descent beyond turns inland to avoid dangerous terrain at Chapman's Pool. Look out for a unique stone block sign pointing the way to Chapman's Pool at the bottom of the descent. Beyond Chapman's Pool the route climbs out round St Aldhelm's Head, with excellent coastal views west, then descends to old quarries at Winspit. (For those aiming to end at Worth Matravers, which is about a mile/1.6km inland, a path heads inland at the valley bottom at Winspit. The village has a pub, shop and café.)

Durdle Door

OS Maps: Landranger 195; Explorer OL15

	This Walk	Cumulative	This Walk	Cumulative	Grading	Timing
Ascent	657ft	114,415ft	200m	34,874m	Severe then Moderate	4 hours
Distance	6.5mi	622.7mi	10.5km	1,002.1km		

For detailed directions see our Walking Guide no. 69, Worth Matravers to Swanage.

The western part of this Section is dominated by St Aldhelm's Head, a flat-topped headland of limestone surmounted by an old chapel. There are extensive views, especially along the coast to the west. Leaving the valley at Winspit the cliffs become increasingly marked by the remains of old small-scale quarrying activity. The route then passes through the Country Park at Durlston Head before rounding the headland to enter Swanage.

Directions

Numerous footpaths cross the cliffs to the Coast Path from the outskirts of Swanage and the inland village of Langton Matravers. This allows for bus-walks which combine these link paths with the Coast Path.

(For those starting in Worth Matravers village, walk past the cottages in London Row then follow the Path over a field to the track which leads down the valley to Winspit Quarry on the Coast Path.)

From Winspit there is a fine high level walk to Durlston Head. Signing in Durlston Country Park is limited; keep on the low level path all the way round Durlston Head then, coming up on the north side take the second turning right (the first is a cul-de-sac to a quarry). Durlston Castle has now been converted to a Jurassic Coast Gateway Centre and includes refreshment facilities.

After leaving Durlston Castle follow a broad stony path north through the woods for some 760 yards/700m to a barrier and sign. From here there is a permanent diversion following a cliff fall. Turn left on a good path for some 125 yards/115m to reach Durlston Road at a gate. Turn right and in 185 yards/170m turn right again into Belle Vue Road. Follow the road north-eastwards to the grassed open space leading to Peveril Point. In bad weather or at high tides use the roadway and then down to the footpath at the end of the coastal buildings, otherwise use the foreshore. Continue along Swanage's sea front promenade. Swanage has all facilities.

Rest and Admire between Tilly Whim and Swanage

OS Maps: Landranger 195; Explorer OL15

	This Walk	Cumulative	This Walk	Cumulative	Grading	Timing
Ascent	492ft	114,907ft	150m	35,024m	Moderate	3.5 hours
Distance	7.5mi	630.2mi	12.1km	1,014.2km		

For detailed directions see our Walking Guide no. 70, Swanage to South Haven Point.

This is an excellent and scenic Section. The southern, Swanage end comprises increasingly high cliffs, culminating in the length between Ballard Point and Handfast Point, with its offshore stacks. This is an exhilarating length with superb views over Poole Bay to Bournemouth and across the Solent to the matching cliffs of the Needles on the Isle of Wight. The northern end passes along a long sandy beach before arriving at the mouth of Poole Harbour, an enormous enclosed water area and the second largest natural harbour in the world.

Directions

A regular bus service, half hourly in summer and hourly in winter, links Swanage with South Haven Point, making a bus-walk a good option. There are also popular local circuits using the Coast Path in the Swanage-Ballard Down-Studland area.

Swanage has all facilities. The Coast Path passes along the town's sea front, following the main road (Ulwell Road) at the north end by the telephone box where it bears left and on ahead into Redcliff Road at a one-way system. At a shop and post-box turn sharp right into Ballard Way – do not be put off by "Private Estate" signs. Continue forward into the chalet estate and follow signs for the Coast Path, to emerge on a grassed area on the cliff edge. However, from the sea front road, except at very high tides or in severe weather it is possible to keep along the narrow promenade then 200 yards/185m along the beach turn up some rough steps to re-join the official route in a little valley.

The Path climbs out to Ballard Down, then the obvious high-level route continues out to Handfast Point and the much-photographed rocks of Old Harry before turning west towards Studland. Studland has toilets and refreshments. For the pub turn up the road from the toilets, otherwise turn right (east) on the outskirts of the village along the signed stony path to South Beach. On reaching the shore, turn left (north) along a terrace in front of beach huts to a seasonal cafe. The route ahead was diverted in 2013 inland up a track to join the road by the public toilets. Turn right here past the pub and right again to re-join the Coast Path above the beach huts, following the cliff edge past Fort Henry to join the Middle Beach access road by a barrier. Turn sharp right down to the beach then left by another café. During periods of high tides this part of Middle Beach may become impassable but there is an alternative route through the car park and down some steps behind the beach huts.

The final 2.6 miles/4.3km are on the sandy beach. Note that further along this beach a length is used by naturists – do not be surprised if nobody else is wearing clothes! There is an alternative, the Heather Walk, through the dunes, marked by yellow-topped posts, but the soft sand is tiring walking and part of the naturist area is still visible. The beach route curves round to the point at the mouth of Poole Harbour. This is South Haven Point, the end (or beginning) of the Coast Path, with an impressive commemorative marker. A ferry links the Point with Sandbanks on the opposite shore, which is linked to Poole and Bournemouth.

The ferry operates all year daily every 20 minutes, from Shell Bay (South Haven Point) 7.10am to 11.10pm; from Sandbanks 7am to 11pm; Christmas Day every half hour from 8am to 6.10pm – telephone 01929 450203; website www.sandbanksferry.co.uk.

Note that the ferry is usually scheduled to undergo maintenance during late October or November and may be closed for approximately four weeks. If you intend to use the ferry at this time check the Association's website under Path News or the ferry company's website above. For ferry details see page 19.

Postscript

For those who have been with us all the way from Minehead, be it in one go or in bits and pieces over a period, a final few words seem appropriate. Alfred Wainwright, at the end of his work on the Pennine Way, said; "You have completed a mission and satisfied an ambition. You have walked the Pennine Way, as you have dreamed of doing. This will be a very satisfying moment in your life. You will be tired and hungry and travel stained. But you will feel great, just great." Just substitute the South West Coast Path for the Pennine Way and Wainwright's words will doubtless ring true. You will be glad and proud that you have walked and finished Britain's longest and finest footpath. As Wainwright said of the Pennine Way, it's a longer step than most take in their lifetime!

Golden Cap

OS Maps: Landranger 194; Explorer OL15

	This Walk	This Walk	Grading	Timing
Ascent	2,290ft	698m	Moderate	8 hours
Distance	17.1mi	27.5km		

For detailed directions see our South Dorset Ridgeway West Bexington to Osmington Mills Walking Guide.

This is a very scenic walk, parallel to the coast and a varying distance inland. For most of its length quite extensive coastal views are obtained beyond a green and rural foreground. Substantial lengths follow chalk ridges and these give impressive views north as well. Coastal features such as Portland and Chesil Beach are clearly seen, as are the flanks of the enormous Iron Age Maiden Castle inland. This is a quiet route, often feeling quite remote, and with usually no refreshments on its length it requires preparation. It is, nevertheless, a superb experience.

Directions

Bus services link both ends, Swyre (for West Bexington) and Osmington, with Weymouth, making a bus-walk possible, especially using Weymouth as a base.

The Dorset element of the Coast Path is unique in having an official alternative route for part of its length. This was often referred to by the apparently contradictory name of the "Inland Coast Path". It is, however, now known as the South Dorset Ridgeway (SDR) and the signposting now uses that name almost throughout. The waymarking has also been replaced and incorporates the name of the South Dorset Ridgeway. The length of the Section, and the fact that the two ends may be reached by bus from Weymouth, make it an ideal long day's walk. However, be aware that other than one seasonal mobile refreshment van if the timing is right, no facilities are found anywhere along the route other than at the two ends, so it is necessary to be well prepared. A detailed route description is given below.

Leave West Bexington car park by the milestone marked "South Dorset Ridgeway Osmington Mills 17" and turn inland up the road. Where the road bears left continue forward up the stony track, signposted SDR.

Near the top of the hill take the right hand fork signed "5¾ Hardy Monument". Before reaching the layby on the B3157 road there is a bench from which there is a panoramic view of the coast. At the layby go over the stile to the left of the field gate and follow the Path to reach the Limekiln. At the Limekiln bear left following the signed path. After passing through a pedestrian gate go straight ahead (rather than bearing off to the left and up to the signpost just visible in the distance). This takes you past a footpath off to the right signed "East Bexington & Beach 1", should you wish to make a detour. If not follow the signed SDR to reach a National Trust sign for Tulk's Hill adjacent to a kissing gate and field gate alongside the B3157. This time cross the road and go over the style, signposted "Hardy Monument 4".

Follow the Path and a series of steps through the Abbotsbury Castle prehistoric hill fort, passing the trig point with superb views in all directions, including Hardy Monument in the distance. At the end of the hill fort go through a kissing gate and follow the Path

southwestcoastpath.org.uk

down to and across a minor road. Go through a metal pedestrian gate to follow the Path in an easterly direction along the ridge of Wears Hill and the Crest of White Hill, following the signed path. Be careful not to follow any signs indicating routes down to the village of Abbotsbury in the valley below and its adjacent hilltop chapel. At the east end of White Hill bear north-east as signed and leave the field in the north-east corner through a gate on to a minor road. Continue north-east along this road for some 50 yards/46m and then turn right as signposted.

Follow the narrow and rough bridleway along the wire fence above the scrub to a path junction; where the bridleway bears right take the yellow waymarked footpath to the left and cross a stile. At the end of this short section take a headland path north-east. At the far side of the field the track then leads approximately 50 yards/46m to a further gate with a stile and waymark. Immediately adjacent to this gate is a prehistoric stone circle, a scheduled ancient monument. Continue forward on the track, leaving a small wood to the left, to reach the road between Portesham and Winterbourne Steepleton. Turn left along the road for about 60 yards/55m and then turn right over a stile into a field, signed "Hardy Monument". Continue eastwards through four fields. At a small wooded area before Black Down Barn (ruin) turn north at a signpost to Hardy Monument. Climb through the woods to the recently renovated monument. In season it may be possible to find a mobile refreshment van here.

To continue find a roadside signpost 30yards/32m east of the car park entrance. Cross the road and descend eastward on a narrow path. Reaching the same road again, ignore the signpost "Bridleway to Coast Path" and the track opposite and turn left along the road, then in another 30 yards/32m turn right, signposted "Restricted Byway" with a Jubilee Trail disc.

Now there is a good ridgeway path for some 3 miles/4.8km, with excellent views to seaward. At a point some 550 yards/500m after passing under the second set of HV power lines take the gate north of a large tumulus to stay on the north side of the fence running along the ridge. On reaching the B3159 road, marked by the Borough of Weymouth boundary stone, continue across as signposted and towards the A354 road. Cross the bridge over the A354 and follow the signed path alongside the A354 until it bears off to the left towards Bincombe Down.

Continue eastwards, then before the farm, with its adjacent radio mast, take care to go through the gate on the right, marked with a blue arrow. After crossing the field, leaving two tumuli on the left, reach a metaled road and turn right. At the junction at the corner of Came Wood turn right at the signpost "Bridleway to Bincombe". At the end of the Path join a metaled lane and at the road junction turn left, signposted "South Dorset Ridgeway".

Drop down the road into the village of Bincombe and where the road turns right take the track forward leaving the small church on the right. Where the Path splits take the left-hand fork, marked with a blue arrow and acorn. After the overhead HV power lines, pass through a small signposted wooden gate and then proceed forward through one field, into the next to a footpath sign. Here turn left and there is a choice of routes for the next couple of hundred yards/metres.

For the best option, at a waymark post turn sharp right down a steep grassy slope to a stile at a road ahead. Cross the road to go over another stile to follow a grassy path that contours around the south and east sides of Green Hill. On reaching a road at a gate and stile turn left and in 50 yards/46m turn right through a gate signposted "Osmington 2¾".

The Path is now easy to follow with extensive views to seaward over Weymouth and Portland. On passing a ruined building on the left the route reaches a broad track; here turn right, signposted "Osmington" and after about 200 yards/185m go through a gate as signposted. Shortly afterwards pass a trig point on the right and at the next field gate bear left and follow the field boundary along White Horse Hill. Just beyond the next gate fork right, signposted "For Osmington". Warning: the Path leading into Osmington can be difficult to negotiate after heavy rainfall. An alternative is to take one of the signposted routes to Sutton Poyntz and follow the valley route to Osmington.

Descend to Osmington and follow the signs through the village. On reaching the main road (A354 to Weymouth) near the Sly Fox Inn turn left and in about 250 yards/230m turn right at a signpost, over a stile and footbridge. Follow the field boundary on the left through two fields – at the top look back to see the Hardy Monument in the distance and the White Horse on the hillside. Go over the stile to the footpath sign, then turn half right to cross the field at an angle to a further stile. Cross it and turn left along the hedge side to the bottom. At the end of the field there is a very short length of enclosed footpath to the road; turn right along it descending to Osmington Mills.

Towards Osmington Mills

If you enjoy sleeping, eating or drinking at any business on the Path please suggest they join us as Business Members so that we can share their brilliance!

The businesses listed here are all supporters of the South West Coast Path Association, they have joined as business members and it would be great if you could show your support for them too. In addition, businesses are listed with more details on our website: www.southwestcoastpath.org.uk Find them through our walk finder or our accommodation finder tools.

KEY:

GR Grid Reference
DP Distance from the Path
NT Nearest Town

🐕 Dogs Welcome
🍴 Evening Meal Available
3 Number Of Rooms

🛒 Grocery Shop On Site
📶 Wifi
🚗 Parking

Bed & Breakfast and Hotels

NAME	OTHER INFO
Quentance Farm Salterton Road, Exmouth, EX8 5BW ☎ 01395 442733 ✉ palleandrose@hotmail.com 🌐 www.quentancefarm.co.uk	GR: 036 820 DP: 1.75miles NT: **EXMOUTH** Offers one night stays 🚗 📶 🐕 Other info:
Southcombe Guest House Vicarage Road, Sidmouth, EX10 8UQ ☎ 01395 513861 ✉ southcombeguesthouse@gmail.com 🌐 www.southcombeguesthouse.co.uk	GR: 127 880 DP: 0 miles NT: **SIDMOUTH** Offers one night stays 8 🚗 📶 🐕 🍴 Other info:
Westleigh Bed & Breakfast Fore street, Beer, Seaton, EX12 3EQ ☎ 01297 23267 ✉ info@westleighbeer.co.uk 🌐 www.westleighbeer.co.uk	GR: 229 892 DP: 0 miles NT: **SEATON** Offers one night stays 2 🚗 📶 🐕 🍴 Other info:
Bay Tree House 11 Seafield Road, Seaton, EX12 2QS ☎ 01297 21966 ✉ info@baytreedevon.co.uk 🌐 www.baytreedevon.co.uk	GR: 242 900 DP: 0.2 miles NT: **SEATON** 5 🚗 📶 Other info:
Beachcroft B&B Burrow Road, Seaton, EX12 2NF ☎ 01297 599022 ✉ bookings@beachcroftseaton.co.uk 🌐 www.beachcroftseaton.co.uk	GR: 249 899 DP: 0.05 miles NT: **SEATON** Offers one night stays 3 🚗 📶 Other info:
Higher Bruckland Farm Musbury, Axminster, EX13 8SU ☎ 01297 552371 ✉ sandie.holmes@btconnect.com 🌐 www.higherbruckland.co.uk	GR: 283 932 DP: 4 miles NT: **LYME REGIS** Offers one night stays 3 🚗 📶 🐕 🍴 Other info:
Westley B&B Lyme Road, Uplyme, Lyme Regis, DT7 3UY ☎ 01297 445104 ✉ westleybandb@btinternet.com 🌐 www.westleybedandbreakfast.wordpress.com	GR: 324 934 DP: 1 miles NT: **LYME REGIS** Offers one night stays 3 🚗 📶 Other info: Single occupancy in double/twin room available

NAME	OTHER INFO
Lucerne View Road, Lyme Regis, DT7 3AA ☎ 01297 443752 ✉ lucernelyme@btopenworld.com 🌐 www.lucernelyme.co.uk	GR: 339 923　DP: 0.25 miles NT: **LYME REGIS** Offers one night stays 4 �car 📶　Other info: Holiday Apartment available weekly lets
Chideock House Main Street, Chideock, DT6 6JN ☎ 01297 489242 ✉ annachideockhouse@yahoo.co.uk 🌐 www.chideockhouse.co.uk	GR: 426 927　DP: 0.75 miles NT: **CHIDEOCK** Offers one night stays 3 🚗 📶 🐕　Other info:
Warren House Main Street, Chideock, DT6 6JW ☎ 01297 489996 ✉ stay@warrenhousechideock.co.uk 🌐 www.warrenhousechideock.co.uk	GR: 421 928　DP: 0.7 miles NT: **CHIDEOCK** 4 🚗 📶　Other info:
Cliff Cottage B&B West Cliff, West Bay, Bridport, DT6 4HS ☎ 07791373419 ✉ info@cliffcottagedorset.co.uk 🌐 www.cliffcottagedorset.co.uk	GR: 456 910　DP: 0 miles NT: **WEST BAY** Offers one night stays 3 🚗 📶　Other info:
Eype's Mouth Country Hotel Eype, Bridport, DT6 6AL ☎ 01308 423300 ✉ info@eypesmouthhotel.co.uk 🌐 www.eypesmouthhotel.co.uk	GR: 448 913　DP: 0.25 miles NT: **WEST BAY** Offers one night stays 17 🚗 📶 🍴　Other info:
Broadlands B&B Chideock, Bridport, DT6 6HX ☎ 01297 489543 ✉ tuckfamily@btinternet.com 🌐 www.broadlandschideock.co.uk	GR: 427 927　DP: 1 mile NT: **BRIDPORT** Offers one night stays 1 🚗 📶　Other info:
Southfield B&B Marsh Gate, Burton Road, Bridport, DT6 4JB ☎ 01308 458910 ✉ angela@southfield-westbay.co.uk 🌐 www.southfield-westbay.co.uk	GR: 466 913　DP: 0.5 miles NT: **BRIDPORT** 🐕 🍴　Other info:
Number Five B&B 5 Church Street, Abbotsbury, DT3 4JT ☎ 01305 871882 ✉ candcrawlings@gmail.com 🌐 www.abbotsbury.co.uk/number-five	GR: 578 851　DP: 0.15 miles NT: **BRIDPORT** Offers one night stays 1 🚗 📶 🐕　Other info:
The Seaside Boarding House Cliff Road, Burton Bradstock, DT6 4RB ☎ 01305 897205 ✉ info@theseasideboardinghouse.com 🌐 www.theseasideboardinghouse.com	GR: 489 888　DP: 0.1 miles NT: **BURTON BRADSTOCK** Offers one night stays 9 🚗 📶 🐕 🍴　Other info: Hotel, restaurant and bar
Cowards Lake Farmhouse B&B 13 West Street, Abbotsbury, DT3 4JT ☎ 01305 871421 ✉ cowards-lakebandb@btconnect.com 🌐 www.abbotsbury.co.uk/cowardslake	GR: 571 853　DP: 0.33 miles NT: **ABBOTSBURY** Offers one night stays 2 🚗 📶 🐕　Other info:
East Farm House B&B Rosemary Lane, Abbotsbury, DT3 4JN ☎ 01305 871363 ✉ eastfarmhouse@uwclub.net 🌐 www.eastfarmhouse.co.uk	GR: 578 853　DP: 1.5 miles NT: **ABBOTSBURY** Offers one night stays 3 🚗 📶 🐕　Other info:

NAME	OTHER INFO		
Peaches B&B 6 Market Street, Abbotsbury, DT3 4JR ☎ 01305 871364 ✉ enquiries@abbotsburybandb.co.uk 🌐 www.abbotsburybandb.co.uk	GR: 577 853 DP: 0.5 miles NT: **ABBOTSBURY** Other info:		
Harbour Lights Guest House 20 Buxton Road, Weymouth, DT4 9PJ ☎ 01305 783273 ✉ harbourlights@btconnect.com 🌐 www.harbourlightsguesthouse.com	GR: 672 877 DP: 0.1 miles NT: **WEYMOUTH** Offers one night stays 🚗 📶 Other info: Single night stays when available. Grocery shop nearby		
Moonfleet Manor Hotel - LFH Fleet Road, Weymouth, DT3 4ED ☎ 01305 786948 ✉ info@moonfleetmanorhotel.co.uk 🌐 www.moonfleetmanorhotel.co.uk	GR: 617 806 DP: 0.8 miles NT: **WEYMOUTH** Offers one night stays 36 🚗 📶 🐕 🍴 Other info:		
Swallows Rest B&B Martleaves Farm, South Road, Wyke Regis, DT4 9NR ☎ 01305 785244 ✉ info@swallowsrestselfcatering.co.uk 🌐 www.swallowsrestselfcatering.co.uk	GR: 661 769 DP: 0.18 miles NT: **WEYMOUTH** Offers one night stays 5 🚗 📶 Other info: Hot tub for guests to use		
Wheelwright's Cottage 14 Rodden Row, Abbotsbury, DT3 4JL ☎ 01305 871800 ✉ suenigel@wheelwrights.co.uk 🌐 www.wheelwrights.co.uk	GR: 578 852 DP: 1 mile NT: **WEYMOUTH** 1 🚗 📶 Other info:		
Windmill Cottage B&B Laurel Lane, Weymouth, DT3 5LZ ☎ 01305 814428 ✉ paule47@gmail.com 🌐 www.windmillcottagebnb.co.uk	GR: 670 845 DP: 4 miles NT: **WEYMOUTH** 📶 Other info:		
Mariners Cottage 181 Brandy Row, Chiswell, Portland, DT5 1AP ☎ 01305 826665 ✉ christina181@live.co.uk 🌐 www.portlandbandb.com	GR: 683 733 DP: 0.05 miles NT: **PORTLAND** 🐕 Other info:		
1 Old Coastguard Cottages Osmington Mills, Weymouth, DT3 6HQ ☎ 01305 832663 ✉ hope.horvath68@live.co.uk 🌐 www.southwestcoastpath.org.uk/1-old-coastguardsosmington-mills	GR: 736 817 DP: 0 miles NT: **OSMINGTON MILLS** Other info: 2 📶		
Ebenezer Cottage Silver Street, Sutton Poyntz, DT3 6LL ☎ 07778 524199 ✉ info@ebenezercottage.co.uk 🌐 www.ebenezercottage.co.uk	GR: 706 837 DP: 0.25 miles NT: **SUTTON POYNTZ** Offers one night stays 3 🚗 Other info:		
Wynards Farm B&B Winfrith Newburgh, Dorchester, DT2 8DQ ☎ 01305 852660 ✉ enquiries@wynardsfarm.co.uk 🌐 www.wynardsfarm.co.uk	GR: 801 845 DP: 3 miles NT: **DORCHESTER** Offers one night stays 3 🚗 📶 🐕 Other info:		
The Dairy House B&B East Chaldon, Chaldon Herring, DT2 8DN ☎ 01305 852138 / 07968225269 ✉ joanneselfe@hotmail.com 🌐 www.southwestcoastpath.org.uk/dairy-house-bb-chaldon-herring	GR: SY795834 DP: 2 miles NT: **WEST LULWORTH** Offers one night stays 2 🚗 📶 🐕 Other info:		

NAME	OTHER INFO		
Chiltern Lodge 8 Newfoundland Close, Worth Matravers, BH19 3LX 📞 01929 439337 ✉ densor@btopenworld.com 🌐 www.chilternlodge.co.uk	GR: 97591 77745 NT: **WORTH MATRAVERS** 🚗 📶 🍽	DP: 1 mile	Other info:
Alford House B&B 120 East Street, Corfe Castle, BH20 5EH 📞 01929 480156 ✉ info@alfordhouse.com 🌐 www.alfordhouse.com	GR: 963 816 NT: **CORFE CASTLE** Offers one night stays 🚗 📶 🐕	DP: 2 miles	Other info:
Knoll House Hotel - LFH Ferry Road, Studland, BH19 3AH 📞 01929 450450 ✉ info@knollhouse.co.uk 🌐 www.knollhouse.co.uk	GR: 030 832 NT: **STUDLAND** Offers one night stays 71 🚗 📶 🐕 🍽	DP: 0.1 miles	Other info:
Acorns Guesthouse 264 Wimborne Road, Poole, BH15 3EF 📞 01202 672901 ✉ enquiries@acornsguesthouse.co.uk 🌐 www.acornsguesthouse.co.uk	GR: 016 927 NT: **POOLE** Offers one night stays 4 🚗 📶 🍽	DP: 3 miles	Other info:
The Laurels B&B 60 Britannia Road, Poole, BH14 8BB 📞 07837 737368 ✉ info@thelaurelsbandb.com 🌐 www.thelaurelsbandb.com	GR: 032 913 NT: **POOLE**	DP: 2 miles	Other info:

Campsites and Holiday Parks

NAME	OTHER INFO		
St Gabriels Campsite Golden Cap Shedbush Lane, Morcombelake, Bridport, DT6 6DR 📞 0356 800 1895 ✉ enquiries@nationaltrust.org.uk 🌐 www.nationaltrust.org.uk/golden-cap/features/ st-gabriels-campsite-on-the-golden-cap-estate	GR: 408 927 NT: **CHIDEOCK** Offers one night stays 🚗 🐕	DP: 1 mile	**Other info:** 12 pitches. Open Feb-Sept
Tom's Field Campsite & Shop Tom's Field Road, Langton Matravers, Swanage, BH19 3HN 📞 01929 427110 ✉ tomsfield@hotmail.com 🌐 www.tomsfieldcamping.co.uk	GR: 995 785 NT: **SWANAGE** 🛒	DP: 1 mile	Other info:

Self Catering and hostels

NAME	OTHER INFO		
The Granary Larkbeare Grange, Talaton, Exeter, EX5 2RY ☎ 01404 822069 ✉ granary@larkbeare.net 🌐 www.larkbearegranary.net	GR: 067 976 — DP: 12 miles NT: **SIDMOUTH** [2] 🚗 📶 🐕 — Other info: Accessible NAS level 1. Excellent drying facilities		
Higher Wiscombe Higher Wiscombe, Southleigh, EX24 6JF ☎ 01404 871360 ✉ info@higherwiscombe.com 🌐 www.higherwiscombe.com	GR: 180 933 — DP: 3 miles NT: **SOUTHLEIGH** 🚗 📶 🐕 — Other info:		
Lyme Holidays Lyme Barn, Morcombelake, DT6 6DL ☎ 01297 441222 ✉ enquiries@lymeholidays.com 🌐 www.lymeholidays.com	GR: SY407939 — DP: 1 mile NT: **LYME REGIS** [1] 🚗 📶 — Other info:		
Shedbush Farm House Shedbush Lane, Morcombelake, Bridport, DT6 6DR ☎ 0347 800 1895 ✉ enquiries@nationaltrust.org.uk 🌐 www.nationaltrust.org.uk/holidays	GR: 405 934 — DP: 2 miles NT: **BRIDPORT** [3] 🚗 📶 🐕 — Other info: Open All year		
The Woodland Studio Arden, Eype, Bridport, DT6 6AL ☎ 01308 422595 ✉ info@woodlandstudioeype.co.uk 🌐 www.woodlandstudioeype.co.uk	GR: 447 915 — DP: 0.3 miles NT: **BRIDPORT** Other info:		
Dorset Seaside Cottages Silverbridge Farm House, North Chideock, DT6 6LF ☎ 01297 480882 ✉ info@dorsetseasidecottages.co.uk 🌐 www.dorsetseasidecottages.co.uk	GR: 424 927 — DP: 0.75 miles NT: **SEATOWN** [4] 🚗 📶 — Other info:		
Graston Farm Cottages Annings Lane, Burton Bradstock, DT6 4NG ☎ 01308 897603 ✉ info@grastonfarm.co.uk 🌐 www.grastonfarm.co.uk	GR: 503 899 — DP: 1.5 miles NT: **BURTON BRADSTOCK** [18] 🚗 📶 🐕 — Other info:		
Upton Grange Holiday Cottages Upton, Ringstead, DT2 8NE ☎ 01305 853970 ✉ uptonfarmholiday@aol.com 🌐 www.uptongrangedorset.co.uk	GR: 742 831 — DP: 1 mile NT: **RINGSTEAD** Other info:		
Swanage Footsteps 38 Quarry Close, Swanage, BH19 2QY ☎ 01929 421441 ✉ swanagefootsteps@gmail.com 🌐 www.southwestcoastpath.org.uk/swanage-footsteps-swanage	GR: 022 787 — DP: 1 mile NT: **SWANAGE** [1] 📶 — Other info:		

NAME	OTHER INFO	
Wyke Dorset Cottages 137a, High Street, Swanage, BH19 2NB ☏ 01929 422 776 ✉ bookings@dorsetcottages.com 🌐 www.dorsetcottages.com	GR: 027 786 NT: **SWANAGE** 🚗 📶 🐕	DP: Other info:
Allnatt Stop and Stay Joseph Allnatt Centres Ltd, 35 Ulwell Road, Swanage, BH19 1LG ☏ 01929 421075 ✉ enquiries@stopandstay.co.uk 🌐 www.stopandstay.co.uk	GR: 029 801 NT: **SWANAGE** Offers one night stays 9 🚗 📶 🐕 🍴	DP: 0.5 miles Other info:

Eat and Drink

NAME	OTHER INFO	
The Ilchester Arms 9 Market Street, Abbotsbury, DT3 4JR ☏ 01305 873841 ✉ info@theilchester.co.uk 🌐 www.theilchester.co.uk	GR: NT: **ABBOTSBURY** 🍴	DP: 2 miles Other info:

Do

NAME	OTHER INFO	
West Dorset Taxi 42 Flaxhayes, Bridport, DT6 5DT ☏ 07876 798770 ✉ puegot409@hotmail.com 🌐 www.westdorsettaxis.co.uk	GR: 462 935 NT: **BRIDPORT**	DP: 1.5 miles Other info:
Coastal Walks UK 10 Court Barton, Portland, DT5 2HJ ☏ 0333 567 8041 ✉ contact@coastalwalks.co.uk 🌐 www.coastalwalks.co.uk	GR: 682 715 NT: **ISLE OF PORTLAND** 🐕	DP: 0.3 miles Other info:
Jurassic Coast Guides Lakeshell, Dorchester Hill, Milborne St Andrew, DT11 0JG ☏ 07900257944 ✉ guide@jurassiccoastguides.co.uk 🌐 www.jurassiccoastguides.co.uk	GR: 801 976 NT: **RINGSTEAD** 🐕	DP: 0 miles Other info:

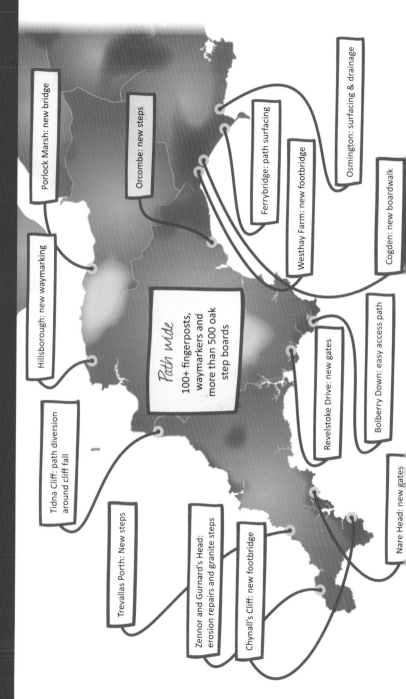

Porlock Marsh: new bridge

Orcombe: new steps

Ferrybridge: path surfacing

Westhay Farm: new footbridge

Osmington: surfacing & drainage

Cogden: new boardwalk

Hillsborough: new waymarking

Path wide
100+ fingerposts, waymarkers and more than 500 oak step boards

Tidna Cliff: path diversion around cliff fall

Revelstoke Drive: new gates

Bolberry Down: easy access path

Nare Head: new gates

Trevallas Porth: New steps

Zennor and Gurnard's Head: erosion repairs and granite steps

Chynall's Cliff: new footbridge

Map not to scale. For illustrative purposes onl

Money raised by the Association from individuals and local businesses has resulted in hundreds of improvement projects being carried out around the Path. Without the generosity of our members and supporters, none of this would be possible.

To learn how to donate to the Association please see page 198.

Ferrybridge

Coleton Camp

£250 can help buy a finger post to ensure you don't get lost while out on the Coast Path

10 could help us create a green corridor for wildlife along the path

Revelstoke Drive

k gates help ensure easier access to path for pushchairs and those with less mobility.

Westhay Farm

Trevellas Porth

Gurnard's Head – Before and After

southwestcoastpath.org.uk

Zennor Head

Orcombe
Before and Aft

Oak and granite steps allow people to
enjoy the Coast Path safely

Bolberry –
Before and After

COAST PATH

COAST PATH
DARTMOUTH
VIA FERRY

Levelling and installing drainage channels mean visitors to the Coast Path
can enjoy the beautiful scenery while they walk more securely on the Path

Pardoe Bridge

Cogden

Town	Address	Phone	Website
Minehead	The Beach Hotel, The Avenue, Minehead TA24 5AP	01643 702624	www.visitminehead.org
Porlock	West End, Porlock TA24 8QD	01643 863150	www.porlock.co.uk
Lynton	Town Hall, Lee Road, Lynton EX35 6BT	01598 752225	www.lynton-lynmouth-tourism.co.uk
Combe Martin	Museum, Cross Street EX34 0DH	01271 889031	www.visitcombemartin.com
Ilfracombe	Landmark Theatre, Ilfracombe EX34 9BZ	01271 863001	www.visitilfracombe.co.uk
Woolacombe	The Esplanade, Woolacombe EX34 7DL	01271 870553	www.woolacombetourism.co.uk
Braunton	Bakehouse Centre, Caen Street EX33 1AA	01271 816688	www.visitbraunton.co.uk
Barnstaple	The Square, Barnstaple EX32 8LN	01271 346747	www.staynorthdevon.co.uk
Bideford	Burton Art Gallery, Kingsley Rd EX39 2QQ	01237 477676	www.northdevon.com/tourist-information-centre/bideford-tourist-information-centre
Bude	The Crescent, Bude EX23 8LE	01288 354240	www.visitbude.info
Boscastle	The Harbour, Boscastle PL35 0HD	01840 250010	www.visitboscastleandtintagel.com
Padstow	North Quay, Padstow PL28 8AF	01841 533449	www.padstowlive.com
Newquay	Marcus Hill, Newquay TR7 1BD	01637 838516	www.visitnewquay.org
Perranporth	Westcott House, St Pirans Road TR6 0BH	01872 575254	www.perranporthinfo.co.uk
Hayle	Hayle Library, Commercial Road, Hayle TR27 4DE	01736 754399	www.hayle.co.uk
St Ives	The Guildhall, Street An Pol TR26 2DS	01736 796297	www.stivestic.co.uk
Penzance	Station Approach, Penzance TR18 2NF	01736 335530	www.purelypenzance.co.uk/tourism
Falmouth	Prince Of Wales Pier, 11 Market Strand TR11 3DF	01326 741194	www.falmouth.co.uk
Mevagissey	Hurley Books, 3 Jetty St, Mevagissey PL26 6UH	01726 842200	www.visitmevagissey.co.uk
Fowey	5 South Street, Fowey PL23 1AR	01726 833616	www.fowey.co.uk
Looe	The Guildhall, Fore Street, Looe PL13 2AA	01503 262072	www.visit-southeastcornwall.co.uk
Plymouth	3-5 Plymouth Mayflower, Barbican PL1 2LR	01752 306330	www.visitplymouth.co.uk
Salcombe	Market Street, Salcombe TQ8 8DE	01548 843927	www.salcombeinformation.co.uk
Kingsbridge	The Quay, Kingsbridge TQ7 1HS	01548 853195	www.welcomesouthdevon.co.uk
Dartmouth	The Engine House, Mayors Ave TQ6 9YY	01803 834224	www.discoverdartmouth.com
Brixham	Hobb Nobs Gift Shop, The Quay TQ5 8AW	01803 211211	www.englishriviera.co.uk
Paignton & Torquay	5 Vaughan Parade, Torquay TQ2 5JG	01803 211211	www.englishriviera.co.uk
Shaldon	Shaldon Car Park, Ness Drive TQ14 0HP	07546 995623	www.visitsouthdevon.co.uk
Teignmouth	Pavillions, Den Crescent, Teignmouth TQ14 8BG	01626 215665	www.visitsouthdevon.co.uk
Dawlish	The Lawn, Dawlish EX7 9PW	01626 215665	www.visitsouthdevon.co.uk
Exmouth	42 The Strand, Exmouth, EX8 1AL	01395 830550	www.exmouth-guide.co.uk
Budleigh -Salterton	Fore Street, Budleigh Salterton EX9 6NG	01395 445275	www.visitbudleigh.com
Sidmouth	Ham Lane, Sidmouth EX10 8XR	01395 516441	www.visitsidmouth.co.uk
Seaton	The Underfleet, Seaton EX12 2TB	01297 300390	www.seatontic.co.uk
Lyme Regis	Guildhall Cottage, Church Street DT7 3BS	01297 442138	www.lymeregis.org
Bridport	Town Hall, South Street, Bridport DT6 3LF	01308 424901	www.visit-dorset.com
Swanage	The White House, Shore Road BH19 1LB	01929 766018	www.visit-dorset.com
Poole	Poole Museum, 4 High Street, Poole BH15 1BW	01202 262600	www.pooletourism.com
Not on Coast Path			
Truro	Municipal Buildings, Boscawen St, Truro TR1 2NE	01872 274555	www.visittruro.org.uk
Weston Super Mare	VIC The Tropicana, Marine Parade BS23 1BE	01934 888877	www.visitsomerset.co.uk
Ivybridge	The Watermark, Ivybridge PL21 0SZ	01752 897035	www.ivybridgewatermark.co.uk

Gifts & Souvenirs

Give treasured memories of the Path as a gift

Everything you buy contributes to Coast Path conservation, improvement projects and charitable activities - making the Path known to lots and enjoyed by many.

Please visit **www.southwestcoastpath.org.uk** to discover our full range of products or phone **01752 896237**.

PRICES INCLUDE P&P

Oak Pens from £9.50
Using locally sourced wood,
including oak finger posts.

**Oak Finger Posts
£20.00 & £48.00**
Beautifully crafted. Small: 25cm x 5cm x 2cm
Large: 50cm x 13cm x 2cm
We can also personalise.

Donations
Donate online at
http://shop.southwestcoastpath.org.uk or by
calling 01752 896237

**Tea Towel
£7.00**
Fun and
colourful 100%
cotton.
Dimensions:
73cm x 43cm.

Clothing

We have some great clothing and accessories to help you keep dry, cool/warm and comfortable. All embroidered with the South West Coast Path Association logo.

There's no such thing as bad weather, only unsuitable clothing

Alfred Wainwright

Headware from £11.00
Snoods, Caps, Beanie and Bobble Hats in a range of colours.

Polo Shirt £22
Available in a wide range of colours and sizes.

Sleeveless Fleece £28
Ideal for evenings or walking during those colder months.

Light Weight Jacket £39
Waterproof and windproof jacket, with concealed hood. Available in various colours.

South West Coast Path
Association

CHALLENGE

What will your Challenge be?

It costs at least £1000 to every year to look after one mile of Coast Path

Keep an eye out for Challenge details on Facebook and Twitter!